IMPACT
INVESTING

IMPACT
INVESTING

Transforming How We Make Money
While Making a Difference

Antony Bugg-Levine   Jed Emerson

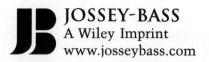

JOSSEY-BASS
A Wiley Imprint
www.josseybass.com

Published by Jossey-Bass
A Wiley Imprint
989 Market Street, San Francisco, CA 94103-1741—www.josseybass.com

Jossey-Bass books and products are available through most bookstores. To contact Jossey-Bass directly call our Customer Care Department within the U.S. at 800-956-7739, outside the U.S. at 317-572-3986, or fax 317-572-4002.

Wiley also publishes its books in a variety of electronic formats and by print-on-demand. Not all content that is available in standard print versions of this book may appear or be packaged in all book formats. If you have purchased a version of this book that did not include media that is referenced by or accompanies a standard print version, you may request this media by visiting http://booksupport.wiley.com. For more information about Wiley products, visit us at www.wiley.com.

Library of Congress Cataloging-in-Publication Data
Bugg-Levine, Antony
  Impact investing : transforming how we make money while making a difference / Antony Bugg-Levine, Jed Emerson.—1st ed.
    p. cm.
  Includes bibliographical references and index.
  ISBN 978-0-470-90721-4 (hardback); ISBN 978-1-118-10066-0 (ebk); ISBN 978-1-118-10067-7 (ebk); ISBN 978-1-118-10068-4 (ebk)
  1. Investments—Social aspects. 2. Investments—Environmental aspects. 3. Social responsibility of business. I. Emerson, Jed. II. Title.
  HG4515.13.B84 2011
  332.6—dc23

                                                                                      2011021818

Printed in the United States of America
FIRST EDITION
HB Printing   10 9 8 7 6 5 4 3

To Ahadi, Antony's anchor and lodestar
and
To Mia, Jed's fellow traveler and partner in all

Try not to become a man of success, but rather try to become a man of value.

—*Albert Einstein*

Contents

Preface

Welcome to our Preface, wherein authors set expectations and explain why we wrote what we did and why you should read it. Just to make sure we are all on the same page (as it were), we would like to make a few things clear at the outset.

This book does not tell you how to invest your money in a responsible way.

And to be fair, we don't tell you how to invest your money irresponsibly either. We figure there are already enough books out there to help you do that.

These pages do not present a how-to guide for those interested in strategic philanthropy or becoming a better donor.

We do not offer you the top ten tips to:

- Making more with less

- Doing well and doing good

- Valuing that which stands beyond valuation

- Pursuing profit with purpose

This book is not an invitation to a picnic. We do not offer the intellectual equivalents of a crocheted blanket to lie on, a chilled bottle of wine to sip, and your favorite breads and spreads.

Instead, we invite you into a dark wood, beyond the comforting confines of your established routines and secure homes. Something exciting is going on out here. There are creatures many have never seen before. They are moving about and working together in fascinating new ways. They are building structures of beauty we could not before imagine, and they will not be confined to these woods for very long.

These creatures are the pioneers of impact investing for blended value, a set of investment strategies that generate financial return while intentionally improving social and environmental conditions. They have left the fields and the cities where people assume the only purpose of investing is to make money and the only way to solve social problems is through charity. Impact investors are showing what we can achieve when we take an integrated approach to the pursuit of financial, social, and environmental performance—in other words, how for-profit investments can help address social problems.

We wrote this book to share our excitement about what is happening. Despite the bug bites and the cold nights and the wet socks, exploring these woods has been a great adventure. We have been inspired by the people we met and what they are up to. And we want to share some of this excitement with you.

A picnic basket will not do you much good out here, so instead we have put into this backpack of a book everything you will need for your adventure:

- With the flashlight, we spotlight some of the most interesting creatures and let you see the lives they have created and the value they are building.

- With the floodlight, we illuminate how these creatures are interacting in an increasingly complex ecosystem and becoming more powerful through this collaboration.

- The map identifies both where you can find creatures to join and where you can find empty spaces if you want to build something new.

These woods are exploding with life. Every week, it seems, we hear about new investors who are taking an integrated approach to the management of their assets—not trading off between social and financial results but recognizing the complement of components that aggregate together to generate a blend of value for shareholders and stakeholders alike. With so much happening, it seems that every chapter has become out of date by the time we finished drafting it!

We are not so arrogant to think these woods sprang up only in the years since we coined the phrases *blended value* and *impact investing*. These woods have been around at least since the seventeenth century when Quakers articulated a blended value vision of faith, commerce, and community. We gratefully walk along paths laid down over the years by those who have made eloquent and passionate calls for investors, philanthropists, businesspeople, and social entrepreneurs to take an integrated approach to the generation of social and financial value.

We're not going to overstate the case for impact investing. For many people, the traditional model of separating financially focused investment and charitable giving will no doubt continue to appear coherent and attractive. We admit that much money and activity will remain in traditional, mainstream investments for decades to come, managed and measured in the traditional ways. And the existing incentive structures will continue to lead many traditional investment advisors and philanthropic consultants to advocate for the traditional, bifurcated approach to wealth management and charitable giving.

Perhaps most important, we fully recognize that markets (whether of capital or products or services) will not meet all our community needs or address each of our demands. This is not a vision of civil society versus market-based solutions. Charity and government support are crucial and will remain so. They are just insufficient to the task at hand.

With these considerations in mind, impact investing for blended value provides a unified approach that will make us better able to create sustainable, long-term value than we could with civil society organizations, government, and mainstream markets operating separately and alone. And the best impact investors are showing us how much more we can reasonably demand from both investment and philanthropy.

The growth in scale, breadth, and collective recognition of the emerging market for impact investing is poised to disrupt the traditional systems that organize enterprises, investment, and charity. And these disruptions will increasingly create opportunities for institutions and entrepreneurs whose approaches provide new solutions.

And that's not all:

- Investment advisors already face clients demanding advice on how to make investments that generate social return as well as financial performance.

- Entrepreneurs are developing business models and funds at the intersection of profit and purpose, despite the difficulty of accommodating them within current regulatory and capital-raising systems.

- Talented young people increasingly hunger for employment opportunities that allow them to address social and environmental benefit, a hunger no longer satiated by participating in the annual corporate charity run or pro bono assignment or the classic nonprofit approach that ignores the positive potential of business.

- Governments are slowly catching up to these entrepreneurs and investors by adapting existing regulations to support their blended value vision.

As a shared vision of blended value emerges and impact invest-ing capital markets grow, participants will increasingly come to realize their collective power and see the opportunities available to those who adapt existing systems to serve the new demand for both maximum justice and economic performance.

Think of these investment pioneers as birds. When they were off on their own, they were interesting to watch but easy to ignore. But as any fan of Alfred Hitchcock knows, when they flock together, they are a potent and disruptive force. And what about when the flocks leave the woods? Farmers and city dwellers alike better take notice. The systems that have kept our farms and cities stable and prosperous are not going to work the same way after this flock arrives.

Now, before we get hopelessly lost in these metaphorical woods, here's how this book unfolds.

Part One describes what is going on in the world of impact invest-ing, looks at how we got here, and anticipates where we're going.

Chapter One offers reflections on the evolution of investing for impact. In a wide range of sectors and regions, the core concepts of impact investing have been at work for years in many markets and communities. These experiences affirm that we can address social and environmental problems while investing in ventures that generate profitable returns, allowing subsidy to play its rightful role together with private investment. We may learn from these experiences in order to improve our performance and accelerate the development of this evolving capital market.

Chapter Two examines the international development field where impact investing experiments have been undertaken over the past fifty years, with mixed results and fascinating lessons.

Chapter Three looks at microfinance, an idea that germinated in the scorched earth of market and government failure in some of the world's poorest countries, hailed by some as the exemplar of the power of capital and others as the scourge of mercenary capitalism run amok. We explore both perspectives for what they can teach about the broader impact investing industry.

Chapter Four shows how impact investing is creating both opportunities and complexity for social entrepreneurs and the people who back them, as social enterprises must navigate the sometimes chaotic options of donors and investors.

Chapter Five describes a framework for predicting where impact investing could expand to next and highlights areas where adventuring investors and entrepreneurs could turn their attention to get out ahead.

Part Two explores how impact investing for blended value is galvanizing the creation of new systems for organizing investment and philanthropy. Our current systems and practices work well for those who stay safely on either side of the bifurcated world, involved in traditional charity or investment. But to generate sustainable blended value requires new approaches and operating systems. By understanding the challenges facing impact investors and their responses, we can begin to understand the systems that will be created to support their aspirations.

Chapter Six turns to the new regulations and policy we will need because existing rules created for mainstream investors and charities inhibit rather than facilitate the effective allocation of resources.

Chapter Seven considers what types of leaders the impact investing industry requires and how we're going to cultivate them now that we are moving beyond the phase where charismatic individuals could lead alone.

Chapter Eight examines the new tools required for measuring and valuing the social impact of investments.

Chapter Nine shows how impact investing creates opportunities for individual donors and foundations to harness all their assets to address the issues they care about but highlights the organizational and leadership challenges required to capture this potential.

Chapter Ten addresses the critical question of capital markets and how they operate. It then maps the most promising capital pools and what it will take for impact investors to tap into them.

We do not claim to present a comprehensive account of conceptual frameworks, intellectual tradition, or investment practice. There are obvious gaps in our approach. Most notably, we do not discuss in detail the fascinating evolution of impact investing as a crucial tool in the community development and low-income housing markets in the United States. This gap results from our lack of relative expertise, not the relative importance of this sector. In general, our map of the impact investing landscape is admittedly more Galileo than Google Earth. But we hope that the range of practice we describe gets the big story right even if we have not filled in all the details.

At the end of this journey, our reward is a fundamentally optimistic vision of capital, community, and corporation. It is a unifying vision about what we can achieve when all of our assets work in unison with our values and beliefs. Understanding this vision can show us new tools and ways of thinking about how to build the life we seek for ourselves, our families, and our communities.

Examples and stories about and from impact investing pioneers populate this book. These barely begin to describe the diverse and rapidly growing impact investing industry. Others have documented individual stories more fully than we attempt to within these pages. We have opted to limit our examples to a small representation of those advancing this work and offer our apologies to the many whose work we were not able to reference, much less profile.

To realize this vision will demand awareness on each of our parts that the goal—the purpose of our having lived—is not our successful buttressing of various silos of market-oriented philosophies or civil society practice or global corporate or development agency success. Rather, the goal is that at the conclusion of our life, each of us can look back on the path we took and say not that we contributed to the creation of our small part but that we worked together, building on our relative strengths to create a greater, more sustainable whole.

We know how to engage in strategic philanthropy. We understand how to manage portfolios for competitive financial returns. What we are learning to do better is to manage it all—our capital, our companies, our compassion and our communities, indeed, our very selves—and maximize the total value of each when taken together. We hope this book reveals something of the new opportunities that exist as this latest evolution of capital markets and social change practice continues accelerating.

How We Got Here

This book marks the confluence of our personal and professional experience. After having discussed and refined these ideas in more organizational management meetings, speeches, and panels than we can count, we wrote this book to share what we have learned with a wider audience.

Jed's Story

My story began twenty-some years ago. After an early career in social work, I spent five years running a venture philanthropy fund in San Francisco with George R. Roberts, founding partner of the private equity firm, Kohlberg Kravis Roberts & Co. In 1996, we produced our first major publication on social entrepreneurship, venture philanthropy, social capital markets, and social return on investment.[1] Melinda Tuan had joined in our reorganization as the Roberts Enterprise Development Fund, the book was out, and I hit the road, working the conference and speaking circuit to explain to the nonprofit sector what we'd learned, were doing, and advancing toward.

Except that a funny thing happened on my way to the next nonprofit gig: I began to receive invitations to speak to for-profit folks. It turned out our ideas resonated with investors, CEOs, and free enterprise types, especially with the new money beginning to flow out of Silicon Valley controlled by people for whom charitable giving and nonprofits were much less compelling ideas than venture philanthropy, new metrics, and social enterprise.

In the course of these discussions during the late 1990s with a wide cross-section of those in both the nonprofit and for-profit sectors, I realized what they all had in common was a notion of the value they sought to create as being "both-and" instead of "either-or." Whatever specific language they used to express it, they were thinking of value as a function of maximizing some level of financial discipline and performance, together with the pursuit of a defined measure of social impact or environmental promotion.

Although each set of actors viewed it differently, often using different terms in this conversation, I felt they were all basically exploring a vision of value as being whole—a blend of these various elements. The stepping-stone toward this new understanding of value may have initially been described as double bottom line or, later, triple bottom line, but they understood that corporate form was simply a shell game and that nonprofits had economic value just as for profits could drive social impact and environmental performance. They ultimately came to see value as a blend of elements that resulted in driving a full, integrated notion of investing and enterprise development. When framed within the context of a business or investment proposition, I came to think of this as the blended value proposition. Starting with my publication of a Harvard Business School Social Enterprise working paper in 2000, I put my focus and energies over the next decade on exploring and defining various aspects of this evolved notion of value and value creation.[2]

Antony's Story

My journey has followed a simple question: How do we get capital from where it is to where it can be used to end poverty?

When I graduated from college in the mid-1990s, I was convinced that anyone who went to work for an investment bank or consulting company was a sellout. So I returned to South Africa, where I was born and spent my early childhood, to work on a book of political biographies. I eventually landed at the South African Human Rights Commission, where I saw how economic power and human dignity are inextricably interlinked. For poor farmers without any resources to press their claims, constitutional protections were little more than ink on paper. And, as the Commission's researchers uncovered, rural landowners exerted the power their wealth accorded them to terrible effect.

Later, when I was working with officials of the ruling African National Congress, I saw how the language of economics could trump the most articulate and passionate social advocacy. "Comrades," the representatives from the Treasury Department would explain, "we just cannot fund the housing program without undermining the macroeconomic austerity that the international capital markets demand."

I returned to the United States to study development economics, determined never to be silenced by economists again. From there it was a relatively short leap for me to a gig at the consulting firm McKinsey & Co., where I set out to learn how big business thinks and talks.

Almost four years later, I sought to integrate my ongoing interest in development work with my newly found appreciation of the creativity and value that business can unlock. My wife and I moved to Kenya, where I headed up the local office of an international nongovernmental organization, TechnoServe, which focused on developing business solutions to rural poverty. Across Kenya and Uganda, inspiring colleagues and clients helped me understand the power of markets and capital. A tiny loan and mechanism to access markets efficiently was all the dairy farmers in the Great Rift Valley needed to unleash their potential and take control of their economic destiny. But capital did not reach these farmers. Having advised some of the biggest global companies, I knew there was no lack of money in the world. It just wasn't getting to the farmers and the businesses that could support them.

When I returned to New York and a job at the Rockefeller Foundation, I set about trying to understand why. I began to cold-call investors who appeared to have related interests and asked them all: What will it take for you to address more social and environmental challenges more efficiently with for-profit investment? With introduction following introduction and interest in this area exploding, I soon found myself in the middle of a global network of inspiring innovators tackling this question. In late 2007, my colleagues at Rockefeller and I convened twenty people for a meeting to discuss how we could work together to address the challenges we faced in this field. By the end of the meeting we had coined the phrase *impact investing* to describe what we were about: making investments that generate a social and environmental impact and that have an impact on investment practice itself. The following year, we launched a formal initiative at Rockefeller: "Harnessing the Power of Impact Investing."

In the end, it all comes together. We have come to see, along with a growing number of others, how impact investing for blended value unites the power of business with the purpose of philanthropy, opening up new possibilities for our societies and ourselves.

June 2011	Antony Bugg-Levine	Jed Emerson
	New York, New York	*Grand Lake, Colorado*

Acknowledgments

It is clear a project such as this is not the result of any one person's work. We first and foremost offer our thanks to those who have worked so hard to pioneer the strategies we describe in these pages. We have learned so much from each of you and are extremely grateful for your willingness to share your lessons with us, whether from the perspective of a commercial market investor, a sustainable private equity fund manager, a social entrepreneur, a mainstream investor open to discussing new ideas, or a customer of an impact investment–financed enterprise. Too many have contributed to our thinking and fed our passion to name everyone, but we offer our sincere thanks to each of you for inspiring us to write this book. We genuinely thank you for your contribution to the field as a whole and respectfully acknowledge our own work has been made possible through your dedication and labor.

Thanks are due to our editors: Jesse Wiley, for his enthusiasm to get us started and patience through the false starts and dead-ends of our writing process, and Alison Hankey, for shepherding us to the finish line. Mike Kubzansky and Anamitra Deb of Monitor Inclusive Markets provided the framing and content for Chapter Four on social enterprise. All of our contributors took time from their busy jobs to share their personal reflections, and we thank them deeply for that. We also thank Nick Jourdan for his solid contributions as our research associate during the first stage of working on this project and Danielle Walker for her good ideas and insights as we worked on the second stage.

Antony: I specifically thank Jed for his pioneering vision to see the blended value woods when they still lay beyond the horizon of most people's imagination, his courage to venture into them, his patience to stay during some long, cold nights, and his generosity to share the knowledge of what he has found. (And his willingness to withhold the expletives—most of the time—when dealing with a new adventurer who showed up acting as if he was the first person to discover these woods!). Under the leadership of Judith Rodin, my colleagues at the Rockefeller Foundation have pushed me down this path over the past four years and kept me on it with camaraderie and conviction. Fred Ogana and Erastus Kibugu, and the rest of our colleagues at TechnoServe in Kenya and Uganda, brought me into their inspiring work with generosity and grace. Sandra Navalli and Ray Horton at Columbia Business School's Social Enterprise Program created the opportunity for me to hone these ideas with unfailingly enthusiastic students.

The insights I have had about impact investing have come from conversations with hundreds of investors, many of whom have become friends. Katherine Fulton, John Goldstein, and Jason Scott have been particularly inspiring and supportive. The management team and board of the Global Impact Investing Network have generously shared their enthusiasm and insights, revealing the creative, passionate, and values-driven side of investment. My parents, Sandy and Janet Levine, set me on the path, and my brother, Roger Levine, has helped cut a clearing ahead of me. And finally, none of this would be possible without the support and patience of my wife, Ahadi, and her unfailing love and wisdom.

Jed: My thanks to Antony for his enthusiastic leadership in the field of impact investing and his passion for telling a story that links great narrative with meaningful analysis. His role in advancing this work has been significant, and I deeply appreciate his partnership in writing this book. I thank Jason Scott and the members of The Group (an informal circle of friends who, when finding ourselves at the same conferences but never with enough time to truly engage, began meeting once a year in places around the world) for their unwavering support; Tim Freundlich, an early thought partner and source of constant affirmation; and my friends in Colorado who help me maintain a grounded perspective on life. I thank my wife, Mia Haugen, for her incredible words to me personally over some very tough months and, more important, for her passion for living and realizing its fullness in nature, family, community, and self. I offer my fond thanks to Adam and Bella, who have given me a level of personal challenge, joy, and millennial perspective I have missed for the better part of my life. I also thank my brother and sister, John Emerson and Lynne Phillips, for their ongoing good wishes and support. And, finally, I acknowledge the great love and backing of my parents, Migs and Jim Emerson, whose witness to living a spiritual life of open inquiry is what set me on this path to begin with. Celebrate the struggle and live in the journey!

We offer this book to all of these people for their contributions to the value we hope it contains.

IMPACT
INVESTING

Part One

THE TERRAIN OF IMPACT INVESTING

Chapter 1

A MIGHTY WAVE

- An investor in Hong Kong wants to secure her children's economic future. But she also wants to use her wealth to address the social and environmental challenges she cares about and thereby leave a deeper legacy. She becomes convinced that simply giving her money away cannot be the only way she can make a difference. So she redirects her assets into investments that preserve her wealth and also directly tackle problems of poverty and environmental degradation.

- A group of friends volunteering for a nonprofit organization look for ways to help reduce poverty in rural Mexico. They stumble onto the idea of lending small amounts of money to poor people who cannot access loans from banks. But they struggle to secure donations and instead take on loans. When their success exhausts their available charitable capital, they convert to a for-profit enterprise and eventually hold an initial public offering on the Mexican stock market that raises more than $300 million. Suddenly they find themselves in the middle of a global media storm, lionized as saviors and vilified as greedy capitalists.

- A senior investment banker in New York decides to shift career tracks to contribute to the fight against global poverty. But instead of leaving Wall Street to do it, she sets up a unit in one of the world's leading finance firms to provide banking services to enterprises around the world that tackle the issue of poverty. Within a week of the announcement of the unit's creation, nearly a thousand employees of the investment bank contact her to offer to collaborate in this work.

It's easy to miss these pioneers in the crowded and complex worlds of investment and traditional philanthropy. After all, a lot has been going on in both worlds recently. And maybe these individuals are just eccentrics we can easily ignore. Perhaps they are just barely visible and unimportant ripples atop the roiling waves we seem to find ourselves in so often these days.

We believe they are something more. These ripples are related and part of a shifting tide. These three people are pioneers in the rapidly evolving global industry of impact investing, as are the many other people you will meet in this book. Each of them is discovering a new realm of possibility. They are maximizing the total value of their investments and organizations, creating a high-octane blend of economic performance and sustained environmental and social impact. And their discoveries are upending long-held and jealously guarded beliefs that profit-making and charitable activities must be kept separate in isolated silos of thinking and practice.

These are the early signs of a long-forming undercurrent that is poised to reshape how society deploys its resources and solves its problems. As Robert Kennedy famously noted, even tiny ripples can become a powerful current that sweeps aside the established order when they are multiplied and brought together. Powerful in its simplicity, the idea of impact investing for blended value—investment strategies that generate financial return while intentionally improving social and environmental conditions—is disrupting a world organized around the competing principle that for-profit investments should seek only to pursue financial return, while people who care about social problems should give away their money or wait for the government to step in. But one person's disruption is another's opportunity. Impact investing pioneers are jumping into these fast-flowing waters, creating new enterprises, ideas, and approaches to match the aspirations of investors and entrepreneurs eager to harness the full power of capital.

This book describes how impact investing is rising around us as the various ripples come together, the disruptions it is causing, and the opportunities it presents. The grand global swell of impact investing is growing as the dynamics that precipitated the movement gather force. We cannot predict what will happen when this water crests. But we will all be well served to develop the insights and strategies that can ready us for the changes it will bring.

Impact Investing for Blended Value: A Definition

Impact investing recognizes that investments can pursue financial returns while also intentionally addressing social and environmental challenges. Despite, or perhaps because of, this simplicity, it can seem threatening to some people. Many mainstream investors reject the idea that they should pay attention to the social impact of their investing, insisting instead that these considerations be left to governments and charities. And for their part, most traditional philanthropists reject the idea that they should use their investments to advance their mission or that businesses generating profits have a right to stand alongside philanthropy and civil society in the noble work of promoting equality and justice.

But impact investing is not a modern aberration. The idea that our investment decisions can have an impact on the wider world beyond financial return did not begin when Jed first described "blended value" in 2000 or when Antony was part of the group that coined the phrase "impact investing" seven years later. In many ways, it reconnects with a centuries-old tradition that held the owners of wealth responsible for the welfare of their broader community. It is a story that goes back at least to the Quakers in seventeenth-century England who sought to align their investment and purchase decisions with their values. It is linked as well with the Shaker congregations in the 1800s that launched businesses in alignment with social values and to fund religious communities. It traces its arc through the environmental movement of the 1970s, the anti-apartheid divestment campaigns of the 1980s, and the modern fair trade consumer and socially responsible investing movements. In one form or another, aspects of impact investing have been playing themselves out on the global stage for centuries. What we see before us today is simply its latest iteration, linking economics with social and environmental aspects of the human experience.

What *is* new is that impact investors are profoundly optimistic about the role business can play in advancing the common good and the leverage that social enterprises can achieve by applying financial tools. We see business practices as a powerful force that can be harnessed for good rather than a necessary evil that must be curtailed. This optimism is not ideological: we are not capitalist triumphalists, eager to spread the gospel of free market greatness to the far corners of the world. Moreover, we are not ignorant of the limits of market-based strategies for social change. But we have observed what is going on in diverse corners of an increasingly connected planet. And we cannot help but marvel at how many people in both rich and poor countries enjoy a better life because of successful profit-seeking investment.

We also know that new challenges require new approaches. Every one of us is confronting the shared reality that regardless of who is in political office or what the latest social trend is, our social and environmental challenges are too vast and our financial resources too limited for our current approaches to work. We can no longer afford to waste capital and talent by organizing ourselves around the separate poles of financial return and social good, which forces us to play the middle against itself. Instead blended value offers a new way to integrate our activity around the recognition that we do not seek appropriate wealth *or* social justice; rather, we seek both.

We are neither purely economic creatures nor social beings. By extension, all of our organizations have elements of financial, social, and environmental performance embedded within them, regardless of whether they are for profit or nonprofit. The sooner we recognize that and organize our public persona and institutions around this basic, seemingly self-evident truth, the sooner we will be able to move beyond the bifurcated approaches to both investing and social change that have dominated our world over past centuries. They have locked us into supposed solutions that have failed to consistently move our communities into a sustainable, just, and personally powerful future.

What's in a Name?

When Jed first heard the term *impact investing,* he cringed and thought, *Yet one more buzzword created by newcomers without the patience to understand what the existing terms and practices really mean.* He felt it was just a new addition to the litany of terms having greater and greater importance to ever decreasing slices of an isolated community where empty words and rhetoric were growing like weeds, making it difficult for others to move through the thicket and on to a clearly defined path. He felt *impact investing* to be just one more reason to spend more time hiking and less time in meetings, conferences, and strategy workshops. We imagine others may share that initial reaction, and so it's worth pausing to explain why we use the term here and how we think it is different from labels of the past.

This current use of the term *impact investing* came out of a set of discussions Antony held with a group of investors in 2007, all of them making impact investments before the term existed. They were early investors in green technology and the first institutional investors who placed equity into microfinance funds. They had launched creative loan structures for low-income housing developers in U.S. cities and were managing public equity investments on a sustainable basis. What unified all of them was an interest in assessing the potential and real performance of their capital through more than a passive financial lens. They wanted to use their capital to do something positive.

And terms in use did not capture fully these investors' interest in defining investing as an active verb. *Socially responsible investing* and *ethical investing* seemed burdened with moral obligation or personal, normative judgment and a history of negative screening that focused on what type of firms to avoid. *Sustainable finance* seemed narrowly focused on environmental concerns rather than the full array of social justice and development issues and seemed also to muffle the excitement these investors felt regarding their possibilities. And although *community development finance* resonated with some Americans, it did not capture the breadth of global investing in which these actors engaged, did not connect with locally focused investors outside the United States, and did not reflect the premium many place on environmental issues or investment opportunities.

Impact investing, however, evoked the optimism and action orientation of this group. The term provided a broad, rhetorical umbrella under which a wide range of investors could huddle. The microfinance investor, the green-tech venture capitalist, the low-income housing lender: all could now see their affinity in a broader movement and begin to collaborate to address the similar challenges they faced. With an intentional double meaning, the term has also cast a wide net. Some impact investors are content just to make investments that directly create social and environmental impact. Others want their investments ultimately to have an impact on how all investment is conducted. The term has resonated as well with a new set of investors who have sensed a desire to integrate their investment and philanthropy but previously lacked the language to articulate it.

What an Impact Investment Is

Defining exactly what is (and what is not) an impact investment has become increasingly important as the term has taken off. And, unfortunately, many people approaching this task are still locked in old language and mind-sets. They are used to orienting themselves around financial return and therefore define impact investments as below-market-rate investments that trade off financial return for social impact. Although these investments certainly form part of the impact-investing universe, the heart of the movement is the reorientation around blended value as the organizing principle of our work: using capital to maximize total, combined value with multiple aspects of performance.

For now, the industry is coalescing around a definition that focuses on intention and the attention an investor pays to blended value returns: impact investors intend to create positive impact alongside various levels of financial return, both managing and measuring the blended value they create.

What does this mean in practice?

All investments are capable of generating positive social impact, but some are closer to the action than others. Public equity investors can generate impact, for example, through a shareholder advocacy campaign, and investors pursuing this approach have had meaningful impact on some corporate practices. Indeed, virtually all the impact investors we know place a portion of their portfolio in impact-oriented public equity funds. In this way, impact investing is a strategy across all asset classes. But the shortest line we can draw between our investment choices and their social impact is to place capital directly into companies and projects and make loans and private equity investments as the vehicles to do so. Therefore, the impact investing movement tends to focus on venture investing, private equity and direct lending because of the unmatched power of these investments to generate social impact.

Of course, not all venture or private equity investments are impact investments, even when they seem to focus on high-potential sectors or geographies. Simply putting capital to work in a poor country does not qualify an investor as an impact investor. Funds and firms earning a seat at the impact investment table focus on strategies that intentionally seek to uplift rather than exploit poor customers and treat impact reporting as a central business management practice—not an afterthought for external reporting and marketing. Similarly, a clean energy investment that inadvertently destroys critical habitat could destroy rather than create value. These distinctions matter to impact investors who are developing strategies to allocate capital where it can generate the most integrated, blended value.

What Blended Value Is

If impact investing is what we do, blended value is what we produce. Value is what gets created when investors invest and organizations act to pursue their mission. All organizations, for-profit and nonprofit alike, create value that consists of economic, social, and environmental components. All investors, whether market rate, charitable, or some mix of the two, generate all three forms of value. But somehow this fundamental truth has been lost to a world that sees value as being only economic (created by for-profit companies) or social (created by nonprofit organizations or government). And most business managers, as well as investors, miss out on the opportunity to capture their total value potential by not managing for blended value on an intentional strategic basis.

The concept of blended value reintegrates our understanding of value as a nondivisible combination of these three elements. Blended value is its own distinct force to be understood, measured, and sought. It is not just something we can achieve by adding up its component parts because it is more than the sum of the parts of a triple-bottom-line analysis. At the same time, blended value does not mean one loses the distinct taste and flavors of the component ingredients of value creation. It is not a blurring of these components, and the components do not lose their unique attributes and characteristics. It is not a weaving together of separate parts, but rather a recombining of core elements that, through their natural integration, transform into a new, stronger, and more nuanced organizational and capital structure. Blended value is the recognition that capital, community, and commerce can create more than their sum and is less a math exercise of zero-sum pluses and minuses than a physics equation of an expanding universe of investments in organizations, people, and planet.

The Coming Disruption

Impact investing has gained its foothold following an historic period of upheaval in the capital markets. In fact, the financial crisis of 2008 precipitated the largest impact investments of all time. Just like pioneering impact investors, governments around the world recognized the need and opportunity to go beyond donations in their scramble to protect jobs and social stability by shoring up private companies. They invested tens of billions in loans, equity investments, and guarantees, the basic tools of the impact investors that we describe extensively in this book. And the forces that set off the first ripples of the impact investing movement continue to grow:

- With gathering intensity, wealthy investors and philanthropists have become impatient with old approaches in the face of intractable and increasingly visible environmental damage and poverty.

- A new generation of business and socially savvy entrepreneurs is launching ventures across an array of geographies and sectors that creatively structure investment capital to tackle society's challenges and pursue new market opportunities.

- Cash-strapped governments are redefining their relationships with private business as demographic realities force a reexamination of fundamental components of the social contract.

- The rise of online social networking platforms creates the potential for thousands of investors to talk, share, and engage with each other as they identify, vet, and place investments in social entrepreneurs the world over.

These forces are finding their outlet in impact investing for blended value. Implementing this simple concept is not easy. Although impact investors see the opportunities in an integrated approach, our systems have not yet caught up. Frustration abounds as the old only grudgingly gives way to the new.

The current of impact investing is washing along the shores of a bifurcated world still organized to separate profit making from social and environmental problem solving. For now, this bifurcated world channels the energy of impact investors into the hidden pools and underground rivers on the margins of mainstream investment and philanthropic activity. But water has a powerful ability to reshape the world it flows through. The gathering weight of impact investment activity is wearing away the bedrock of seemingly immovable institutions and investment practices.

Impact investors will not long be content to force-fit their aspirations into a set of systems created to support a bifurcated vision. Instead, these systems will inevitably change under the collective weight of a new generation of investors, entrepreneurs, and government officials flowing together in the pursuit of blended value:

- In the bifurcated world, established for-profit and nonprofit business models facilitate separate profit-maximizing investments and philanthropic contributions. In the world of blended value, a new class of social enterprises will organize to maximize the full blended value of investment.

- In the bifurcated world, laws and regulations clearly define and protect traditional entrepreneurs, investors, and philanthropists. But they are ill suited to understand, yet alone guide, enterprises and investors seeking to maximize blended value. In the world of blended value, governments will determine how to harness impact investment to complement public resources in capitalizing the solutions to society's most pressing challenges.

- In the bifurcated world, leadership development systems and support services create clear pathways for talented people to navigate separate careers in charity or business. In the world of blended value, we will need new approaches to find and develop the professionals who want to apply their business savvy to create wealth and tackle social and environmental challenges together.

- In the bifurcated world, we know how to measure the value of financial investments and are getting better at describing the social impact of charity. In the world of blended value, we will create common language and measurement systems that can ensure we steer our capital and attention to the enterprises most adept at creating profit together with social value.

- In the bifurcated world, a vast array of institutions constitutes the capital markets that separately facilitate exchange between the donor and the charity and the investor and the business. In the world of blended value, these capital markets will turn to the task of connecting impact investors and social entrepreneurs.

We do not seek to overstate the changes that are occurring or the challenges in sustaining that innovation. The bifurcated world will certainly linger. For many people, separating investing and charity will continue to make sense. But some established systems will inevitably adapt. And others will become increasingly isolated as they fail to evolve in response to the new conditions, replaced by new systems that do.

The Opportunities That Impact Investing Brings

Throughout this book, we describe the disruption that impact investing for blended value is causing. For us, this disruption is exciting. What a privilege to live in a moment of fundamental transformation as people remove the blinders of habit and stale conviction. Opportunities abound for the innovators who can see clearly what is happening around us and build the enterprises and systems for the future.

In this book, you will meet some of these innovators:

- An entrepreneur building a successful business that identifies and structures impact investments for family offices and foundations

- An investment banker harnessing international capital markets to accelerate the vaccination of children in Africa

- A social entrepreneur raising rural incomes across the world by making loans that connect isolated farmers to global supply chains

- A policy advocate creating a new corporate form that allows a business to honor its social purpose while pursuing profit

- A graduate student rejecting the advice of his parents and professors to make money first and worry about the world later, and instead applying his business skills to address social challenges from the beginning of his career

You will also learn alongside these and other pioneers as they explore the principles and approaches that will flourish in this new world. By bringing together two previously separate worlds, impact investing is forging unlikely collaboration and friendships between philanthropists and venture capitalists, between investment banks and nonprofit organizations, between wealth advisors and their clients.

We hope they inspire you to join their ranks. But we do not assume you will necessarily quit your job and jump head-first to swim alongside these pioneers fording rivers into unexplored terrain. Understanding how the current of impact investing is poised to change the world is relevant even if you stay on the shore. This is your world, and you will have a stake in it regardless of where you live or how much you have to invest.

Devastation or Renewal?

First taking shape out of the sustainable investing and divestment campaigns of the 1970s and 1980s, the waves of socially responsible investing have begun to alter how executives in many industries engage with customers, regulators, and society. Impact investing grew out of the conditions these waves created and has the potential to be even more disruptive.

Currents can create devastation when they wash ashore, but they can also be forces for renewal. The annual flooding of the Nile Delta has brought sustenance to millions of people for centuries. And the pioneers of wave energy are turning ocean currents into a sustainable source of renewable power.

What will result from the current of impact investing? Will it undermine support for philanthropy and draw resources away from more productive investment? Will it bring the renewal and energy that enable us to tackle the seemingly impossible challenges we face? Or will it just fade as so many other currents have in the past before making much difference at all?

The answer will come from how we direct the current and prepare to harness its power. We will need to see the ripples for the mighty current they can become. Actors on both sides of the checkbook—investors and those receiving investment—need to recognize we are all part of something potentially more powerful than we can be alone. This is easy to affirm but difficult to put into practice. Many individual participants are only beginning to understand the full extent to which they share a basic set of approaches and values that unite them in this newly emerging capital market. We will be called on to take the leap of faith that supporting this new industry will serve us and the rest of the world better than preserving our small niches.

We must also collectively resist the danger that impact investing will become merely a marketing tool. The resonance of the term is its greatest threat. Tempted by the good intentions of clients, institutional asset managers may co-opt the spirit of impact investing by structuring investment product that appears to create value but avoids the hard work required to generate more than just nice stories with pictures.

And just like a flowing river, the current of impact investing will create opportunity that we must organize to capture. New laws, new systems for measuring value, new capital markets' innovators, new approaches to cultivating leadership: these will be the hydropower stations and the sustainable fisheries that convert this current into a powerful force. To build them will require all of us to abandon our assumptions and our self-righteousness and to collaborate with people and institutions we may have comfortably ignored in the past.

The Power of Capital

We have seen the true power of capital:

- It is the green of heavy banana bunches on the slopes of Mt. Kenya in the dry season, watered with irrigation equipment funded by a microloan.

- It is the anticipation on the face of the woman on Chicago's South Side who tapped a local community development fund to launch her bakery.

- It is the professional pride of a foundation program officer whose investment in an educational services company in New York has helped provide teachers with the tools they need to raise students' performance to heights that grants alone never could.

- It is the satisfaction of a family in India that has just moved out of a slum into a new brick home purchased from an equity-backed, low-income-housing developer.

- It is the light shining through the window of a home in rural Nicaragua that is powered by a micro-hydropower plant built with investment from a renewable energy fund.

- It is the investment banker in London signing the closing documents for a new fund that will channel client capital into businesses that provide affordable, essential services to poor people.

These are the realities we can create when we remove our blinders and realize the potential for blended value all around us. There are some clear paths and promising trails but no one way to go or right way to execute the strategy. Through this book, we invite you to come with us, to see something of the terrain, to explore parts of this promising landscape and to cut your own path.

Chapter 2

IMPACT INVESTING IN INTERNATIONAL DEVELOPMENT

Of Cows, Calling, and Capital

A farmer awakes before dawn near Kinangkop, Kenya, on the edge of the Great Rift Valley. She walks outside her mud-walled hut to milk her two cows. From the light of her kerosene lantern, she sees that one of her cows is sick and realizes she will need to contact a vet.

Five years earlier, she would have had to walk along a dirt path to wait along a dirt road to catch a mini-bus taxi into the nearest town. Once there, she would have sought out the local vet, perhaps waiting hours for him to return from a house call. If she was lucky, she would have cash to cover his visit. More likely, she would need to negotiate an expensive payment plan. If she could not afford his services, she would go home and pray her cow became healthier. A few weeks later, when the monthly cash supplement arrived from her son in Nairobi via long-distance taxi or Western Union, she might have had enough left over after paying the money transfer fee to pay the vet. His service would be just as expensive but too late to save her cow.

But now her world has changed. When the farmer sees her cow is sick, she takes out the mobile phone her son brought her from

Nairobi. She checks the balance in her mobile money account and then sends a text message to her son, who transfers ten dollars into her account. She then sends a text message to the vet explaining the problem with the cow. The vet arrives later that morning, carrying the medicine he predicted he would need. After he injects the cow, the farmer sends a text message transferring the payment of ten dollars for this service from her mobile phone to his. A text message appears on the vet's phone confirming payment. In the meantime, a farmer from a neighboring village has sent a text seeking the vet's advice. He puts his phone in his medical bag, gets back on his motorcycle, and rides off. Within weeks, the cow heals fully, having received the medicine when she needed it. The farmer's investment in her health paid back.

This illustrative story is just one vignette in the multifaceted history of the global mobile phone revolution. The potential of mobile phones to support development is now widely recognized. And the business potential of a product that has won over hundreds of millions customers in Africa and generates billions in revenue annually seems obvious now. But it was not obvious in 1998 when a Sudanese engineer named Mohammed Ibrahim sought to build a cell phone company targeting sub-Saharan Africa. Despite his track record as an engineer and business builder, mainstream investors across Europe ignored his pitch for start-up capital, wary of investing in a cell phone company in a region where few people had ever heard a dial tone.[1]

But one investor was different. The London-based Commonwealth Development Corporation (CDC), which operates under a mandate to make private equity investments in emerging markets, had been investing in Africa for more than fifty years. In 1998, it invested $22.5 million in Ibrahim's company. It subsequently provided three more rounds of expansion capital as the company, eventually named Celtel Africa, expanded to more than 6 million customers and annual revenue exceeding $1 billion. In 2005, Celtel Africa sold itself to Kuwaiti mobile operator MTC for

$3.4 billion, in a deal still lauded by many as the greatest exit in African private equity. The CDC's 9.3 percent stake was valued at more than $300 million.

Ibrahim became a billionaire. Like many newly minted billionaires before him, he set up a foundation, in his case most famously creating the Ibrahim Prize, a $5 million award to promote non-corrupt practices by African leaders. But he also used his windfall to create Satya Capital, a private equity fund focused solely on making investments in Africa.

The next Mo Ibrahim with a vision for building a multinational company in Africa will find at least one door that is more welcoming than she might have found in the past.

Investing for Development

A complex set of actions and interactions by many people operating across the private sector and government were required for the story of the cow and her owner to end happily. One crucial element, the timely investment CDC made into Celtel, exemplifies how important impact investing can be to efforts to promote economic development in places like Kenya. Development-focused investment has shaped sectors ranging from agriculture, to healthcare, to financial services, in countries from Brazil to Burkina Faso to Bangladesh.

Impact investing for development grew out of the recognition that donations to governments and nonprofits alone will not spur long-term economic growth and poverty alleviation. Initially governments and multilateral organizations pioneered this approach to complement their official donor aid programs. Investing for development impact is now evolving into a complex ecosystem of public and private endeavors. Impact investment is moving into poor countries through a diverse array of financial institutions and investment products—from private equity firms, to loan guarantee companies, to bond-issuing special investment vehicles. Investment banks such as Goldman Sachs and Morgan Stanley have entered the field. So too have relatively new philanthropists such as George Soros and Bill Gates, who are increasingly making use of impact investments to complement their grant-making activities.

While impact investing for development has brought capital to cash-starved businesses in poor countries and innovations to global capital markets, it has also proven complicated to measure and manage. The rapid flow of foreign investment into many developing countries previously ignored in the backwaters of the global capital markets has troubled the waters of impact investing for development. Measuring what constitutes an investment with true impact is difficult in a world in which many people without development intent are making investments in poor countries. And as we discuss in this chapter, in the wake of spectacular initial public offerings and public controversy, determining how much profit is enough is increasingly contentious.

Engaging Private Investors to Complement Government

Impact investing for development began as a tool for governments that realized donations alone could not spur sustainable poverty alleviation in poor countries. After World War II, the victorious Allied powers set up the International Bank for Reconstruction and Development, precursor to what is now the World Bank. This entity made loans primarily to the governments of Europe and Japan (what we prefer to think of as intergovernmental impact investments).[2] Sixty years later, the World Bank group annually makes more than $60 billion in grants and highly concessionary loans to very poor governments and market rate loans to less poor governments.[3]

The World Bank's founding governments soon recognized that private companies also needed investment support, and the bank thus launched the International Finance Corporation (IFC) in 1956 to invest directly in the private sector. In recent years, IFC has invested approximately $10 billion annually into projects in more than one hundred countries.

Following the example of the World Bank and IFC, similar development finance institutions have proliferated. Many regional multilateral banks, such as the Inter-American Development Bank, have opened up to investment in private companies. National governments have also embraced impact investing through state-financed investment funds, typically referred to as bilateral development finance institutions. These range from the British CDC, created in 1948 to promote industry and agriculture in the capital-starved parts of the British colonies, to the $5 billion China-Africa Development Fund, launched in 2007 to capitalize African investment projects, though primarily for Chinese companies and joint ventures.

In the United States, the Overseas Private Investment Corporation (OPIC), created in 1971, pioneered political risk insurance to facilitate U.S. company investments in emerging markets and now commits billions in insurance, loan guarantees, and lending capital. In 2011, OPIC launched its first program to provide low-interest loans explicitly to impact investing fund managers. (Table 2.1 shows the prominent development finance institutions.) The traditional donor arm of the U.S. government's international development effort, the U.S. Agency for International Development, has also taken advantage of a tool of impact investment, setting up the Development Credit Authority in 2000. This authority provides loan guarantees, mostly to encourage banks in poor countries to lend to targeted groups such as poor farmers. In its first ten years, approximately two hundred guarantees in sixty-two countries unlocked $1.8 billion in lending.

Table 2.1. Top Five Development Finance Institutions, by Capitalization, 2010

Institution	Total Capital ($ billion)	New Disbursements, 2010 ($ billion)	Year Established
International Finance Corporation (multilateral)	61	7	1956
FMO (Netherlands Development Finance Company)	7.8	1.4	1970
DEG (German Investment Corporation)	7.2	1.6	1962
Overseas Private Investment Corporation (United States)	7.1	2.4	1971
Commonwealth Development Corporation (United Kingdom)	3.8 (2009)	0.5 (2009)	1948

Note: Disbursement and assets in dollars are approximations based on average exchange rates for FMO, DEG, and the Commonwealth Development Corporation, which account in euros and British pounds.

Private Philanthropists Entering the Field

Impact investing for development is no longer just a public sector game. For today's private philanthropists, their billions of charitable dollars are tiny compared to the vast capital flowing from international donors and, perhaps more important, international and local capital markets. Against this reality, some are increasingly attracted to impact investing as a new tool to amplify their capital and take advantage of this operating context.

Some donors are developing for-profit investment funds to complement their international development grant making. For many, this approach grows out of their personal experience of the power of for-profit business models. Financier George Soros has set up the Soros Economic Development Fund, an investment vehicle committing up to $200 million to impact investments. E-Bay founder Pierre Omidyar has committed almost $500 million through his "philanthropic investment firm," Omidyar Network, with an almost even mix between grants and impact investments. And the Aga Khan Development Fund, the private investment arm of the economic development network associated with the leader of the Ismaili Muslims, has for decades pursued a business-based approach to promoting development. Portfolio companies in Africa and Asia generate more than $1.5 billion in annual revenues, with profits ploughed back into further investment.

Some of these impact investors are not idly waiting for market opportunities to emerge; instead, they are moving into frontier markets and emerging industry segments not yet ripe for mainstream investment and creating new fund management companies where none exist. In 2008, Soros, Omidyar Network, and Google.org jointly invested $17 million to launch SONG, an investment fund in India focused on investing in small- and medium-sized companies. And where private philanthropists do not find companies that serve their development goals to invest in, they are building them from scratch. For example, British philanthropist Lord Sainsbury capitalized Aquifer Ltd., an agriculture-focused investment company in Mozambique to which his charitable trust has committed $50 million. These investors are also using loan guarantees to unlock substantial private investment, a tool they have borrowed from the development finance institutions.

Here Come the Investment Bankers

Investment bankers are also entering the impact investing arena. Mainstream behemoths and entrepreneurial boutiques across the financial services sector are providing products and services to impact investors focused on international development.

Goldman Sachs, certainly not known as a development bank, helped structure and market the International Finance Facility for Immunisation (IFFIm), a multibillion-dollar bond issue that

provides front-loaded finance for emerging market vaccine campaigns. Securing sovereign guarantees from seven countries, the
facility launched in 2006 with a AAA credit rating and was placed
with institutional investors from Germany to Japan by Goldman's
bankers.

One year after the launch of IFFIm, Goldman's rival, Morgan Stanley, joined microfinance boutique bank BlueOrchard in
placing the first rated microfinance bond offering with European
institutional investors, raising more than $100 million for micro-
finance banks in twelve countries from Nicaragua to Cambodia.
And despite the market downturn in 2008, impact investment
banking specialist ShoreBank International raised a $62 million
bond offering that year to capitalize the expansion into East Africa
of the Bangladeshi microfinance leader BRAC.

Challenges to Integrating Performance

Pioneering impact investors are scouring developing markets for
the next great investment that can generate the kind of profits
and social impact of CDC's investment in Celtel mobile phones in
Africa. This is not easy. As if making traditional development assistance work was not hard enough, impact investing faces additional
and unique challenges. Beyond the investors' usual challenge to
source and manage deals, impact investors must also ask:

- What business model works best to ensure a fund manager
  will make the most productive investments that generate
  the most blended value?

- How can an investor know her capital is targeted to where
  it's needed, and not just where it's easiest to invest?

- How will we know when an investment is in fact an impact
  investment?

Defining the Business Model

The core promise of impact investing for development is that we can marry the incentives and discipline of private investment to the passion and purpose of development aid. That sounds all well and good, but how do we create a sustainable organizational structure?

Many of the early development-oriented impact investment funds were linked closely to the government aid agencies that capitalized them. As the histories of FMO and CDC exemplify (detailed later "Marrying Profit and Purpose: Happily Ever After?"), approaching investment with the mentality of a donor agency has often led to slow-footed decision making. Politically motivated investment mandates have also proven to be financially unsustainable in the long run.

In response to the challenges of these government-run business models, private sector fund management structures are becoming increasingly common. These promise to harness the scaling capacity and incentives that come from enabling management teams and private investors to receive an appropriate level of profit from the fund's success. Actis, a leading private fund manager, actually spun out of the old CDC (the firm that made the initial investment in Celtel). The Swiss development agency spun out its investment arm in a management buyout in 2005. Microfinance fund managers are also entering the broader impact investment for development space. Bamboo Finance, a for-profit venture capital fund, spun out of pioneering microfinance asset manager BlueOrchard. Start-up funds are also proliferating. One of many examples, the Sierra Investment Fund, was founded in 2006 by a former private sector consultant to the local United Nations Development Programme. It makes equity investments that, among other benefits, have helped revive Sierra Leone's ice production, crucial for the many families that rely on income from fishing.

Marrying Profit and Purpose: Happily Ever After?

The rocky histories of the Netherland-based FMO and the British CDC typify the challenge of integrating the development mission and the profit imperative for impact investors in emerging markets.

FMO's History

Like many other bilateral development finance institutions, FMO began as a fund to capitalize the foreign operations of companies from its own country (in the case of FMO, to provide an investment lifeline to Dutch firms in 1970 after their expulsion from Indonesia). FMO took on a broader development mandate in 1977 when it began investing in non-Dutch companies. The early FMO, however, failed to balance development and financial sustainability, investing in high-risk projects and incurring politically untenable losses.

A reorganization in 1991 sought to redress this imbalance by partially privatizing the company and allowing outside investors to take an ownership stake. With the Dutch government providing financial backing, FMO achieved a AAA credit rating that has allowed it to borrow from capital markets to support its operations. Its owners are the Dutch government, Dutch banks, and institutional investors. Completing the transition from government agency to international finance player, FMO secured a bank license from Dutch regulators in 2008.

CDC's History

The CDC has engendered its own controversies through its transition from an agent of the British colonial administration to an independently run development finance institution. By 1995, the

CDC began funding its operations entirely from its own earnings. As the private equity industry matured and developed clearer business models for aligning incentives of managers and investors, CDC sought potential advantages in stepping out of the fund management business. Instead it now backs independent fund managers to invest on its behalf. In 2001 it entered into a joint venture with the Norwegian development finance institution Norfund to create an independent fund manager, Aureos Capital, to manage its small- and medium-enterprise portfolio. With the launch of Actis Capital three years later through a CDC management buyout of the large-scale private emerging markets portfolio, the CDC exited fund management. The CDC is now an independent company (though wholly owned by the British aid agency), placing its approximately $4 billion with sixty-five fund managers in seventy-one countries in 2010.

As in the Netherlands, finding a practical and politically feasible balance of profit, development, and politics has not been easy. The Actis privatization engendered controversy in 2007 when opposition politicians criticized the government for selling Actis to its managers for only £373,000. With Actis managing more than $2 billion by 2007 and reaping the benefits of the lucrative Celtel initial public offering among other investments, the sales price recalled other controversial privatization deals.

Actis employees proudly brandish the company logo, "The Positive Power of Capital." Their critics lambaste them as money-grubbing, globe-trotting investment bankers. Who is right? And which is better for development: the old CDC of government bureaucrats or the new Actis of private investment professionals? Without standards for measuring the social impact of investment and clear benchmarks to compare performance, the answer still says more about the convictions of the judge than the facts we can bring to the case.

Many similar initiatives that originate within private philanthropic organizations are spinning out as commercial operations.
One prominent example is the recent trajectory of Growth Finance,
commonly referred to as GroFin. Initially incubated by the Shell
Foundation with in-kind subsidies and low-cost capital, GroFin has
become a leading force in the small- and medium-enterprise lending sector across Africa, now managing more than $250 million. It
is building an operational base and expertise that could ultimately
see it become a viable investment for institutional money managers seeking exposure to African small-scale debt. And nonprofit
investment pioneers Root Capital, Acumen Fund, and E+Co. are
similarly considering spinning out more commercially oriented
fund operations.

Unfortunately, the benefits of the private sector fund management model can also obscure a fund's focus on generating
development outcomes. The potential to share personally in the
fund's profits can distract managers from the social mission.
The institutional imperative to meet investing targets can similarly skew management incentives. It should come as no surprise
that the average deal sizes of Aureos and Actis Capital have
increased substantially since their management buyout (given how
much more difficult it is for fund managers to profit from smaller
investments). These challenges are spurring calls for standardized metrics and impact reporting practices, along with efforts to
draft principles of practice for both social entrepreneurs and impact
investors in order to help ensure that those who talk the impact talk
are actually walking the impact walk.

Ensuring Investment Capital Targets Development

Figuring out whether an investment in an emerging market is
profitable is relatively simple: read the audited financial state-
ment. But impact investors also need to know if the investment is
generating development outcomes. Having faced this issue for
longer than most of the rest of us, the development-focused

impact investment industry has developed two approaches that are worth considering for their more general applicability: the principle of additionality and the practice of impact measurement.

The Principle of Additionality: Don't Be Redundant

Simply put, the principle of additionality calls on impact investors to target businesses that would not otherwise be capitalized by private investors. This may seem like an obvious principle and an easy one to apply. But often the most capital-starved countries, sectors, and institutions are capital starved for a reason: they are the most difficult ones in which to make financially profitable investments. Investors motivated to focus on financial returns may well shy away from these difficult environments, yet these are often the places where impact investment is most needed.

In international development finance, additionality takes a multilayered and evolving form, focused around three questions:

- *Do you invest in an undercapitalized place?* Many investors seek additionality by committing to invest only in particularly poor countries or poor regions. The CDC in 2009 established a new investment policy mandating that 75 percent of investment must be in low-income countries and 50 percent in Africa, thereby limiting investments in Eastern Europe and increasingly middle-income countries such as Brazil and India. The IFC has also committed to a "frontier country strategy" that is steering capital away from more commercially attractive markets and substantially increasing its exposure in Africa. A relatively small but extreme example of this principle has been the launch of IFC SME Ventures, an investment fund targeting small companies (hence, "SME" in its name, signifying small and medium enterprises) in eight low-income emerging markets, including Sierra Leone,

Central Africa Republic, Bhutan, and Bangladesh. Entrepreneurs from any of these countries receiving $500,000 loans from the IFC through this fund will certainly be enjoying an unusual opportunity!

- *Do you invest in an undercapitalized sector?* Some impact investors also seek to achieve additionality through investments in undercapitalized sectors. Under this approach, investors increasingly target companies that provide basic services to poor communities, for example. Even in relatively well-off countries, these sectors could be undercapitalized by mainstream investors unconvinced that poor people can be reliable customers. Mexico-based IGNIA Fund typifies this focus on bottom-of-the-pyramid investment. Other impact investors target the missing middle, providing capital to medium-sized enterprises—companies that are too large to benefit from microfinance loans and too small to gain the attention of mainstream investors. Without capital, small and medium enterprises cannot become the jobs-creation engine, source of innovation, and general economic force they are in almost all rich countries. Highlighting the importance of this subsector, impact investors and other organizations targeting pro-development SMEs banded together to form the Aspen Network for Development Entrepreneurs in 2008 to coordinate this activity.

- *What asset class do you focus on?* Beyond targeting a specific geography or sector, some impact investors consider the asset class they target as an important component of additionality. Debt capital is becoming more readily available in many poor countries. Therefore, some impact investors argue that development-focused impact investors should provide the equity finance that is still harder to come by. For example, European development finance institutions pride themselves for putting half of their capital to work in private equity investments, and private investors, such as the U.K.'s Sainsbury Trust, are similarly focusing on providing precious equity to complement increasingly available debt.

Although these tactics are useful to inform the debate about additionality, they do not resolve it. Lessons from the microfinance industry are instructive to this additionality debate. In a widely discussed paper in 2007, the nonprofit organization MicroRate argued that given the entry of private capital into the microfinance industry, public development finance investments were not just superfluous but worse because they crowd out private investment.[4] The authors argued that most of these investments went to top-tier microfinance institutions and accused investors of "trophy lending" to fulfill political rather than development objectives.

This argument is not new (and is not limited to microfinance). For decades, institutions such as the IFC have steered capital to regions and countries where the absorptive capacity of the private sector made investing relatively easier. Until 1998, IFC investment tended to follow in proportion to a country's per capita income and the presence of private finance flows—not the other way around, as we would expect for a fund focused purely on its development potential.

What is new is the amount of private investment capital now flowing into many countries where development finance institutions used to operate without competition. Especially since the Goldman Sachs research department popularized the phrase BRIC in 2001 to highlight the distinct economic prospects of Brazil, Russia, India, and China among emerging markets, private capital has flooded in. Riding this wave, private and public members of the Emerging Market Private Equity Association manage more than $500 billion in investment capital. Within the context of these increasing private capital flows, what does it take for an impact investor to be truly additional?

Innovations in Integrating Profit with Purpose in Emerging Markets

Across public and private business models, in increasingly crowded markets like Brazil and frontier markets such as the Gambia, impact investors are pioneering new approaches to integrating the pursuit of profit with purpose. These innovations break free from traditional understandings of the separate realm of investor and philanthropists. They show how making investments alongside subsidies and grants can unlock greater total value to shareholders and society. They also point out the challenges and tensions that impact investors face in applying these innovations in new settings with new ambitions.

Providing Technical Assistance

Even the most diligent impact investors will be hard-pressed to make productive investments unless they have strong entrepreneurs with good business prospects to back. But without investment that can generate economic growth, an entrepreneurial class is unlikely to emerge and business prospects will remain dim. Some impact investors are dealing with this chicken-and-egg problem by providing what they refer to as technical assistance alongside investment capital. Technical assistance can entail helping an entrepreneur prepare a more viable business plan or providing accounting services or strategic consulting advice for investees.

In mainstream venture capital, supporting entrepreneurs in this way is part of the work that private sector investors undertake. But in many emerging markets, potential deals are scarce and small enough that an investment fund cannot afford to offer these services as part of its investment practice. Philanthropic or governmental subsidies for technical assistance are therefore an important complement to investment capital in making impact investments work in poor countries.

In deciding where to put their capital, impact investors must navigate a complex set of technical assistance setups. Which subsidies create highly leveraged development outcomes? Which ones just mask the inefficiency of an investor? There are no easy answers but substantial work is underway to understand what technical assistance is most effective and efficient.

Creating Social Incentive–Based Compensation

Greed might not be good, but it exists and it motivates. Rather than hide from this reality, how can we harness it? For-profit fund managers will be a central part of the impact investing story in emerging markets. But they struggle to resist the temptation to withdraw from markets and sectors where profitable deals are hard to find, even if they could generate substantial social good. Can we change this tendency by changing management incentives (without trying to change human nature)?

Still in its infancy, the concept of tying fund manager compensation to social outcomes is an exciting innovation. This will become easier when social impact reporting standards become widespread and facilitate performance benchmarking. Until then, some investors are creating more rudimentary fund-specific targets to keep their investment managers' eyes on the social impact ball. Set up by, among others, the IFC and Gates Foundation in 2009, the $100 million Africa Health Fund, for example, pegs fund manager compensation to attainment of verifiable social targets in its investment portfolio. True, this approach does not claim to measure development outcomes. Instead, it uses simple proxy metrics such as deal size and customer income levels. Still, it represents an encouraging commitment by the investors and fund manager to integrate social performance into financial incentives.

Creating and Implementing an Integrated Reporting System

Measuring blended value is difficult under the best of circumstances. It is even more so for an investment fund operating in an emerging market where even rudimentary financial statements are hard to find. But how then will impact investors maximize their contributions to development?

The socially responsible investment movement has offered one overriding guideline for investors: "Do no harm." The additionality principles add a second: "Don't be redundant." Is any investor who follows both principles good for development?

Unfortunately, little evidence exists to answer this question. Instead, most government and private investors have traditionally accepted on faith that profitable investment is good for development. This seems to make sense. After all, investments in profitable, law-abiding companies can create jobs, increase the tax base, and cause the economy to grow. Many investors tend to resist running academically rigorous studies or engaging in regular econometric review of their social performance. They are busy enough trying to make businesses succeed in these difficult markets, they say, echoing the business owners, who similarly resist demands to measure social performance.

But with purely profit-motivated investors crowding into the traditional domains of impact investors in emerging markets, governments and private investors are increasingly seeking to understand whether their impact investments are generating something more than just financial return. To be honest, few standards have emerged for measuring and reporting the social impact of investment deals. Social impact reports are still largely self-reported and anecdotal. Nevertheless, they are becoming standard issue for development-oriented investors and fund managers.

A set of initiatives is now underway to build a more stable infrastructure for measuring the social (and development) impact of investment. These include the Global Impact Investing Rating System (GIIRS), the Impact Reporting and Investment Standards (on which GIIRS is built), and the SROI Network. All now have emerging markets-focused components to their global networks (we discuss them in Chapter Eight).

Investors and fund managers are increasingly looking to create social management information systems to assist them not only tracking performance and impacts but also assessing the relative value of the impacts they generate. A common standard for measuring the social impact of investment will be necessary for impact investing to complement aid and mainstream investment in generating sustainable and equitable economic growth.

These innovations in targeting investment, measuring development outcomes, and aligning the business model of fund managers with incentives to make money and promote development are important innovations, if initial steps, in harnessing the power of impact investing to contribute to the cause of ending poverty in our lifetimes.

Defying Oversimplification

The story at the start of this chapter of how a sick cow in Kenya was healed weaves together a whirl of history. Impact investing has been part of this whirl. Without an impact investor willing to back Mohammed Ibrahim in his dream of bringing mobile phones to Africa, perhaps the farmer would not now own an affordable and reliable cell phone in her village on the edge of the Great Rift Valley.

A powerful example of the potential of impact investing, the story also defies oversimplification. Impact investing capital may have kick-started the mobile revolution in Africa and helped put a phone in the farmer's hand. But the technology that allowed her to receive an instant money transfer from her son and to pay the vet has its genesis in a more traditional development tool. Largely lost in the hype of the runaway success of the money-transfer business was the approximately $1.5 million grant that the British Department for International Development (DFID) awarded mobile giant Vodafone in late 2003 to develop M-Pesa.

Whether taxpayer-supported development aid should enable multinational companies to develop profitable products is a debate for another book. Regardless, this detail highlights the continuing impact that donor aid still has, even in a world of substantial private capital flows.

Whatever your political tendencies, we hope it is clear that effective international development initiatives increasingly need to engage important private sector actors with greater savvy. As large companies and private investors move capital, ideas, and products around the world at an unmatched pace and scale, impact investing for international development offers an exciting and demonstrated opportunity to harness the power of these capital flows and more efficiently fill the gaps that remain.

Nowhere else has both the promise and the pitfalls of impact investing for development been made clearer than in the modern microfinance industry. In its forty-year arc from obscure development innovation, to capital markets' darling, to lightning rod of controversy, we can trace the contours of the likely development of the broader impact investing industry. The next chapter explores this arc and its implications in detail.

Chapter 3

MICROFINANCE

Still the Best Brand
in Development?

The Fruit Seller and the Office Worker

In London in July 2006, an office worker received her pay stub. It noted that her employer had contributed £400 to her pension fund managed by a local institutional investor.

A world away, in Cuzco, Peru, an *ambulante* (fruit seller) sets up in the local outdoor market. She had returned the previous night from a trip to Lima where she had used a loan of one thousand nuevo sols (approximately three hundred dollars) to purchase the fruit she would be selling in her stall that day.

These two women never met, but they were connected nevertheless. Through global capital markets, the savings of the London employee contributed to the capital that the fruit seller borrowed. Specifically, the British fund that invested the office worker's pension bought bonds from Morgan Stanley issued to fund twenty-two banks in thirteen countries, including Mibanco in Peru, which provided the three hundred dollar loan.

The following year, a similar bond offering raised an additional $110 million, this time with a rating from Standard and Poor's.

Though they may not know it, bank customers and pension-ers from Europe to the United States are now being paid to make their savings available to cobblers, tailors, and women sup-porting their families by selling basic goods in makeshift stores and open-air markets from Peru to Cambodia.

This story illustrates the global phenomenon of microfinance, an industry that by 2010 served more than 100 million clients with more than $50 billion in loans. How a set of unrelated experiments in the 1970s grew into a global force that could successfully link the savings of the British worker to the Peruvian microentrepreneur offers important lessons for the broader impact investing industry—as do the tensions that integrating these social and economic forces have created.

The $50 Billion Phenomenon

While specific definitions and methodologies may vary, the basic premise of microfinance is simple: lend small amounts of money (typically less than a thousand dollars and sometimes as little as fifty dollars) to poor borrowers who often lack any assets to pledge as security for the loan.

The idea of microfinance is not new. Various efforts to provide basic lending services to poor people have included the Irish Loan Fund set up by pastor Jonathan Swift (author of *Gulliver's Travel*) in the early eighteenth century, the German rural banking cooper-atives a century later, the West African network of small-scale *susu* lenders, and various credit unions and savings cooperatives around the world. Building on this legacy, the modern microfinance indus-try emerged from a cluster of initially unrelated experiments in the 1970s in Bangladesh, India, and Brazil.

In different ways, these experiments upended conventional wisdom about how to run a bank. They revealed that people (especially women) without material assets to pledge as collateral could be reliable borrowers if they borrowed as part of a group responsible for each member's repayment. Peer pressure substituted for the threat of losing pledged collateral to induce borrowers to repay their loans. The group members' knowledge of their peers substituted for credit reports or loan officers to determine who was creditworthy.

Modern microfinance was initially a donor-funded development project. These experiments attracted initial grants from private foundations and governments—the traditional backers of development aid and relief projects. At this point in the story, microfinance could have ended up as another in a long list of development innovations that seemed promising to some but ultimately never reached substantial scale or impact. But as word spread about the success these organizations were having, similar initiatives rose across the developing world, and some of the early pioneers grew substantially. Over succeeding years, nonprofit and government-run microfinance operations proliferated.

Eventually donor funding allowed pioneers to refine the operating model enough that some microfinance institutions could not only lend sustainably but also make substantial profits. Over the past ten years, these lucrative microfinance businesses began to attract commercial attention and investment capital. Commercial microfinance is now a vast industry engaging an array of institutions ranging from mainstream investment banks like Morgan Stanley and Citigroup, to large pension funds, to specialist bankers and advisors, and to government-sponsored development finance institutions.

For many people, microfinance is now the flagship of how for-profit investment that is managed effectively can be put to work to address poverty productively. Others, however, see it as just another way in which investors and greedy businesses exploit poor people. But for all its success and controversy, microfinance is an archetype of impact investment for multiple returns.

Managing the Brand

At least until the turmoil of 2010, microfinance had been arguably the most successful recent brand in international development. It enjoyed a rare appeal across the political spectrum, seen as a business and market-led approach that the right can embrace and a tool for empowering low-income women that inspires the left. This brand connotation has underpinned wide support. Over thirty-five years, an estimated $15 billion in direct grants and subsidized loans has flowed from government donor agencies and foundations to the wide range of microfinance businesses and nonprofit organizations. This brand value has, for example:

- Enabled kiva.org, to raise more than $200 million in no-interest loans through its online platform that allows individual lenders to make loans to borrowers in poor countries.

- Allowed ResponsAbility, the Swiss-based asset manager, to raise more than $1 billion primarily from wealthy Europeans for its microfinance funds

- Helped motivate Citibank to form its global microfinance unit in 2005

- Spurred the campaign to award microfinance pioneer Muhammad Yunus the Nobel Peace Prize in 2006

The successful transition of microfinance from donor-funded niche innovation to international phenomenon resulted from collaboration among media-savvy industry leaders. Though his Grameen Bank was neither the first nor the largest of the modern microfinance lenders, Yunus served as the international face of this new brand-building agenda, quietly charismatic as he tirelessly gave speeches and sat for interviews, often in traditional Bangladeshi dress. A 1989 profile of Grameen on the U.S. news show 60 *Minutes* ushered in a new era of heightened attention to microfinance strategies as an effective tool in addressing poverty.

Eight years later, with Yunus's support, the first Microcredit Summit Campaign meeting brought 2,900 people to Washington, D.C., and launched the attention-grabbing goal of reaching 100 million people by 2005 with credit to support self-employment or small business growth. The summit helped galvanize industry-wide advocacy and gave impetus to the campaign to have the United Nations declare an International Year of Microcredit, which it did in 2005. The following year, the industry reached the international advocacy pinnacle with Yunus awarded the Nobel Peace Prize.

Collective Leadership to Build Industry Infrastructure

Through this brand-building work, the poor woman bettering her lot through microenterprise has become an iconic image of microfinance in the popular imagination. But as important as individual initiative may be, collective leadership has also been crucial to microfinance's success. A spectacular initial public offering (IPO) or Nobel Prize for a pioneer tends to obscure the importance of this less glamorous but crucial work. Those seeking to draw broader lessons from the evolution of microfinance need to consider the full story standing behind the most visible successes. In the case of microfinance, collective leadership has spurred the development of critical industry infrastructure such as dedicated ratings agencies, targeted donor groups, advisory services, data depositories, advocacy organizations, training centers, and peer networks.

While bold experiments in the early 1970s kick-started the modern microfinance movement, in the 1980s networks formed to help link and promote these experiments internationally. Women's World Banking, an international nonprofit network connecting thirty-nine microfinance institutions that focuses on ensuring women have access to microfinance, grew out of an international women's summit in 1980, and the Small Enterprise Education and Promotion Network was launched five years later, primarily to enable practitioners to share experiences and lessons. In Latin America, regional organizations with operations in multiple countries increased the industry's visibility and proved critical to its expansion.

These networks laid the groundwork for broader infrastructure development and industry expansion in the 1990s. The launch in 1995 of the Consultative Group to Assist the Poorest (CGAP) brought together donors from multilateral finance institutions such as the World Bank, national development finance institutions, and private foundations. CGAP has proven instrumental as a coordinating mechanism and fulcrum for industry leadership.

By consolidating donors and industry leaders under one organization, with an annual budget at times exceeding $20 million, CGAP has achieved the critical mass needed to identify gaps in the global industry infrastructure and fill them. To provide a central portal for information about the industry, CGAP launched the Microfinance Gateway, an online information resource for the global microfinance community. In 2002, CGAP helped facilitate the merger of two data projects to create the MIX Market, a data clearinghouse on financial performance of individual institutions that has underpinned subsequent investments by private investors. CGAP also helped spur the development of financial ratings systems for microfinance, launched a fund to subsidize information system investments, and created Microfin, a business planning support tool. The industry group has partnered with research arms of established investment banks, such as Deutsche Bank and J.P. Morgan, to issue investor reports on topics ranging from long-term market sizing to equity valuation.

Together these collective action platforms and resources have enabled microfinance to become a coherent industry. Instead of working in isolation, professionals in one microfinance organization can benefit from the experience and networks of their peers. Research agendas are financed and executed. Talent markets are beginning to clear as young professionals can more easily chart a career path within the field of microfinance. In this way, success for one microfinance provider creates demonstration value that eases the path for the next.

Riding the Wave of Commercial Capital

With a strong brand and supporting networks and infrastructure, microfinance has rapidly expanded in scale and variety. But as impact investors are finding across geographies and subsectors (and as the other chapters in this book make clear) integrating doing good with doing well is not easy. The microfinance industry's success in engaging mainstream capital markets in the past decade has brought a disruptive current of both opportunity and controversy into the formerly quiet waters of nonprofit microfinance. The microfinance industry is still struggling to find its new center.

As proponents of microfinance commercialization have long hoped, the ability to raise debt and equity from the multitrillion-dollar global capital markets has liberated top microfinance institutions from exclusive reliance on the vagaries of philanthropy and government-backed finance. The $100 million deal that connected the British office worker and the Peruvian fruit seller in 2006 is only one example of this trend. It was followed in 2007 by a similar $110 million capital raise. International investors operating through more than one hundred microfinance investment vehicles invested more than $6.5 billion by the end of 2008, a figure that grew 35 percent that year, despite the collapse of mainstream credit markets.[1] Swiss-based funds ResponsAbility and BlueOrchard were both managing approximately $1 billion in their microfinance funds by 2010. Even venture capital funds are now active within microfinance, most notably with Silicon Valley venture capital legend Sequoia Capital's entry into the Indian microfinance market with a series of equity investments into India's largest microfinance company, SKS, before its IPO in 2010.

Beyond capital, microfinance institutions can access an array of financial services now that banks are treating them as customers and not just charity cases. Citibank launched a global unit in 2005 dedicated to providing these services. In India, local financial services firms such as IFMR Capital are structuring bond placements and securitizations for microfinance institutions.

Without philanthropy, modern microfinance would not exist. But without this integration into the global investment system, microfinance would likely not have exceeded so spectacularly the Microcredit Summit's goal of extending microfinance to 100 million families. But at what price?

To some people, the industry has lost its way in pursuit of mainstream capital. They argue that profit-seeking investors distort the social purpose of the microfinance companies they back, whether with venture capital investment or through buying stock after an IPO. They also point out how access to global capital markets has created a segregated industry. The fifty largest and most savvy microfinance institutions, which are concentrated outside the poorest countries and regions, have access to investment resources and attention, while the many thousands of institutions that are too small or not profitable enough to meet commercial investment standards are largely ignored.[2] With scant evidence on social impact to resolve them, passionate discussions regarding the effects of commercial capital in microfinance fester.

For mainstream investors, debates about capital-raising strategies and growth take place in the business press and the boardroom. They are the concern of investment analysts and corporate strategists who assess the claims of competing business models and invest capital and resources accordingly. But as an impact investment, microfinance is about more than profits. Socially motivated private and public investors are making capital available to microfinance institutions at least partly because they believe this is in the long-term interest of poor people. Regulators consider the poverty-alleviating potential of microfinance when creating the rules that govern how it operates. Professionals are leaving their mainstream jobs to join microfinance operations and investment funds to pursue blended value in their own careers. And these debates are now taking place on the front pages of newspapers and the halls of governments. The implications are profound for the future not only of microfinance but also of impact investing more generally.

What Impact Investors Can Learn from Microfinance

As this brief tour of the evolution of modern microfinance shows, the industry has benefited from thoughtful collaboration and brand management. It has also encountered many challenges that increasingly will become commonplace in the broader impact investing field. The transition of microfinance from a donor-funded innovation to a capital-market-driven business has been particularly rocky, marked by private infighting and public controversy. These rifts highlight the danger of overselling the social impact of investment and underestimating the lingering skepticism that many people have about the moral legitimacy of for-profit businesses that sell basic services to poor people.

On an increasingly prominent stage, industry leaders are left to debate what microfinance is—a social innovation or a new business model for profitable investment—and who gets to determine its future.

Three questions in this debate are particularly relevant for the broader impact investing industry:

- Who controls the brand?

- How do we sustain collective leadership?

- How much can investment really contribute to ending poverty?

A Tale of Two IPOs

Just as the woman in an open market selling basic goods may be the archetypal image of microfinance, the initial public offering, with a triumphant company owner ringing the bell at a major investment exchange, may be the archetypal image of modern capitalism. The collision of these two iconic images, however, has proved combustible. With IPOs of microfinance companies in Mexico and India in recent years, simmering debate about the effects of profit and commercial investment in microfinance has boiled over, providing important lessons for the broader impact investing industry.

First, the Mexican microfinance bank Compartamos went public on the Mexican stock exchange in 2007. Its offering price was significantly enhanced by its consistent profits, strong growth prospects, and investor appetite for Mexican financial services stock. The initial listing, which valued the company at $1.5 billion, was oversubscribed thirteen times. Early private investors, who had invested $6 million between 1998 and 2000, saw the value of their investment grow 250 times.

The Compartamos IPO woke up institutional investors to the opportunity to invest in microfinance. After the IPO, we started noticing a new group showing up at our public speeches about impact investing. In addition to the usual development professionals and social enterprise enthusiasts, mainstream private equity investors and finance students had heard about Compartamos and wanted to know how they could get in on similar lucrative investment opportunities.

Then, in 2010, India's largest microfinance institution, SKS, went public on the Mumbai stock exchange. Aided in part by a series of investments beginning in 2007 from legendary U.S. venture capital firm Sequoia Capital, SKS had grown rapidly. By the time of the IPO, it had almost doubled its customer base in the previous year to more than 6.5 million people. The IPO raised $347 million from investors. Oversubscribed like Compartamos, the share price rallied, leading

SKS to reach a market capitalization of $2 billion in the weeks after the IPO.

The SKS IPO awakened the global media and Indian politicians to the great profits being made in microfinance. Consumer rights advocates pointed to the coercive claims processes and dishonest lending practices of some Indian microfinance institutions. Politicians and the media highlighted the contrast between reports of a spate of debt-induced suicides and the multimillion-dollar payday for the SKS founder and investors. In Andhra Pradesh state, the center of Indian microfinance, rapidly drafted regulation effectively shut down commercial microfinance.[4] By December, SKS's share price had dropped 50 percent.

With stories about the chaos in Andhra Pradesh making front-page news in the world's leading newspapers, we started fielding more frequent questions about whether making money selling basic products to poor people is in fact morally legitimate.[5] Board members in institutions considering a move into impact investing pointed to this controversy when asking us whether impact investing is really worth the reputational risk.

Before their spectacular IPOs, both Compartamos and SKS had started as donor-funded nonprofits. In its ten years as a nonprofit, between 1990 and 2000, Compartamos received $4.3 million in grants and a further $30 million in concessionary loans and guarantees from public development agencies. SKS's first institutional "investor" was the U.S. nonprofit Echoing Green Foundation, which awarded its founder a two-year fellowship in 1997. Both also benefited from a range of microfinance industry infrastructure, including management training and technical support. For example, the data collection efforts at CGAP enabled institutional investors to become more comfortable with their investment in the public offerings.[6]

From their similar origins as nonprofits, both subsequently attracted substantial commercial investment. To some people, this transformation was a triumph to celebrate. For the nonprofit network ACCION, which had helped Compartamos convert from a nongovernmental organization to a finance company in 2000 (and which made more than $100 million on its initial investment in Compartamos), the IPO was the clearest vindication that the strategy to support microfinance institutions could make profits for investors and therefore attract the billions of dollars needed for long-term growth. For others, however, the arrival of commercial investors in the halls of microfinance was a distressing signal that capitalism had corrupted a once-noble institution. After the IPO, Muhammed Yunus labeled Compartamos a new form of exploitative "moneylender."[7] In India, some politicians urged SKS customers to default on their loan repayments.

In the end, neither extreme position is accurate or useful. Undoubtedly the arrival of commercial capital in microfinance has

Who Controls the Brand?

With microfinance receiving increased attention as both a lucrative investment option and a powerful development innovation, the debate over how it should be perceived is also becoming increasingly contentious.

As the precursor of a challenge that will likely occur across the impact investing industry, microfinance leaders are splitting into two camps. From one corner, people see nonprofit microfinance as a tool for economic development aimed at reaching the poorest of the poor. They resist the intrusion of commercial capital that does not seek social return. They worry that greedy investors and business managers will exploit poor customers and undermine support for all microfinance operators among donors and politicians. In the other corner is a commercially focused group emphasizing the profitability of microfinance institutions as the linchpin to enable them to reach more customers more rapidly by tapping into global capital markets. They generally no longer emphasize the development potential of microfinance and worry that stories of poor women and social purpose could scare off mainstream investors.

greatly expanded the opportunity for microfinance to reach the many more millions of poor people who could benefit greatly from having access to small loans. It has also certainly created opportunities for greedy business owners to profit from exploiting poor customers.

The heated debate that has surrounded both IPOs will continue as impact investing takes new forms in areas beyond microfinance. These IPOs reveal the danger in overselling any impact investing as a silver bullet against poverty and highlight the need to work with the media and government regulators. How one company's business decisions can transform the reputation of the entire industry also points to the importance of better self-regulation and collaboration among industry leaders.

For those who are keeping score, Yunus is the increasingly adamant flag-bearer of the nonprofit approach, while ACCION, a leading microfinance advocate, and its affiliates, together with CGAP, make the best case for the commercially focused approach.

Credible data and analysis showing how commercial microfinance firms do or do not create development impact along with profits would help defuse this debate. So would clear evidence that more development-focused, nonprofit institutions create relatively more (or less) social good. These data could justify ongoing philanthropic support that steers resources away from other funding priorities or other innovative strategies. But the microfinance industry has in many ways been late to recognize the importance of measuring social impact. Initial social measures have focused on simple proxies for understanding development outcomes, such as the percentage of women borrowers and the average loan size—the assumption being that smaller loans represent better targeting to poor people. But no major academic study has yet been able to demonstrate a clear link between providing microfinance and long-term economic development.

In a roundabout way, the commercial successes of some microfinance investors have spurred efforts to measure and prove the social impact of microfinance because of the public controversies they have precipitated. CGAP has launched the Social Performance Taskforce to develop a standard set of measures for microfinance institutions to track and report. And for its part, Grameen has been promoting its Progress Out of Poverty Index. These and other efforts seek to go beyond simple customer profiling to examine the effect of microfinance on development outcomes.

The broader impact investing industry can mobilize now to avoid having to play a similar game of social measurement catch-up later. The microfinance industry's intellectual ice-breaking in the area of social impact measurement is creating open water that benefits other impact investors. The innovations we describe in Chapter Eight are a good start, and especially encouraging is the spirit of collaboration that many standard-setting activities currently benefit from. But sustained attention to impact measurement will be necessary to ensure the impact investing industry's long-term relevance.

How Do We Sustain Collective Leadership and Industry Infrastructure?

The recent growth in microfinance demonstrates the importance of leadership, coordination, and investment in public goods infrastructure, which are themes we explore in Part Two. But the dual nature of microfinance—an increasingly profitable activity for investors and a tool for pursuing multiple returns including economic development for poor people—has raised important questions about who should pay for and maintain this infrastructure. Whether the microfinance industry continues to sustain its infrastructure will have important implications for the development of impact investing over the coming years.

When microfinance was only a nonprofit development project focused on poverty alleviation, supporting this infrastructure with donations made sense. Hundreds of millions of dollars in government-funded dollars and private charity helped create the scaffolding for the microfinance industry. These subsidies helped build data platforms, ratings agencies, and coordination bodies, not to mention many of the leading microfinance institutions themselves. If microfinance becomes just another commercial business model, then its profit-seeking participants should figure out how to pay collectively for this infrastructure. That is what companies and investors in other industries do through trade associations, fee-for-service, and licensing business models.

But what if microfinance forges a new path between these two extremes? Highly profitable microfinance companies like Compartamos and SKS will be able to pay for collective infrastructure. But these companies will coexist with microfinance nonprofits that cannot afford to pay for these services; nevertheless, they can take advantage of them to create substantial social benefit. Should donors continue to spend precious philanthropic dollars on a microfinance sector that is enriching investors—or abandon the nonprofits that still rely on subsidies? A cross-subsidy model, in which more profitable institutions pay fees that help support less profitable peers to use these services, seems reasonable. But establishing this approach has proven difficult in a sector where very few organizations are willing to pay full fees for these historically subsidized services.

This debate in microfinance is a preamble to the longer story likely to be told about the interplay between subsidy and profit in the broader impact investing industry. As we discuss in the next chapter, the mix of profit and purpose inherent in many components of the industry can create confusion. Pioneers are learning by doing as we navigate this confusion. We are finding that some philanthropists are willing to subsidize industry infrastructure even if profit-focused investors benefit. We are putting together coalitions of investors who recognize the need to cross-subsidize less-well-off industry participants. And we are finding some donors willing to subsidize the innovation that more commercially minded investors can bring to scale. But these are not easy coalitions to build and maintain or conversations to have. An honest discussion about the complex interplay between financial and social motives in the production of blended value will serve us all well to create a more stable foundation for the impact investing industry.

From Silver Bullet to Silver Buckshot

As the difficulty in proving social impact shows, microfinance is potentially powerful but is not a silver bullet to end poverty. Overselling whom it can reach and what it can do will only disappoint impatient investors looking for simple and quick fixes to the complex and entrenched problem of underdevelopment.

The question of whether microfinance can and should serve all people, including the poorest, has been a lightning rod for tension between the commercial- and development-focused camps. CGAP's decision in 2003 to change its official name from Consultative Group to Assist the Poorest to the Consultative Group to Assist the Poor, and the controversy that ensued, with Yunus and CGAP president Elizabeth Littlefield trading barbs in the press, is indicative of this debate.[3]

Beyond the debate about whom microfinance can reach is the broader question of whether microfinance is really a poverty eradication tool for the customers it does serve. To solve this debate may require reframing the question. As long as microfinance is marketed as a poverty eradication tool, then lingering poverty will indict microfinance leaders for failing to meet their obligations. When their customers remain poor, they will be accused of letting greed distract them from their social mission.

Instead, perhaps it is better to think of microfinance as a tool that can direct economic opportunity to poor communities, but one that must be used in concert with broader economic development strategies. In many communities, access to finance has proven to be a necessary but insufficient component of a broader development strategy. In this sense, perhaps microfinance is less about finding a silver bullet than it is about finding a component of the silver buckshot to be used in hunting for successful approaches to addressing the challenge of poverty.

In this vein, impact investing will add additional pieces of shot to the cartridge. Beyond making loans available to previously unbanked people, impact investors are designing business models to sell affordable health care, education, and housing to customers previously left adrift by conventional businesses and government. But none of these activities in isolation will be enough to eradicate poverty. Just as microfinance pioneers are learning now, impact investors will need to set expectations clearly and work effectively with the governments, nonprofits, private charities, and mainstream businesses that must all function effectively to create the conditions of development that will allow all people to flourish.

Microfinance in a Blended Value World

From its modern origins in the experiments of nonprofit organizations in South Asia and Latin America to its spectacular IPOs and transactions that brought hundreds of millions of dollars into the sector, microfinance has become both a useful and a dangerous exemplar of impact investing for multiple returns. It's useful because it has shown how well-honed business models that combine profit and purpose can reach millions of poor people with a valuable service and link them, for the first time, into global capital market flows. And it is dangerous for two reasons. First is that the visibility of its current success tends to obscure the four decades of subsidy and careful infrastructure building required to bring the industry to this point. Second, the diverse range of investors and business owners that this success has attracted includes those who focus exclusively on personal profit rather than social purpose and whose business practices can easily foment criticism and backlash.

REALIZING A DREAM
Carlos Danel Cendoya, Cofounder, Compartamos,
Mexico City, Mexico

Back in the early 1990s, Mexico was on its way to become a developed country, or so we were told. However for a group of us, college student volunteers for a nongovernmental organization (NGO), it was clear that many Mexicans still lacked opportunities for development.

We stumbled into microfinance, an idea well developed in Asia and South America but absent in Mexico and other large middle-income countries. Two things stood out: its potential for scale and the idea of using business principles to solve social problems. We set ourselves to start Compartamos with the dream to serve 1 million clients.

We had no banking or finance background, little capital, and no connections to microfinance. But we were determined to do it, to learn as we went along, and to take it one step at a time. We were driven by the idea of building a "social company," committed to creating social value (access to financial services for as many people as possible in the shortest time), financial value (allowing for profitability to fuel growth), and human value (for all stakeholders to become better individuals).

However, microfinance was still far from mainstream, and funding our NGO to grow was challenging. The donor community, so present in other countries, was absent in Mexico. But we were starting to make our first connections to the microfinance world, and we were impressed with how much had been achieved elsewhere. Following the footsteps of the pioneers, we came to see commercial microfinance as both an effective way to harness business principles and a means to grow more quickly.

By the late 1990s, we converted to a regulated financial company. We raised money among leading social investors active in microfinance like ACCION and ProFund Internacional and development finance institutions like the International Finance Corporation. We also tapped private investors who were willing to take a risk on us.

Slowly investors were starting to see microfinance as investable. We also learned that raising investment capital required us to embrace full transparency, good governance, and accountability.

In April 2007 we took Compartamos public in an IPO. We had anticipated that the IPO would be controversial, but underestimated the shock waves it would send throughout the microfinance industry. Some critics worried that our new investors would influence us to abandon our social mission. Many were also uncomfortable, and still are, about the role of profits as a means to build an industry. Vigorous debate followed, and perhaps the best result has been to force people to take a stance. Clearly there is no single right answer or model, but it's hard to argue that commercial microfinance has not served the purpose of reaching millions.

Almost four years after the IPO, we still serve the same clients, have sustained our growth, kept our asset quality stable, and increased our efficiency. Most important, a spur of innovation and competition has changed the market. In our first ten years in operation, we served sixty-four thousand clients. In the next ten years, we reached almost 2 million.

But the industry still has plenty of challenges. Among them is to really understand what exactly it does for its clients. Early on, microfinance advocates routinely claimed they could eradicate poverty. Today those claims have moderated, but there is still a sense that the industry has overpromised its social impact. We have come to understand that financial services are important, but they are not a silver bullet. This is of special concern to donors and philanthropists.

And the challenge of reaching global scale remains. Many people are still unserved, and the products the industry delivers are still limited and supply driven. So the race for growth, especially in the context of commercial microfinance, should consider not only prudent regulation, but good management, excellent governance, and sound ethical and business principles. Without it, the industry could falter.

Compartamos certainly has its work cut out for the future as we aspire to keep contributing to our deepest aspiration: to help create an industry to serve those who need it the most.

And what does the emergence of impact investing as a broader industry bode for the pioneers in microfinance? It could prove a boon. Many microfinance investors are well placed to use the skills, networks, and business models that have been developed to serve microfinance clients and investors in expanding into the broader impact investing market:

- Established microfinance players are launching new impact investing products such as Swiss-based BlueOrchard, whose founder created Bamboo Finance in 2007 to invest in medium-scale enterprises in poor countries.

- Others are diversifying offerings within existing microfinance vehicles, such as ResponsAbility, which launched a broad impact investing fund in 2010.

- Gray Ghost Ventures, a U.S. pioneer in setting up microfinance investment vehicles, has broadened its $200 million investment funds beyond microfinance, including with investments into affordable private schools in poor countries.

- Unitus, whose second equity fund includes an allocation to investments beyond microfinance, has announced it is leaving the microfinance field altogether to shift its attention to new areas of impact investment.

At the same time, the growth of the impact investing industry will break the near monopoly that microfinance has until recently enjoyed over investors who are interested in generating positive financial returns while promoting economic development in emerging markets. With social enterprises pioneering business models that allow impact investors to support commercial solutions that provide basic services such as health care, education, clean water, and electricity to poor families, microfinance leaders will have to justify why their business model creates the most blended value. Impact investing in social enterprises will require investors to develop new levels of sophistication and savvy in forming unusual partnerships and innovating the investment model. The next chapter discusses this challenge and the opportunities emerging at the intersection of these two potentially transformative ideas.

Chapter 4

IMPACT INVESTING IN SOCIAL ENTERPRISES

Flourishing in the "Confusing Mess"

Dial 1298 for Ambulance

Shaffi Mathur and Ravi Krishnan discovered their calling when their mothers became sick and needed emergency medical care. Ravi's mother fell ill in New York City, called the 911 emergency number, and was rushed to the hospital in an ambulance. Shaffi's mother fell ill in Mumbai and spent a scary night without any medical care. There was no emergency number to call.

Inspired by these different experiences, Shaffi and Ravi set out to bring emergency ambulance service to India. Partnering with two friends, they created a company, Ziqitza Healthcare. With $400,000, Ziqitza launched Dial 1298 for Ambulance in Mumbai in 2005. They received free training and equipment from the London Ambulance Service and donations from a range of supporters. But rather than rely on donations, they also looked to generate revenues that could help them pay for more ambulances and expand the

This chapter draws on an earlier draft written by Mike Kubzansky and Anamitra Deb of Monitor Inclusive Markets.

service to new cities. They set up a variable-pricing system in which patients who asked ambulance drivers to take them to private hospitals paid more than patients who asked to go to public ones. They also sold ad space on their ambulances.

By 2007, Dial 1298 operated ten ambulances, but these ambulances barely began to meet the need for emergency services in a city of more than 15 million people. With an unusual business model, a strong social focus, and limited collateral, Dial 1298 could not win over skeptical commercial investors or secure a bank loan. But they did attract the interest of the Acumen Fund, a New York–based nonprofit set up to invest in enterprises that used business approaches to deliver basic services to poor people. Acumen invested $1.5 million in Dial 1298 in 2007 and seconded a staff member to provide strategic planning advice.

Dial 1298 used this investment to buy new ambulances and bolster its senior management team. The investment gave the company time to refine its operating model and gain market traction. It also joined a national advocacy campaign to convince state governments to support emergency medical service. A second round of equity financing in 2009 brought in another $1 million from Acumen Fund and strategic investment from a commercial health care provider. By 2010, Dial 1298 operated more than 240 ambulances and had secured $80 million in state contracts to expand the service beyond Mumbai.

The citizens of Mumbai and other cities now have a reliable number to call when they need emergency services.

The Two Sides of the Velcro

As this story typifies, solving social and environmental problems is no longer the exclusive domain of traditional, grant-funded nonprofit organizations or government. Instead, social entrepreneurs like the founders of Dial 1298 are using the best of business thinking and practices to pursue value creation that is integrative and not exclusively either socially or financially directed.[1] Many social enterprises require grants and subsidies to scale up, but increasingly others adopt business models that can generate financial returns for investors as well. These social entrepreneurs embody the blended value proposition in their mentality and approach. They are comfortable adopting whatever tools of corporate form and capital they can get their hands on. Instead of asking, "What is the 'right' way to address a social challenge?" they ask, "What works?"

And that's why things are getting interesting. Both social entrepreneurs and impact investors have gained new opportunities from the explosive convergence of the social entrepreneurship movement with the evolving industry of impact investing. Social entrepreneurs can be, as Root Capital founder Willy Foote likes to say, the "other side of the Velcro" to impact investors who are seeking enterprises to back that can convert capital into blended value.

But this expanded opportunity to match social entrepreneur and impact investor brings greater complexity. As the story of Dial 1298 shows, impact investors in social enterprises face the adventure that comes from investing in evolving business models in frontier markets, often in sectors without broadly accepted practices for generating or measuring results.

By putting capital to work in businesses focused on delivering blended value, social enterprise investment crystallizes both the potential and challenges of impact investing. Impact investors are enabling companies like Dial 1298 to expand services to poor customers in India. Innovators like Root Capital are improving income opportunities for farmers in poor countries around the world. But investing in social enterprise is not easy. Successful impact investors must navigate complex partnerships and capital structures that bring together grants, subsidies, and commercial investment capital. They must forge new approaches to collaboration, build a supportive ecosystem (beyond the narrow focus of their specific investments), and take an active role in refining investee business models and measuring the full spectrum of their blended returns. These are the skills and traits that will characterize successful investors in other areas of the impact investing industry.

Origins on Both Sides of the Checkbook

Before we focus on the specific convergence of social entrepreneurship with impact investing, it is worth highlighting a few of the threads that have come together to create the social entrepreneurship movement. Trying to assign the origins of social entrepreneurship is like trying to say that one person invented the modern automobile; like the car's inventors, many individuals in countries around the world had a vision of social entrepreneurship. Generally the concept began to take hold internationally in the late 1980s when Bill Drayton, founder of Ashoka: Changemakers and the Ashoka Foundation, began identifying and supporting "individuals with innovative solutions to society's most pressing social problems." The international work of Ashoka was, in the United States, complemented by the domestic work of Echoing Green and other early investors in individual social entrepreneurs. While proponents highlighted the way these leaders harnessed entrepreneurial principles to run their organizations, these organizations initially focused on the leaders of nonprofit organizations and social or civil society movements.

Soon a more market-oriented approach to social enterprise also began to take hold. In the United States, many social entrepreneurs running nonprofit organizations began to harness the tools of business and market-based strategies to the pursuit of social change and positive environmental impacts: Billy Shore, of Share Our Strength, advocated cause marketing; Jerr Bosche, of the National Center for Social Entrepreneurship, promoted earned income approaches; and Jed, in his role as founding director of San Francisco-based Roberts Enterprise Development Fund

(REDF), worked with social entrepreneurs who were interested in offering transitional employment to formerly homeless individuals through the vehicle of market-based social enterprises supported through venture philanthropy and earned income. These social entrepreneurs expanded upon the practices and vision of such historic innovators as the Salvation Army, Goodwill and others. And so, during the mid-1990s, these individuals and others tirelessly promoted a vision of social entrepreneurship that merged the principles of transformative social improvement with an embrace of market discipline and earned revenue-fueled growth.

In the United Kingdom, Charles Handy, Michael Young, and a host of fellow community innovators led the execution of a number of social enterprise strategies that continue to serve as global models. They also laid the foundation for many of the current initiatives and financing innovations underway in the United Kingdom under the Big Society program.

Social entrepreneurs also emerged within commercial companies. Anchoring this market-oriented subset were individuals—such as Ben Cohen of Ben and Jerry's, Anita Roddick of the Body Shop, Yvon Chouinard of Patagonia, and Gary Hirshberg of Stonyfield Farms, among many others—who launched for-profit ventures that pursued financial returns alongside social and environmental impacts and value creation.

Across the checkbook from these social entrepreneurs, new investors emerged. Venture philanthropy brought new capital and innovative types of organizational support to nonprofit social enterprises. Groups such as REDF, New Schools Venture Fund, Social Venture Partners, and New Profit spent millions of dollars supporting social enterprise nonprofits in the United States while Ashoka, the Skoll Foundation, and others spread this support globally. For-profit investors began making investments in commercial enterprises on the basis of both financial promise and the potential of social and environmental value creation. Angel investors backed pioneering companies and eventually began to collaborate in impact investing angel networks such as Investors' Circle.

By fits and starts, these social entrepreneurs and their early investors have begun to create a new world freed from the old constraints that separated profit making from problem-solving activity. By the early years of the new millennium, social enterprise had become a galvanizing concept for investors eager to back new approaches to solving social challenges and for entrepreneurs, like the founders of Dial 1298, with a strong sense of social purpose and a wide-ranging appetite to try different ways to achieve it.

How Impact Investing Can Fuel Blended Value Creation Through Social Enterprise

Interest in social enterprise has exploded in recent years, and business owners as well as nonprofit leaders take pride in distinguishing themselves as social entrepreneurs. But as Jed wrote a decade ago in the original articulation of the blended value proposition, all enterprises create a blend of social and financial outcomes, both positive and negative. Social enterprises simply organize around social value creation in a more concerted manner.

How Social Enterprises Create Blended Value

The seemingly simple question of how social enterprises create blended value unlocks a powerful framework for understanding not only social enterprises but also how impact investors can work to support their development.

Create a Public Good Externality That Requires Subsidy

Some social enterprises produce substantial value for society in a way that does not allow their enterprise to benefit financially from this activity. An organization that leads a campaign for women's equality, for example, will create social value and financial gains for society but may not be able to pursue an earned revenue approach. In this case, the financial return is what economists would refer to as a public goods *externality*. These are traditional nonprofits that will need funding from donors.

Internalize Enough of the Value They Create to Take On Commercial Investment

Other social enterprises create business models that allow them to participate financially in the social value they generate. They may sell essential goods like clean water or provide essential services such as electricity at a price that improves customers' welfare but with a healthy profit margin. They may source products from previously isolated rural suppliers, creating a lower-cost and lower-churn supply chain that improves their long-term profitability. These enterprises can fuel their growth with for-profit investment capital. And traditional for-profit firms can structure their supply chain management and other operations to directly create social and economic value as well.

Benefit from Formal Subsidies

Of course, markets do not always reward companies that address social problems. The producer of more fuel-efficient light bulbs cannot necessarily charge most customers more just because her product is better for the earth. However, many businesses can take advantage of an increasing array of explicit and implicit subsidies. The most obvious form of subsidy comes from governments that offer tax breaks or other incentives to companies that contribute to addressing social issues. These subsidies can tip a social enterprise into the position where it can generate enough profit to attract investment capital.

Benefit from Informal Subsidies

Beyond formal subsidy, consumers and employees can also change the economic prospects for investors. The willingness of fair trade consumers to pay premium prices rewards a fair trade business for providing the social good of higher wages and better environmental stewardship. The willingness of senior managers to work for below-market wages also enables businesses to succeed in areas where customers' price sensitivity may otherwise threaten long-term sustainability. On the margins, both formal and informal subsidies can tip a solution from needing philanthropic backing to one that can take on investment instead.

Create a Hybrid Capital Structure

Between the social enterprise that relies on philanthropy and her sister enterprise that can internalize enough financial return to secure market rate investment lie fascinating hybrids. These are the enterprises that can internalize some of the value they create in the form of financial return but not enough to operate and scale with investment capital alone. Two pathways are available to them.

First, they can combine subsidies and investments simultaneously. Some social enterprises generate enough financial return to pay some of their capital providers but not all of them. They can create a hybrid finance structure where different investors receive different mixes of blended value. In India, Naandi Foundation provides clean water in villages by charging customers enough to cover operations and maintenance after the government has built the basic system for free. Or grants may provide ongoing subsidy to a business model that is generating revenue but not enough to make it solvent without subsidy. Many of the REDF portfolio companies received grants that enabled them to employ individuals with higher training and supported employment requirements than would have been possible in a purely market-based venture. Similarly, Root Capital raises both grant funding and low-interest debt that allow it to lend to poor farmers and train them to handle the loans. Dial 1298 for Ambulance exemplifies the complexity of the hybrid capital structure. It has combined grants and free advice from ambulance associations and hospitals, received concessionary capital from the Acumen Fund, won government contracts, and received investment from a commercial emergency services company—truly a blended value enterprise.

The second pathway is to blend subsidies and investments sequentially. Often a grant is initially necessary to demonstrate the viability of a new business model or enable the social entrepreneur to refine the strategy until it proves commercially viable. For example, many microfinance institutions that today function as profitable banks sank their roots with the support of grant funding—for example, SKS Microfinance in India, Equity Bank in Kenya, and Compartamos Banco in Mexico. Similarly, as we saw in Chapter Two, a grant from the U.K. government enabled mobile phone giant Vodafone to develop M-Pesa, a product that allows mobile phone subscribers to transfer money across the mobile phone network. Vodafone has subsequently rolled out M-Pesa as a commercial product that constituted an estimated $150 million of the company's enterprise value in 2010 (while contributing substantially to economic development in many countries).

Of course, these categories are not static. The financing of social enterprise business models frequently moves along this capital spectrum. And the hybrid approach is not for the weak of heart. The experience of Root Capital highlights both the growing opportunity and complexity of this hybrid model. The model brings together under one roof investors who may seek social impact first and foremost with investors seeking mainly a financial return—and managing such hybrid ventures can create real challenges for investor and entrepreneur both.

The Most Promising Social Enterprises for Impact Investors

Organizing our understanding of social enterprise around the question, "How does the enterprise create blended value?" helps us understand how these enterprises can grow with three types of capital: philanthropy, commercial investment, and a hybrid structure. We are also starting to understand that certain clusters of approaches are most amenable to investment:

- *Those that provide essential goods and services affordably to poor communities unreached by existing commercial businesses.* A focus of social enterprises operating in poor countries, this is the essential promise that microfinance revealed and now applies to a range of other social enterprises, from those that sell clean drinking water (such as Voltic in West Africa), to solar lanterns (D. Light), and affordable housing finance (MFHC in India). Typically these enterprises adopt a high-volume, low-cost business model.

- *Those that organize supply chains to enable poor producers to benefit from trade.* These social enterprises, such as Root Capital, FabIndia, and Divine Chocolate, participate in the global fair trade movement and provide more equitable supply chains for local consumption. By cutting out middlemen or selling into premium markets (or both), these business models create enough economic surplus to produce blended value by increasing the income for primary producers (typically poor farmers and artisans) and selling at a margin that provides investors with a financial return.

- *Those that provide support for delivery of public goods by government and nonprofits.* Social enterprises can carve out opportunities to participate profitably even in areas of social services that governments and donors ultimately take responsibility for providing themselves. This opportunity exists wherever the distribution (by donors and government) can be separated from the service and manufacture. While the distribution of antimalarial bed nets is increasingly a donor-driven activity, the

Tanzanian-based A to Z Bednets has taken on impact investment capital to expand its capacity to manufacture bed nets primarily for sale to donor agencies. This approach also has great potential in developed countries where social entrepreneurs are building organizations that provide services such as training and standards monitoring to a range of public services such as schools and hospitals.

What Impact Investors Are Learning About Social Enterprises

If you are an impact investor, you need to separate the social enterprises that can absorb investment capital from those you might support with grants and subsidies. If you are a social entrepreneur, you need to figure out what type of capital fits your current state best. You may be surprised how many investors and entrepreneurs don't make these distinctions well, and along the way, they may leave the world worse off. The lure of investment capital is driving some well-functioning nonprofits to take on debt that their business model cannot support. This can create dire consequences for the people who are relying on the services they provided.

What It Takes to Invest Effectively

Impact investing can be powerful fuel for the right social enterprise at the right moment. Impact investors are developing skills and approaches to avoid both the rocky shoals of financial ill discipline and the whirlpools of mission drift. They are figuring out how to get the most out of hybrid capital structures and are getting comfortable with the early-stage investing that social enterprise requires. They are becoming more realistic about the returns they can generate and more effective at measuring them. Their experience is helping to fill in details about this new world of impact investing for blended value.

Getting the Most out of Hybrid Capital Structures

Despite the hype that comes from celebrating successful outliers, most social enterprises cannot rely entirely on commercial investment. Social enterprise business models are hard to perfect and usually require time and patience to refine. They sometimes require specialized strategy and development support that is expensive to provide. Given this constraint, many social enterprises need grant funding or highly concessionary investment to hone their business models and determine which components may be financed with investment. Willy Foote's experience with Root Capital is typical of the complex interplay between impact investment and subsidized funding. In the Root Capital example, providing accounting training for farmer groups requires subsidy; providing working capital to the most successful of these groups need not.

Successful impact investors in social enterprise know how to structure their investment into a stack of capital from a range of funders. They often arrange loan guarantees from government programs, concessionary investment capital from government-sponsored development finance institutions, and grant money from foundations. They also help investees negotiate contracts from government, strategic investors, and other capital sources. Dial 1298 for Ambulance secured in-kind support from a U.K. trade association and U.S. hospitals, donations, a concessionary investment and strategic support from Acumen Fund, substantial government contracts, and commercial investment. This complex capital structure is not atypical.

To make the complex capital stack work, impact investors need to become effective at collaborating with donors and governments. But the providers of these subsidies typically focus on maximizing only public goods and social outcomes and fail to recognize (or even find suspect) the profit an enterprise could create. Many impact investors underplay the importance of this support and dismiss the legitimate claims that donors have to ensure an enterprise maximizes the social value it can generate.

One specific conflict that often arises between donors and investors is how to treat proprietary information. Donors often seek to place the intellectual property an enterprise creates (best practices, challenges, and process innovations, for example) into the public domain as quickly as possible. Focusing on social impact, they want the enterprise to build bridges to entry for other social entrepreneurs to replicate the model widely. In contrast, most private investors want to maximize their financial return by building barriers that prevent others from adopting a new business model or technology. Neither approach maximizes blended value. Instead, impact investors need to find new ways to integrate the imperative to replicate models for maximum social impact with the need to generate profits and achieve investment exits.

Getting Comfortable with Early-Stage Enterprises and Staged Investments

With a few notable exceptions, many social enterprises tend to be both small and relatively complex. Impact investors enjoy few opportunities to invest in proven business models; they often must finance start-ups. This dynamic is likely to endure, especially in emerging markets. Monitor Group research in India and Africa in 2009–2010 found that average investment sizes are usually less than $2 million.

Social enterprises tend to take many years of business model refinement and long walks down strategic dead ends before they are ready to scale. Their investors must adopt a venture capital mentality that recognizes investees' need to experiment with their business models. Structuring investments to phase in capital over time is essential in many cases to manage risk even as it fragments already small investment opportunities.

And while they tend to be small and early stage, many social enterprises are also relatively complex. Early-stage investors typically support investees in implementing basic processes and systems. Impact investors in social enterprises have to do this work and often more. They may also have to support the investee to organize a value chain from end-to-end, because so many social enterprises operate in areas with sparse supporting systems for business to draw on. This often requires add-ons beyond the initial investment to develop and refine tailored business models, fund start-ups that can complement the core investee, or organize partnerships to fill in the ecosystem gaps. As Monitor Group's Mike Kubzansky points out, in the areas where social entrepreneurs often operate, especially in businesses providing goods and services to poor customers, if you want to be Google, you usually have to build the Internet yourself first!

Being Realistic About Financial Return

Of course, as is true in both traditional investing and philanthropy, many impact investments do not succeed. Enterprises fail, impact investors lose their money, and business models do not achieve their intended social goals. Nevertheless, unrealistic expectations abound. The social enterprise sector suffers from an acute case of *premature celebrationitis* that causes the community to heap praise and glory on entrepreneurs with exciting ideas before they have achieved much at all. Few people pay attention long enough to see that these enterprises often fail to live up to expectations. By the time results come in, we're on to the next big thing. Investors counting on easy financial returns in the social enterprise sector are headed for disappointment. Impact investing in social enterprise is hard, and investors need to be realistic about the financial returns they can expect and the patience needed to realize them.

Measuring Blended Return

Especially when social enterprises adopt a hybrid capital structure of impact investments, grants, and subsidies, measuring value becomes crucial to answer important strategic questions:

- How do impact investors willing to make a below-market loan to, say, Root Capital know if Root Capital generates enough social value to offset the opportunity cost of investing their money in a more lucrative investment?

- When a social enterprise provides a service to purely commercial entities (as Dial 1298 for Ambulance does by taking patients to private hospitals), how do investors know they are generating social good with their investment rather than just subsidizing corporate profits?

- When does the need to repay impact investors prevent a social enterprise from the innovation and scale it could reach with pure subsidy?

Answering these questions is new territory for many investors. Many steer away from rigorous impact measurement because they fear it may raise already high transaction costs. But investors need to ask for information that can inform these answers. We also need to share it. Developing these answers alone is both inefficient and ultimately unsatisfactory because it leaves investors without the benchmarks and standards necessary to underpin judgment about potential investees. Projects such as the Global Impact Investing Network's Impact Reporting and Investment Standards (IRIS) and the international SROI Network are organizing a collective response to the measurement challenge.

However, as we discuss in Chapter Eight, investors should not assume that necessary impact and social reporting systems are in place within the social enterprise sector. We also cannot assume that social enterprises will independently invest in measurement infrastructure. If investors are going to take seriously the vision of creating social and environmental impacts, then we also have to take seriously the challenge of building meaningful information systems at the enterprise level.

What It Will Take to Foster Impact Investing in Social Enterprise

Impact investors who want to see the social enterprise field flourish have a vested interest in doing more than just making deals. We must work toward building a more coherent marketplace. Rather than sitting back and waiting for good business plans to come across our desks, we need to support efforts to encourage the launch of social enterprises and nurture their early growth even before they are investable. Impact investors also need to fight our tendency to operate as lone cowboys and instead pool investments to enable fund managers to develop unique expertise. Finally, we need to develop new approaches to making investments that recognize and adjust for the unique characteristics of social enterprise.

Seeding the Pipeline

The few readily investable social enterprises are generally well known thanks to a vigorous social enterprise industry and media focused on unearthing success stories, but deal flow is not keeping up with the proliferation of impact investors who are targeting these enterprises. As a result, impact investors often find ourselves chasing the same deals. While the resulting negotiating power this gives to investment targets would be an irritant for mainstream investors, it is fundamentally more problematic for impact investors. For many impact investors, simply making an investment that generates decent returns and produces social impact is not good enough. Following the principle of additionality (discussed in Chapter Two), we want our capital to make a difference by enabling businesses to grow that otherwise would not.

If our capital is going to be additional, we need to expand the pipeline so we are not chasing deals that could be financed in other ways. Who is going to seed and cultivate the start-ups today that can be investable tomorrow? Investors need to build on early examples of collaboration in launching mentoring programs, business plan competitions, and joint pools of seed-stage funding. We also need to use our relationships with donors and governments to integrate subsidy and donations more thoughtfully.

From Cowboys to Collaborators

At this time, effective social enterprise investing requires specialization because the nuances of investment opportunities are often market specific, location specific, and sector specific. The same operational models that may work in a certain part of peri-urban India are unlikely to work across all of India, with its vast cultural and linguistic differences, let alone in sub-Saharan Africa or the United States. But specialization is hard for any single investor to develop when the deals are small and the business models so complex.

Pooling capital through funds would allow specialization, but many social enterprise investors want to make direct investments. They relate personally to the stories of social entrepreneurs and seek the excitement that comes from direct connection to their investees. Yet if they want to help the social enterprise field reach its potential, these investment cowboys need to give up at least some of the thrill of being out on the range alone.

Since few impact investors invest enough to become specialists in many areas, if they want to invest across geographies or sectors they will need to coordinate with other like-minded investors. One way to coordinate is through participation in investment funds. An investor can spread her capital across a range of fund managers who each develop expertise in a specific area that she alone could not. When funds do not exist, investors may have to create them, as the Soros Economic Development Fund, Omidyar Network, and Google did in launching the SONG fund targeting Indian social enterprises. Formal or informal investment clubs that share information and deal flow can also be a good way to tap into collective expertise. And nonprofit financial services firms such as ImpactAssets are emerging to act as intermediaries in the introduction of multi-manager investment funds and other vehicles which can bring impact investors together.

Evolution of the Investment Model

Compared to mainstream businesses, social enterprises typically take longer to scale, require smaller investments that drive up transaction costs, and operate in a range of sectors with untested business models that require substantial support beyond capital.

Add to this the sheer complexity of building new systems to track and assess blended value return. Put all this together, and it makes sense that the different world of social enterprises requires a different investment model.

Unfortunately, early social enterprise investment funds have been pressured to adopt mainstream investment models. A typical private equity closed-term fund model distributes all profits after seven years, and the management team takes a 2 percent annual management fee along the way. This fund structure forces the investor in slow-growing social enterprises to liquidate the fund before many portfolio enterprises have taken off. Relying on the standard management fee also limits fund managers' ability to cover the costs of executing the many small deals they find and the additional services they need to provide investee companies.

Some impact investors in social enterprise are moving beyond this cookie-cutter approach by developing innovative investment models. Some are tweaking the traditional fund model, increasing their fund life to ten years or more or even converting their closed-end funds into perpetual holding companies. They are also raising pools of donor capital that can supplement their management fee to enable them to cultivate their pipeline and support their investees.

Others are throwing the entire fund model out, creating radical new approaches to identifying, vetting, and structuring invest-ment deals. Village Capital, a brainchild of microfinance pioneer Gray Ghost Ventures, is applying the group lending principles of microfinance to venture capital in social enterprise. Instead of hiring fund managers to identify and vet investees, this program commits investment capital to groups of social entrepreneurs who decide themselves which business most deserves investment. This approach is slashing the cost of early-stage investment while simul-taneously creating a peer network to support the social enterprises. Further innovation in the spirit of Village Capital will be necessary to create the unique investment models that can rise to the unique challenges of investing in social enterprises.

Celebrating the "Confusing Mess"

When Florence Nightingale (cited by Ashoka as an early model social entrepreneur) set out to create the first modern nursing school in mid-nineteenth-century London, deciding how to fund her social enterprise was relatively simple: she raised charitable contributions from the limited sources (family, friends, church, and state) that would provide them. When Matt Flannery and Jessica Jackley set out to create kiva.org, the pioneer of online peer-to-peer lending in microfinance in early twenty-first-century San Francisco, they faced a "confusing mess," in Matt's words: a dizzying array of potential donors, impact investors, and commercial venture capitalists and lawyers offering advice on the nonprofit or for-profit corporate form they could adopt.[2]

What should they have done?

In recent years, there have been ongoing debates regarding whether it is "right" to be a for-profit mission-driven business or a nonprofit with a compelling business model. But the fact is that there is simply no "right way" to create blended value. Forcing normative judgment onto our understanding of which approach works best is not helpful. Neither is moralizing and self-righteousness between proponents of grants versus investment and for-profit versus nonprofit organizational forms. This debate doesn't serve any of us. The type of investment that is best and desirable is completely contextual. In each case, the answer will be different based on a host of factors. And ultimately we will judge the success of each enterprise and investment on how well it optimizes its value potential across a continuum of economic, social, and environmental performance criteria.

Some social problems must be addressed with donations and government grants. We would not want to imagine a world where we ask all people, regardless of their financial status, to pay for vaccine delivery, HIV/AIDS prevention and counseling, domestic

ROOT CAPITAL: NAVIGATING THE INCREASINGLY COMPLEX WORLD OF SOCIAL ENTERPRISE FINANCE
Willy Foote, Founder and CEO, Root Capital, Cambridge, Massachusetts

In the late 1990s, I spent two years working on a journalism fellowship in Mexico reporting on the impact of globalization and the collapse of the country's economy following the 1994 peso crisis. While traveling through the countryside, I encountered scores of businesses that were creating viable alternatives to slash-and-burn agriculture and illegal logging but could not grow without access to credit. Juxtaposed to my corporate banking experience on Wall Street just a few years before, this gap in the capital markets was striking: thousands of small businesses were overlooked simply because of their location, the amount of financing they needed, their lack of traditional collateral, and misperception of their risk.

As the fellowship ended, my wife and I drove our truck from southern Mexico to Boston, where we both planned to attend Harvard Business School. As we rolled past hundreds of small family farms, I couldn't shake the idea that there had to be a solution to this failure in the credit markets. These businesses could supply products that were in high demand in North America and Europe, yet they couldn't get a loan to cover their production costs. If credit could reach these rural areas, I was confident that the businesses, their farmer and artisan suppliers, and their families could thrive.

So on a wing and a prayer, I deferred admission and obtained an initial donation to try to address this market failure. Root Capital was born as a nonprofit social enterprise focused on closing the finance gap for small and growing businesses (SGBs) like those I saw in Mexico that build sustainable livelihoods and transform rural communities in poor, environmentally vulnerable places.

From 1999 through 2004, Root Capital gradually expanded by raising two types of capital: concessionary debt that was pooled and loaned to rural SGBs and grant funding to cover overhead costs and build our balance sheet through contingency reserves. In the early days, the idea of an "investment" with a below-market return and a repayment schedule into a nonprofit lending abroad was novel.

Religious institutions, socially responsible investment funds, foundations that were experimenting with program-related investments, and some individuals were the first to embrace it. Others, particularly more traditional family foundations and individual philanthropists, approached philanthropy completely independent of their investments and were skeptical of mixing the two. By the end of 2004, Root Capital had raised $7.9 million in debt from forty-three investors, and that year we made forty-five loans, including our first loan in sub-Saharan Africa.

Prior to 2004, most of our investments were in the range of $25,000 to $125,000 with an average annual return of 2.66 percent. In 2004, we approached Starbucks Coffee Company for the first investment of over $1 million in our fund. We initially secured a $2.5 million note from Starbucks; its investment has since grown to $9 million. Although Starbucks had an active foundation in 2004, it exclusively provided grants. Its investment in Root Capital is drawn from the corporate side of its business, with funds coming off its balance sheet to advance its objectives for supply chain stability as well as more conventional corporate social responsibility.

As Root Capital expanded from $12 million in loan disbursements in 2005 to $80 million in 2010, the impact investment field was evolving, led by large investors with a focus on the long-term organizational sustainability of their investees. Whereas investments greater than $1 million were 32 percent of lending capital in 2004, they accounted for 70 percent in 2010. Tapping into this emerging class of impact investors and blending their capital with investments from the likes of Starbucks and the U.S. government–backed Overseas Private Investment Corporation, as well as grants from individuals and foundations, has enabled us to reach 450,000 small-scale producers with more than $256 million in loans and to provide extensive training services.

While most of our early investors have remained, we have experienced an overall shift in the approach of both original and new funders. It is now easier to articulate our dual need for both below-market investments and grant funding. With traditional donors moving into impact investing, we see trends toward larger investments and an increasing willingness to provide operating support to Root Capital as an organization, with less emphasis on funding a narrow set of restricted activities. This approach mimics equity investments in for-profit companies—investments to support organization-building necessities such as net assets on our balance sheet, loan loss reserves, and upgrades to our loan management and information technology systems—and enables us to

---

abuse support, or other critical services. These are public goods whose access should not be determined by a customer's ability to pay.

However, the fact that subsidy is appropriate in some cases does not negate the importance and legitimacy of investment in others. The argument against for-profit investment in *any* social enterprise is an outdated red herring. Nongovernmental business today *is* big business, a multibillion-dollar commitment of capital to domestic programs and international development efforts.

In a growing number of cases, for-profit, nonprofit, or hybrid social enterprises hold great promise for creating sustained, long-term solutions to what have been the equally long-term and sustained challenges of poverty, injustice, and environmental degradation. In these cases, impact investing is going to be an essential component of the capital structure that brings the best social enterprises to scale. The issue is not which operating model is "right" (a question of morality) but rather which works best to advance the greatest impact and returns for both stakeholders and investors (a question of impact).

Within the "confusing mess" is a powerful combination of entrepreneurial moxie and impact investing savvy that promises to transform the pace and scale at which social enterprise can expand in response to the demand for our services without being overly donor driven.

As Root Capital grows, we cover an increasing portion of overhead costs (72 percent in 2010 and a projected 100 percent by 2013) through interest and fees from our lending operations. Until we reach threshold scale and break-even, we look to impact investors to couple their debt capital with grant support to fill our operating shortfall and feed our balance sheet. In that way, we can maintain a conservative debt-to-equity ratio and build a solid foundation for growth in what is considered a highly risky asset class.

---

generate blended value. Despite the complexity and challenge, investing pioneers are creating the insights, learning the lessons, and developing the innovations that will ultimately enable investing in social enterprise to stand as a crucial component of the impact investing industry, as well as a growing option for mainstream investors looking for financial performance with impact.

We have seen the promise of impact investing in the proliferation of investment-backed social enterprise, the growth of microfinance into an industry serving 100 million poor customers, and the broader application of impact investing in development. But where will the next breakthroughs come? While we can't predict the future, we can hone our capacity to see around the corner. The next chapter provides a framework for recognizing the opportunities that impact investors enjoy and the areas in which they are most likely to capture them.

Chapter 5

WHERE IS IMPACT INVESTING HEADED?

Impact investing has been generating blended value in various sectors around the world, sometimes for decades:

- Small businesses are accessing credit in Cambodia as part of the multibillion-dollar microfinance industry.

- Families are living in affordable homes in U.S. cities that were built by low-income housing developers with backing from dedicated finance funds.

- Green companies are finding eager investors in Europe.

- Hospitals are expanding with private equity investment in Kenya from development finance institutions.

All of this is happening because impact investors have organized an investing ecosystem in these subsectors. The next question is obvious: What similar stories will we be telling in five or ten years? When the next edition of this book comes out, what chapters will we need to add?

To be honest, we cannot predict exactly where impact investing will take off next. Unanticipated success and seemingly inexplicable failure have characterized it as much as they have mainstream investing over the past few years. Whatever we predict will be the next subsectors to watch, we will probably look back a bit sheepishly when we see what was missing from our list. What we can offer is a broad framework so you can determine for yourself what areas are (or are not) ripe for impact investment.

Fundamentally, impact investing will work only where the following conditions all hold:

- Solving basic social problems requires substantial investment that donors and governments cannot source alone.

- Profitable and scalable business models are emerging that can repay lenders or investors (rather than requiring charity).

- Business models are at an early stage of development where they are too fragmented and subscale to attract the attention of mainstream investors.

- Government and society support the idea that private enterprise should be allowed to operate in this market.

Providing basic services to poor customers, the increasingly recognized bottom-of-the-pyramid opportunity, is a rich vein to explore for future impact investing activity. But impact investing is not limited to addressing issues of basic poverty in poor countries. In developed countries, retreating social safety nets are creating space for impact investors to step in and step up.

If even a few of the sectors we explore in this chapter do take off in the next several years, they offer great potential to improve the lives of millions of people and solidify the industry of impact investing for blended value.

Impact Investing Opportunities

In some ways, the current impact investing community has a bit of the feel of the Old West: there are rumors of riches to be found yet plenty of folks looking for the next big gold strike. Prospecting for new areas in which impact investing can flourish is a relatively simple task:

1. Sift through social challenges to identify those that government and philanthropy cannot solve alone, that is, those that need a market-based solution.
2. Sift through potential solutions to identify the ones where a market-based solution is viable and can generate financial return for investors.
3. Throw out the business models that mainstream investors will back.

What's left are those shiny nuggets on top of your sieve: the impact investing subsectors of the future.

A Societal Need for a Market-Based Solution

To love impact investing, you don't have to unconditionally worship traditional capitalism. But you do need to accept that there are some social challenges and many places where the combined effort of governments and charities is not going to be adequate. When you go out prospecting for problems governments are not solving themselves, the "failed state" is an obvious place to start. People living in a place like Eastern Congo already rely on private business for the provision of almost all basic services, from health care to education to electricity. But even in relatively well-functioning countries, government services invariably bypass certain communities. And in this era of widespread resource constraint, these areas of neglect are growing. Even relatively prosperous governments are pulling back from their role in providing basic social services. Room opens up for impact investors to back private sector companies offering basic services when government imposes across-the-board service cuts in places like the United Kingdom.

After you have scanned the world for evidence of state failure or retreat, add to your list solutions that will simply cost too much for states and philanthropists to bear alone. A general rule is that if you are talking about solutions that require trillions of dollars, then private investors need to be at the table. This is why all realistic proposals to address climate change include private sector incentives. Even in good economic times, no government could afford to transform the energy economy to renewable sources. Similarly, building decent housing for the world's 1 billion slum dwellers is a capital-intensive project no government can underwrite alone.

State failure, however, is a moving target, and getting caught addressing a need the state is aiming to fulfill can put you in an awkward position. That's what happened in 2010 to microfinance providers in the Indian state of Andhra Pradesh, the center of India's commercial microfinance boom. When the government's $20 billion program to extend credit to poor communities stalled, microfinanciers became an easy target. Subsequent government-imposed restrictions on microfinance operations and widespread calls by politicians for customers not to repay their loans hobbled the center of India's microfinance industry. While the stand-off between government and microfinance institutions has deescalated, the disruption continues to worry impact investors there. Had the government not been attempting to address the issue of credit in these communities, the microfinance industry would likely have had greater sway to operate independently for a longer time.

A Viable Market-Based Solution

The list of issues and places where government activity and charity alone will not be enough is long. But some items simply cannot be addressed in ways that generate financial return to investors. For example, the problem of domestic violence is big enough to make the list but does not lend itself to any business-based solution we can think of.

But as we saw in the previous chapter on social enterprise, impact investors are figuring out new ways for social ventures to address a growing number of other items. In some cases, they produce products that expand their customers' access to affordable goods or services. In other cases, they provide better income to suppliers or employees.

Figuring out how to create blended value within a business that creates profit and social good may sound easy enough. In practice, substantial work is still required to develop and refine business models that can serve these customers sustainably and at scale. After all, it took more than thirty years of experimentation and failure before the modern microfinance business model took off. Impact investors who can work in sophisticated partnerships with donors and subsidized capital will play an important role in identifying, backing, and scaling future business models.

Eliminate Deals That Mainstream Investors Will Back

We started with a list of problems that need investors' help to solve, then crossed off challenges for which we cannot figure out business models that can pay back investors for contributing to the solution. What remains is still an exciting list of opportunities—but we still need to cross off those opportunities that mainstream investors will seize without any consideration of social impact. This may sound limiting. To those of you who wonder why we would not take advantage of the most lucrative opportunities, we say, "What's the fun of doing the easy stuff?" It's not that we discourage anyone from making investments that mainstream markets have already seized on. It's just that impact investment is too precious a resource to spend on deals where we're not needed. This is not to say that impact investors cannot pursue opportunities for making great financial returns; we just want to follow the principle of additionality to maintain focus where we can make the most difference.

Putting this principle into practice is tricky. Mainstream investors often follow where impact investors paved the way.

What may be a commercial opportunity *now* still required impact investment *then*. Typically mainstream investors tend to focus their attention on a narrow slice of the overall opportunity. The fact that mainstream venture firm Sequoia Capital has invested in the most commercial microfinance institutions in India leaves plenty of deal flow for impact investors who want to invest in other firms there or in microfinance in other places.

What It Will Take to Capture These Opportunities

Impact investors developing these frontier subsectors will benefit from drafting behind systems established by impact investors operating in more established subsectors. The growing interest in impact investing among asset managers, donors, and governments creates a substantial tailwind for the next generation of innovators. In addition, the ecosystem that early impact investing pioneers created—in business models, investment structures, investment banking capabilities, policy considerations, and research—should all enable these new subsectors to scale more quickly.

Despite this promise, many challenges remain. Three stand out:

- Concerns raised regarding the private provision of public goods—a moral issue

- The need to bridge the sectoral divide—a strategic question

- The need to complement government services—a limiting factor

Defending the Moral Legitimacy of Market-Based Solutions

Around the world, substantial stigma attaches to private sector solutions to social challenges. This moral issue fueled the furor over commercial microfinance in India in late 2010. In the face of this stigma, we are not surprised that impact investing has so far flourished in areas that are important, such as access to finance and sustainability, but not universally recognized as basic human rights. Many of the exciting opportunities that made it through our screening process will move us closer to these core concerns. If you think the global condemnation of initial public offerings (IPOs) of microfinance companies has been severe, just wait until the companies going public are in the housing, water, education, or health care industry segments.

Those of us who want society to give impact investors a chance to roll up our sleeves and tackle the core social challenges on our list need to make a stronger case for why we are the good guys. We need to broaden the public understanding of how governments and markets are failing so many people and how the enterprises we back support rather than exploit their customers. We also need to make sure we are the good guys, separating out the true impact investors from the impact imposters more carefully through the application of industry benchmarks and impact performance indicators.

Bridging the Sectoral Divide

Some of the most interesting impact investment innovations will come from creative partnerships among investors, entrepreneurs, and social sector leaders. Bridging the historic gap between investors and social sector organizations will not be easy. Financing housing for shack dwellers in slums, for example, will require investors to partner with slum dweller associations. Early interactions between these groups have been fraught with miscommunication and mutual suspicion. You can probably imagine what happens when Wall Street investment bankers sit down with radical activists living in the slums of Mumbai or Johannesburg. For many social sector organizations, working with private investors also threatens support from current donors who may not share management's excitement about the opportunity to work with a new breed of impact-oriented investors.

On the other side of the equation, impact investors will need to be realistic about how reluctant commercial banks and mainstream investors are to enter these markets. Short-term demonstration projects and loan guarantees generally fail to entice mainstream investors to enter these markets as quickly as impact investors hope. Impact investors will sometimes need unusual patience when we back innovative business models that need to overcome mainstream skepticism or neglect.

Complementing Rather Than Competing with Government

In many areas, well-functioning, centrally provided, and government-run services may well be superior to private sector solutions. Piped clean water, on-grid electrification, effective national school and health systems, and large-scale public housing development: most likely all will eventually provide cheaper alternatives for more poor customers than the private models that impact investors will back in the next decade. And publicly provided and funded services will always be necessary to provide a safety net for people too poor to participate in market-based solutions.

At the same time, impact investors can provide a powerful lifeline to the millions of poor people alive today who cannot wait for government services to reach them or for mainstream investors to wake up to the opportunity to fund businesses that serve them. These investors will invest in the provision of services and products created not by the ideology of either the "free market" or "the welfare state," but rather by the opportunity for generating meaningful, sustained impact in the lives of poor people.

But as we go about backing businesses, impact investors must not lose sight of the fact that impact investment is the means and the solutions to social problems the ends we aim for. We must celebrate when a government extends affordable clean water distribution systems to a rural community even if the extension threatens the social enterprise we have backed that is providing off-grid water in that village. In such an instance, there will probably be even more remote villagers who can use the private sector solution. Or perhaps the enterprise can create value-added services to complement basic water delivery. In general, an improvement in government services should spur innovation rather than lead to resentment or competition.

Welcome to the Future: Subsectors to Watch

We offer the following list of subsectors to watch, with the caveat that the only thing we know about our list is that it is going to be wrong. With that in mind, we suggest these six subsectors are the most promising for rapid exploration by impact investors:

- Health care
- Affordable housing in emerging markets
- Education
- Agriculture
- Distributed utilities
- Restructured social spending

Especially in emerging markets, where their rapid take-up represents one of the most profound social and economic disruptions in decades, mobile phones will serve as a delivery platform for many of these subsectors. We do not list the mobile phone subsector as a particular impact investment because mainstream commercial investment already capitalizes its rollout. But impact investors are already backing entrepreneurs offering service delivery breakthroughs using the mobile platform in various areas we cover here.

Health Care

Health care in emerging markets exhibits all the characteristics on our checklist of impact investing opportunities:

- The International Finance Corporation (IFC) has estimated that meeting basic health care needs in sub-Saharan Africa alone will require $25 billion to $30 billion of private investment between 2010 and 2020. The total annual market for private sector health care will double there to $35 billion by 2016.[1] Governments in most African countries are not in a position to fund this gap themselves. Their counterparts in much of Asia and Latin America face a similar unfundable gap.

- In most poor countries, a majority of the poor population are already buying health services from private sector providers. A good number of these providers are uncertified, and they often exploit ignorance and desperation. But some of these providers are pioneering new business models that provide decent services at increasingly affordable prices to a wide range of customers.

- Although mainstream investors are beginning to invest in emerging-market health care, their sights seldom wander beyond businesses that target relatively rich customers in cities.

Given this reality, impact investors are increasingly supporting innovative entrepreneurs to expand and improve the efficiency of private sector health care delivery. And capital markets are also being harnessed to improve the health impact of international donations for health systems.

Development finance institutions, private foundations, and nonprofit impact investors are leading the way and spurring investment innovation as they do. The IFC, African Development

Bank, Gates Foundation, and German development finance institution DEG launched the Africa Health Fund in 2009 to capitalize small- and medium-scale businesses whose growth can improve health services for poor people. The fund manager, Aureos, will receive financial rewards for investing in companies that target relatively poorer customers. Deutsche Bank, working with the International Association to Prevent Blindness, has launched a $20 million debt fund to invest in eye hospitals in poor countries. And the nonprofit Acumen Fund is also making private equity investments in health care in India, as are impact investing funds IGNIA (in Mexico) and Bamboo Finance.

In addition to making direct investments in companies and private equity funds, impact investors are creating financing innovations within mainstream capital markets that are raising funds for public health delivery. The International Finance Facility for Immunisation is the flag-bearer of this approach. The facility has raised more than $3 billion since 2006 in AAA-rated bonds bought by institutional investors to be repaid over twenty years from annual national donations to global vaccine efforts. This money converts long-term commitments of aid support into immediate and predictable cash flow for the GAVI Alliance to expand vaccine campaigns and improve health systems in seventy-two poor countries. This front-loading tool has widespread potential application in public health for funding training, physical infrastructure expansion and renovation, and improved systems for financing, management, and information.

Affordable Housing in Emerging Markets

By many counts, 2009 marked the first year in human history in which more people lived in cities than rural areas. With more than 1 billion people living in urban slums and the most basic decent house costing at least a few thousand dollars, the investment need in housing and sanitation services runs to trillions of dollars. Over the next fifty years, a demographic deluge is expected to sweep across Africa and South and East Asia as hundreds of millions more people move into cities. Government spending and donor funding alone will not address this critical need. However, the developer who can figure out how to build a decent home for less than five thousand dollars, issue long-term, fixed-rate mortgages, and solve legal titling issues will stand to make millions and generate substantial social good.

Around the world, investors and developers are scrambling to take on this challenge.[2] India especially is awash with innovation in affordable housing development and finance.[3] In Mexico, impact investing fund IGNIA has invested in a housing strategy in Chiapas, one of the country's poorest areas. The international nongovernmental organization Habitat for Humanity and UN-Habitat (the United Nations department that oversees urban issues) are also raising impact investment funds to support affordable housing development.

While addressing specific, local dynamics in unique ways, successful investments in affordable housing also need to solve three near-omnipresent challenges:

- *Limited land title.* In most emerging-market cities, building housing with individual title deeds is difficult or impossible. As Peruvian economist Hernando de Soto famously noted in his book *Mystery of Capital*, this informality complicates project development as well as finance and mortgage provision.[4]

- *Fragmented customer base.* Affordable housing is a market that will be driven by volume, not margins. Successful projects will need to achieve substantial economies of scale in construction and finance. Yet achieving this scale is difficult and expensive. Slum dwellers tend not to be organized through formal aggregation mechanisms such as trade unions, formal sector employers, or retail banks that would facilitate a wholesale sales approach.

- *Political pressure.* In many cities, slums have arisen on prime real estate near city centers. Given the potential value of this land, affordable housing must compete with other potentially more lucrative uses. In addition, affordable housing developers need to stabilize land acquisition costs in areas with volatile land prices.

Impact investors are innovating solutions to these challenges with pilot projects that could scale substantially in the next decade. The movement for land titling reform is gaining momentum as many national and city governments become aware of the need to work with private developers to improve living conditions. Growing organizations of slum dwellers also provide an increasingly potent partner who can help organize potential customers into groups that could be more efficient to serve. Organizations such Slum Dwellers International are establishing microsavings groups and increasingly looking to partner with impact investors to raise new construction loans for their members. Companies that stand to benefit from housing investment, such as cement and paint companies, are also beginning to back experimental approaches to creating a profitable market for low-income housing development.

Education

Government-run school systems in poor countries around the world are being overwhelmed by the twin forces of rapidly growing populations of children and an increasing demand for education. The private sector is stepping up to fill the gap. By some estimates, 75 percent of all students in poor countries attend private schools, even where free public schools are available. From the slums of Hyderabad to Nairobi, parents are willing to pay for their children to attend higher-quality schools. But lack of access to finance prevents many schools from increasing their capacity and quality.

In response, impact investors are pioneering innovative approaches to financing the expansion of these schools. Perhaps the most aggressive innovator here is the U.S.-based Gray Ghost Ventures. A pioneer in the commercialization of microfinance, Gray Ghost has turned its attention to the affordable private schools sector. It launched a nonbank finance company, the India School Finance Company, in 2009 targeting principal-owned schools in India's slums, typically with loans averaging twenty-five thousand dollars. The IFC is also getting into this sector, primarily by using loan guarantees to encourage local commercial banks to lend to private schools. By 2008 IFC had invested $295 million in education projects in twenty-five countries, reaching 700,000 students.

These experiments are demonstrating both the potential and challenges of channeling impact investment capital to fund school expansion. While some entrepreneurs are seeking to create large-scale school companies that can overcome the problems of fragmentation (such as Gyan Shala in India and Bridges International Academies in Kenya), most schools are small-scale operations run by educators rather than businesspeople. Investors need to put substantial time and effort into working with potential borrowers to improve their business and accounting operations.

Beyond the affordable private school sector and its focus on providing primary and secondary education, impact investors are also putting capital to work in financing university education. With undeveloped student loan markets (such as in Mexico, where only 2 percent of students access credit to pay tuition), impact investors are pioneering new approaches to student lending. Web-based lender Vittana.org is working with microfinance institutions to facilitate peer-to-peer lending for college students in Latin America. Other investors have gone even further, offering to pay students' university fees for a share of their future earnings. Lumni covers tuition fees for students who commit to paying a portion of their salaries for the ten years after they graduate. We acknowledge that these innovations push up against both laws prohibiting indentured servitude and the comfort level of most investors. We often hear audible gasps of disapproval when we describe these financing arrangements to audiences in rich countries, but they represent important innovations that could generate social value if appropriately managed.

Finally, impact investing in education is not limited to emerging markets. At least in the United States, where some argue that the government is retreating from its role in providing quality education, impact investors are organizing finance for charter schools and supporting companies that provide services to schools such as teacher training and healthier food. Education finance has been a central component of the Kellogg Foundation's $100 million impact investing program. The Gates Foundation has also highlighted U.S. education finance in the early deployment of its $400 million impact investing commitment. In 2009, it signed a $10 million guarantee that enabled a charter school operator to secure a $67 million bond issue to build new facilities that enabled it to increase enrollment by seven thousand students.

Agriculture

Volatility in the price of staple foods around the world is creating chaos and concern with increasing frequency. Sudden increases in the cost of rice, maize, and wheat precipitated a global food crisis in 2007–2008 that caused food riots from Haiti to Burkina Faso and pushed an estimated 100 million people back into poverty. In 2011, global food prices are skyrocketing again. An outcome of structural dynamics in the global food system, long-term demographic trends, and erratic weather patterns, increased and volatile food prices are likely here to stay. At the same time, farmers and food companies in rich countries are tapping growing consumer attention to the source of their food. Local and organic food movements have emerged in the wake of the wider environmental movement. And seemingly overnight, investment opportunities are proliferating in the long-moribund agriculture sector.

Impact investors will play an important role in determining the social impact this increased investor appetite in agriculture creates. If speculative investors seeking only to maximize financial return dominate the capitalization of agriculture, the world's food needs will likely be met by large-scale commercial farming operations, heavy on the use of poisonous chemicals and light on the generation of development opportunities for local citizens. Recognizing this danger, impact investors are developing business models and investment structures that could rapidly scale up in the coming years.

Engaging Smallholder Farmers

In most poor countries, the poorest people are the subsistence farmers who struggle to grow enough food to feed their families and generate a small surplus to cover basic needs. Market and other inefficiencies abound in the rural economy. Poor transport and storage infrastructure leave as much as 30 percent of the food to rot before it is eaten. Lack of processing facilities reduces the market value of most crops. And even if they had money, many farmers are too far from suppliers to buy basic fertilizer and irrigation equipment. Banks, even those in the burgeoning microfinance industry, are often unwilling to lend to farmers. And government-led attempts to create sustainable rural development have rarely succeeded since the great gains of the Green Revolution in the 1970s.

Against this backdrop, impact investors are creating innovative approaches to capitalizing local farmers by providing loan guarantees to encourage local banks to lend to smallholder farmers. In one example, Africa's largest bank, Standard Bank, committed to lend $100 million to smallholder agriculture on the back of a $10 million guarantee by a Nairobi-based private foundation, the Alliance for a Green Revolution in Africa. Impact investors are also investing directly in farming operations. To maximize social impact, they often provide financing and expertise to local farmers to enable them to process and market their products through anchor commercial-scale farms.

Impact investors are closing the financing gap that remains in the fair trade supply chain. Consumer awareness campaigns have increased the demand for ethically sourced and sustainably produced commodities such as coffee and cocoa. Many major companies now seek to diversify their supply chains to include smallholder producers. But lack of capital from skeptical local banks and the reluctance of multinational food companies to become local lenders leaves many farmers shut out of these markets. Impact investors such as U.S.-based Root Capital are filling this gap. As discussed in Chapter Four, Root Capital is pioneering new approaches to providing loans to farmer cooperatives and marketing companies through relationships with supply chain partners like Starbucks and Nestlé.

Sustainable Agriculture and Slow Money

Investment gaps for agriculture are emerging in rich countries as well. Consumer demand for locally produced and organic food is outpacing mainstream investor interest in the sector. Investment in sustainable agriculture is a major interest for many impact-focused family offices that are beginning to close the financing gap. Organic farmers are also tapping angel investor networks and finance from dedicated private equity funds.

Some philanthropic investors are beginning to organize through the Slow Money movement. Slow Money, based on the core ideas of the Slow Food movement, seeks to secure and invest funds on the basis of long-term, deep-value investing. Coined by Woody Tasch in his book by the same name, Slow Money has created a long-term philanthropic investment fund that will raise funds as charitable contributions from individuals to underwrite infrastructure development in rural areas in the United States.[5] These investments will help local farmers grow and transport crops as well as access needed capital for "hard cost" investments such as irrigation or other equipment.[6] In this way, Slow Money harvests various levels of financial performance by using charitable gifts to make long-term, revolving loans and other investments together with real environmental impact and social capital development—a true blended value proposition.

Distributed Utilities

In an age of technological marvels, it is sometimes too easy for citizens of rich countries to forget how many people still live without access to basic utilities like clean water, electricity, and gas or oil for heating and cooking. In many countries, especially outside major cities, most, and sometimes almost all, residents live without on-grid electricity and piped water, and they cook using open fires or charcoal stoves. Historically, providing these services was seen as a natural monopoly in which a single entity could more efficiently serve more customers. Government-controlled entities have dominated (and often failed) in the delivery of these basic utility services.

Now, technological breakthroughs and shifting costs might upend the dominance of natural monopolies and open space for impact investors to back entrepreneurs offering distributed, or off-the-grid, solutions. Rapid innovation in renewable energy production and storage is expanding the reach of companies offering solar- and wind-powered electricity services. Other companies are creating affordable systems that convert farm waste into cooking gas and plant fertilizer. Community-level water treatment facilities are also proliferating, especially in India, where rural villages tend to have the population concentration necessary to support the cost of installing a water purification plant.

Impact investors have joined donors and governments in backing many of these early demonstration projects. Impact investors like the nonprofit E+Co., which targets communities far from government-sponsored on-grid services. Most people have historically considered these to be stop-gap solutions that will provide the service until the more efficient grid reaches a village or urban slum community. But increasingly, the costs of some distributed solutions are starting to converge with the cost of on-grid solutions as business models develop and benefit from efficiencies of scale and technological advances at the same time as the costs of traditional approaches increase. Impact investors will play a crucial role in providing the bridging finance that will enable distributed services enterprises to innovate until they can compete for cost and service quality with the dominant utilities.

Restructured Social Spending

Impact investing is poised to expand rapidly through the launch of creative finance structures that enable impact investors to work directly with government to bring private capital into basic service provision. One such innovation is the social impact (or pay-for-success) bond. In this approach, a group of investors enters into a contract with a government agency or philanthropy that agrees to pay the investors if a specific social outcome is achieved. The investors then raise capital, which they give to organizations they believe best placed to create the desired social outcome. Although this may seem at first glance to be a standard pay-for-performance agreement, it is in fact a significant financial innovation with profound implications for expanding the impact investing market. Unlike a pay-for-service contract, the social impact bond provides upfront funding to the organizations that will deliver the service. This enables the best organizations to participate in providing community service, not just those that can fund their own working capital. Perhaps more important, by raising the initial bond from private investors, the structure places the risk of success onto the investors, allowing private investors to do what they do best: take calculated risk in pursuit of profit. In turn, the government will pay only for verifiable results and will profit from keeping the additional savings.

The potential of the social impact bond lies in its ability to structure the involvement of impact investors in a wide range of social issues. Social impact bonds could be applied to any social issue in which:

- Preventing a problem costs less than treating it, creating a surplus that can be shared between taxpayers and investors

- Measuring success is relatively easy, making what government owes investors predictable and uncontroversial

- Approaches to intervention are proven, so that investors can be relevantly confident their investments will pay off

The first social impact bond was agreed to between the U.K. Ministry of Justice and the impact investment advisor Social Finance in 2010. Through this investment vehicle, private investors have invested approximately $8 million, which is going to nonprofit organizations working to help recently released convicts stay out of jail. The British government has agreed to pay bondholders on a sliding scale: the fewer prisoners who reoffend, the more money the private investors will receive, with a capped annual return of 13 percent. The payment to investors will represent only a fraction of the money the government will save from having these former offenders stay out of jail.

Reducing obesity in communities with a propensity to develop diabetes, reducing high school dropout rates, and supporting foster families to take in orphans: all of these issues and many others share the characteristics that make them ripe for the social impact bond approach. And this could potentially transform the funding landscape not only for organizations that deliver these innovative social services but also for social enterprises that are pioneering new approaches.

Where Do We Go from Here?

As you know from the legal disclaimers you will have read on your pension plan report or an investment prospectus, past performance is not a good predictor of future success. And predicting the future is dangerous anywhere, especially in the rapidly evolving world of impact investing for blended value.

So, what *do* we know?

We know conditions are set for impact investing to make a substantial mark on transforming the trajectory of the human condition. Hundreds of millions of people are suffering from the failure of both government and markets to provide basic goods and services. Opportunities abound for impact investors who, in pursuing blended value, can see and create opportunity where others see only market failure and government neglect. Governments will be crucial to open space for investors to put their capital to work, even in areas previously considered the reserve domain of government. And don't wait for the multinational companies to lead the way: except under a narrow set of conditions, innovation will be driven by local entrepreneurs for whom figuring out how to serve poor customers at scale is their only business, not a sideline.[7]

What Will Be *Our* "Apple IPO"?

In 1980, the Apple computer company sold shares in a legendary IPO. Beyond its significance in the technology sector, the IPO also transformed the trajectory of a previously unheralded financial innovation. This novel investment strategy proposed the seemingly crazy idea that an investor could profit in the long run by providing start-up and expansion capital to very young companies. Mainstream institutional investors had stayed away from this crazy idea. But the Apple IPO made its early-stage investors very, very rich. Suddenly institutional investors took notice, and what was

BUILDING AN EFFECTIVE INDUSTRY
Alvaro Rodriguez Arregui, Cofounder, IGNIA Fund,
Monterrey, Mexico

After I graduated with a Harvard M.B.A. in 1995, I stayed in Boston while my wife completed her studies. In the midst of the Mexican financial crisis, it was not easy for a Latin American to find a job, so I eventually went to work with the microfinance pioneer ACCION.

My experience at ACCION changed my life. For the first time, I saw poverty firsthand and realized the huge human challenge that lack of access to basic products and services creates. I also learned about the power of business solutions. Moreover, I realized that the nonprofit world was not a good place to learn basic management skills and business discipline.

After a year at ACCION, I went on to a career in business but stayed connected with microfinance. When my business friends asked me why I dedicated so much time to microfinance, I explained that I was passionate about it and was preparing for my life after business. Interacting with microfinance clients, I realized that lending was only one of many services absent in many lower-income communities. I speculated about the existence of entrepreneurs looking to tap into this pent-up demand for capital as well as strategic and managerial support. In early 2007, I began discussing the idea of creating a social impact fund (the term *impact investing* did not exist yet) to fill this need.

When I left my job as the chief financial officer of Vitro in 2007, I was humbled with numerous job offers in the corporate world. But I was really passionate to start this social impact fund myself. I always thought that I would wait until I retired to dedicate my professional life to social causes, but the time had come twenty years early! With my old boss from ACCION, Michael Chu, I launched IGNIA Fund in mid-2007.

At IGNIA, we aim to increase access to basic products and services in an efficient and effective way. The challenge is huge, and the need is urgent. Profits are not the objective, but they are the means to achieve it: profits are necessary to attract both capital and driven and promising entrepreneurs. Both are crucial to create the scale and new industries we need. Because poor people have so few options, we see opportunities for companies to provide a better value proposition while maintaining high margins in various subsectors like health care and housing. We are also excited by the potential for scale with business models that figure out how to reach the vast untapped markets of poor customers.

But capital raising is never easy. IGNIA was an innovative idea in a nascent impact investing field that was seeking change in underserved markets. Moreover, we faced skeptical investors trained to believe that doing good and doing well simultaneously is not possible. We were stuck in a no-man's-land where commercial investors perceived us as "too social" and philanthropists and social investors perceived us as "too commercial." Navigating this territory, we had to be very clear in articulating our ideas. Eventually we closed the fund in 2010 with $102 million from a mix of local investors, development finance institutions, and leading impact investment funds.

While navigating a winding fundraising road, we also had to put together a unique management team. We need people with rigorous financial and analytical skills who are also passionate about social issues and can work in different environments with ease. Our team members need investment savvy to find and structure deals, operating experience to support investee companies, and a strong commitment to social impact so we can maintain our focus and so social entrepreneurs are willing to work with us.

IGNIA Fund is only one part of the larger task to build an effective industry that can use business solutions to address social issues. Single firms are born, they grow, they mature, they get lazy, and they die. But industries prosper over time and reach scale as competition fosters the delivery of better products at lower cost. To build an industry, we need a language for reporting social impact that is homogeneous and adds transparency to the sector, infrastructure to reduce search costs and identify the players, and networks of like-minded individuals to share data and best practices.

But ultimately, we need multiple demonstration cases that will motivate the thirst of capable, driven, and creative entrepreneurs who are attracted by the potential of profits. We have to show strong financial performance. And we have to adopt ways to credibly measure and report on social impact so that we can identify precisely what we do and attract a new class of impact-oriented investors.

---

previously viewed as a crazy approach is now a standard component of investment portfolios, known as the very mainstream concept of venture capital.

What will be impact investing's Apple IPO? In what geography or sector will the concept of impact investing for blended value find a success so compelling that it commands attention, overcomes the skeptics, and propels us into the mainstream? One thing we know is that it's going to be about more than just money. Our Apple IPO will need to create blended value by deploying substantial amounts of capital and substantially addressing a major social problem. This "IPO" will occur when we can point to a compelling social or environmental challenge that impact investment–backed enterprises solved at a level that would not have been possible for government or mainstream markets alone.

We also know a great investment deal alone will not be enough. A great impact investment that occurs in isolation will deliver blended value to some investors and help some communities improve their lot, but it will not be an industry-defining moment. For that, we will require a deal to occur within a well-organized industry that knows how to measure blended value, cultivate leaders who can convey its power, work effectively with government to expand its opportunities, and rapidly identify and replicate successful investment practices.

What will it take to build the systems that will allow our Apple IPO to transform not only investment practice but also our capacity to solve our pressing social problems now and into the future? The rest of this book explores that question.[8]

Part Two

THE IMPLICATIONS OF IMPACT INVESTING

Chapter 6

HOW WILL WE REGULATE IMPACT INVESTING?

The Reluctant Tax Expert

When Canadian entrepreneur Bill Young decided in 2000 to shift his time and resources from building businesses to addressing social challenges, he did what most other people in his position have done for a century: he set up a charitable foundation. And like many other earnest philanthropists before him, he set about conducting research to determine what social issues he should focus on.

After six months, Bill decided to address the issue of unemployment among disadvantaged communities in Canada. But unlike his predecessors, he did not assume that the only way to help people secure sustainable jobs was through donating to nonprofit organizations. Instead, he sought to draw on his experience as a business builder and investor to support social enterprises that could increase employment opportunities by expanding their businesses. To pursue this work, he formed a nonprofit investment fund and advisory firm, Social Capital Partners.

He assumed the government would support this approach to tackling a difficult social challenge in a sustainable model from which he did not profit. He was wrong. To his surprise (and the surprise of his lawyers), the government rejected his application for charitable status. Its six-page explanation detailed the charity regulator's discomfort with the way Social Capital Partners planned to work with for-profit companies in addition to charities and to make investments as well as grants. And with all the money he had to dedicate to his philanthropy tied up in his foundation, he suddenly faced a severe roadblock to the pursuit of this work.

A decade later, Bill has figured out how to build Social Capital Partners into an important impact investing innovator. But he has had to learn more than he ever wanted to know about the charitable regulatory tax system in Canada. And this learning has cost him time, money, and energy he could have more usefully spent helping build businesses that can provide decent jobs to people who need them.

Creating the Enabling Environment

Everyone at some point complains about government regulations and the officials who make them. But as much as public policy will always be a lightning rod for criticism, the legal and regulatory system in well-governed countries provides a basic scaffolding to support investment and business activities. And to varying degrees, most countries are building a similarly useful scaffold to support charitable activity. These systems define and protect entrepreneurs and investors. They also provide a range of incentives to encourage individuals and corporations to use their assets to contribute to social good through charity.

As long as the only purpose of investment is to generate financial return and the only way to pursue social ends is through charity, these systems generally work. For-profit investors and philanthropists can retreat into their safe corners where separate regulation supports their independent activities. But the development of impact investing up-ends this comfortable equilibrium, raising a number of challenging questions:

- If a loan to the Peruvian fruit seller we met in Chapter
  Three is a better way to lift her family out of poverty than a

gift would be, should an investor receive a tax break to lend
to her?

- How do regulators protect the interests of investors in a
  venture capital fund like IGNIA who want the fund
  managers to pursue both financial returns and social impact?

- Should Root Capital be allowed to maintain its nonprofit
  status, and the tax break that comes with it, if it raises
  commercial investment to fund its operations?

- Should taxpayers subsidize microfinance companies like
  Compartamos when they may end up making millions of
  dollars in a public stock sale?

In most places, the regulatory system has not yet caught up
with answering these questions. Bill Young's experience in Canada
is unfortunately more typical than remarkable. But like Young,
other impact investors and entrepreneurs are not waiting idly for
politicians and regulators to answer these questions. They are
already making impact investments that generate blended value
for investors and stakeholders alike. Country by country, sector by
sector, and even, in some cases, city by city, impact investors are
carving out exemptions to corporate and charity law that create
the legal space to enable them to operate.

These exemptions provide safe havens within a fundamentally
hostile legal environment. They are not the basis for sustained
and rational oversight of the impact investing industry. In most
cases, social entrepreneurs and impact investors have been left to
force-fit their aspirations into a regulatory system that pushes them
to pretend they seek to make a difference or make a profit, but not
both. Policy shapes and enables markets. No major innovation in
either investment practice or social change has ultimately scaled
without a supportive policy framework. Getting policy right is
crucial to realizing the potential of impact investing.

Entrepreneurs often ask us whether they should set up their organizations as for-profit or nonprofit entities and whether they should seek to attract investors or donors. For their part, investors often ask us whether it makes sense to run their impact investments out of a charitable trust or a mainstream fund. Currently, our answers are context specific and rarely satisfying. Eventually regulators and politicians will create a holistic framework for harnessing the power of impact investing for blended value. When that happens, we will have a more compelling answer to these questions: "Neither. There's something better that's tailored for you." Until then, we hope this chapter provides a useful outline of the building blocks of a holistic system.

Fitting New Aspirations into Old Systems

The impact investing industry essentially has two sides: the investors who are putting assets to work and the enterprises that can take this capital and convert it into blended value. For both investors and enterprises, the regulatory system remains a frustrating obstacle to generating blended value in an integrated way. While this book focuses on the investment side (and will do so in this chapter as well), observing the regulatory system first from the perspective of the enterprises powerfully reveals the inadequacy of the current system.

The Frustrations of the Impact Entrepreneur

Imagine an entrepreneur setting up a new organization. If she primarily wants to pursue a social purpose, she will register her enterprise as a nonprofit or charitable enterprise. In most countries, her enterprise will receive tax breaks for pursuing a charitable mission. To maintain this benefit, her enterprise must agree to pursue only activities that the tax code deems socially desirable. She will be able to generate income from donors (and increasingly, in many countries, from selling goods and services) but will not be able to raise capital from equity investors. She will face a regulator focused on ensuring the nonprofit organization does not defraud the government by claiming tax breaks it does not deserve.

If our entrepreneur primarily wants to generate profits that could be distributed to outside investors, she will register as a for-profit entity. Her enterprise will be given wide sway to operate as it sees fit (within the bounds of basic human rights, labor, and environmental standards) and will be expected to contribute directly to society only in paying corporate taxes. She will face a regulator focused on ensuring the enterprise does not defraud investors or violate basic standards of corporate behavior.

Historically, this system has worked fine for most organizations and entrepreneurs. But it is easy to see how neither option fits for a social enterprise eager to create blended value in an integrated way by mobilizing impact investment capital. The regulation of nonprofits is premised on the idea that the pursuit of profit (or certainly capital gains) is evidence of mission drift. But that leaves nonprofits restricted in the profit-seeking activities they can undertake. The regulation of for-profit entities is premised on the idea that pursuing a social purpose would distract management from their primary duty to maximize profits. This leaves the for-profit entity restricted in how it can pursue social purpose activities that do not contribute to financial return in the eyes of the regulator.

So what's a social entrepreneur to do? They are finding ways to twist the current regulatory system to the point that they can at least function, if not flourish.

Starting from the Nonprofit Perspective

Let's say our entrepreneur decided to take the nonprofit route but realizes she can pursue business-based solutions that generate revenues and perhaps even equity value. Looking around, she will see others forging two paths to navigate the regulatory system. First, in addition to her primary nonprofit, she could set up a wholly owned for-profit entity controlled by the nonprofit parent. This will allow her the flexibility to undertake profit-generating activity while ensuring that the profits from this work flow back to her social mission, typically by pre-designating profits to fund charitable activity. Impact investing nonprofits such as Acumen Fund, which is focused on international development, and Enterprise Partners, which is working in U.S. community development, have found this approach necessary when seeking to take on investment capital.

But over time, she might find that the nonprofit designation brings restrictions that outweigh the tax and branding benefits. In this case, she could take the second path: flee the nonprofit regulatory regime entirely and reincorporate as a for-profit company. As inspiration, she could look at the journey of organizations like Compartamos in Mexico and SKS in India that converted from nonprofit to finance company status before their initial public offerings (IPOs).

Although these two approaches allow our entrepreneur to pursue blended value, they are work-arounds that bring substantial costs. They will force her to jump through accounting hoops, such as allocating senior management time on an hour-by-hour basis between the nonprofit and for-profit entity, hiring different managers to perform duplicate tasks, and keeping separate e-mail accounts, for example, and to pretend she is not seeking to generate blended value in an integrated way. Her regulators will be able to stay in their comfort zones. But our entrepreneur will be frustrated and distracted.

Starting from the For-Profit Perspective

Proving to a skeptical nonprofit regulator that a business-oriented approach is actually focused on social benefit just doesn't seem worth the hassle. What if our entrepreneur instead sets up her enterprise under for-profit business regulation?

Regulation in this area is constructed to ensure that the management of the enterprise applies appropriate fiduciary duty to protect investors' financial interests. If the manager seeks to use her for-profit business to support social purposes, she will have to jump through hoops to mask these activities so as not to be seen to be violating fiduciary duty. Here she has two options.

First, like her nonprofit counterpart who set up a for-profit subsidiary, she could set up a nonprofit entity linked to the for-profit company. Increasingly, companies in the services sector are adopting this approach, such as the consulting company Bain, which spun out the nonprofit Bridgespan in 2000. The nonprofit allows them to pursue contracts from foundations and government more inclined to hire nonprofits and also to create an organizational and cost structure more compatible with nonprofit work. But regulators will strive to ensure as much separation as possible between the for-profit and nonprofit to ensure the nonprofit is not used as a tax dodge. This setup will not support more creative approaches to creating blended value in an integrated way.

Her second option is to choose over time to convert her company into a nonprofit organization. The idea of making this switch on purpose is rare but not unprecedented. It will require liquidating any equity shares in the company because a nonprofit cannot have equity owners. This move will likely be difficult for our entrepreneur unless she has managed to hold a strong controlling ownership and governance stake.

In addition to these paths that allow the entrepreneur to operate within formal nonprofit regulatory frameworks, she could try to pursue her social mission entirely as a for-profit entity. If she can maintain control of her company, she will certainly have more leeway than she would have starting from the nonprofit trailhead. But when she sells the company, or especially if she decides to take it public, current regulation does not provide a clear pathway to preserve this mission orientation. Some business owners are inserting mission preservation clauses into their incorporation documents, but these remain largely untested. Similarly, public companies that pursue a social mission through the main business have to cloak this activity in the shroud of long-term shareholder value creation for fear of shareholder lawsuits.

Ultimately our entrepreneur will likely find that this path converges on the same mountain peak of inefficiency and frustration. There is no way around the fact that current corporate law and regulation has not caught up to her aspirations to use her social enterprise to create truly blended value.

Frustrations of the Impact Investor

If the journey of the social entrepreneur up the mountain of regulation is treacherous and ultimately unfulfilling, what about the impact investor who wants to back enterprises that can generate blended value? Unfortunately, Bill Young's experiences in Canada are typical of the Frankenstein's monster of corporate entities he may need to cobble together to realize his impact investing vision.

The aspiring impact investor will find that in most countries, governments provide tax break incentives to individuals and corporations that contribute their private capital to solving social challenges. These incentives can be direct (by allowing these contributions to count as expenses or losses for income tax purposes) or indirect (by allowing investors to receive capital gains tax breaks if they contribute the profits of their investments). In many countries, these tax breaks drive charitable giving, especially among very wealthy individuals, and an army of lawyers and accountants has mustered to maximize the tax-avoiding benefits of these incentives for their clients.

Now here's the catch: the regulations governing these incentives almost always equate charitable purpose with donation. To receive a tax break or maintain the charitable status of a private foundation requires giving away money rather than making impact investments with it. With few exceptions, an impact investor who wants to use the tool of investment rather than grant or donation will run afoul of the regulators overseeing these incentives.

And it's not just that he will not have access to tax incentives for the investments he makes. Regulators will likely insist that whoever manages his assets place them only in safe investments that avoid the risk many impact investments may be willing to take on. In this case, the investor will face a regulatory system that ignores the social good of impact investment or treats it as financially suspect.

As long as donations were the only way to make a social contribution, this made sense. But for many impact investors like Bill Young, impact investing is an exciting tool to enable them to make all their assets (not just the excess cash flow their investments generate) available to pursue social good. For them, a regulatory system that ignores or restricts impact investment is anachronistic.

Cracks in the Regulatory Wall

In truth, regulation has been slightly more pliable for investors. Some governments are slowly realizing that impact investments can be a powerful way to harness private sector interest in pursuing social purpose. These innovations build on the incentives many governments have already provided philanthropic giving and their interest in subsidizing and mandating private sector investment into underserved areas.

An impact investor who lives in a country where these adjustments are being made and is interested in a social issue these adjustments cover could find some interesting opportunities to make impact investments that benefit from supportive regulation.

Tax Breaks for Impact Investments from Private Foundations

An impact investor who has set up a private foundation to channel his social purpose assets may be able to receive tax breaks for some impact investments. As we discuss in more detail in Chapter Nine, private foundations in many countries pay little or no capital gains tax as long as they release a set percentage of their assets annually for social purpose. (In the United States, this payout requirement is 5 percent, against which the foundation may charge both administrative and program costs.) Most foundations meet this payout requirement through donations to nonprofits and governments. In the 1960s, however, the Ford Foundation recognized that some of the nonprofits it contributed to could benefit from loans, not just grants. In 1969 the foundation successfully advocated for a change in the U.S. tax code to allow what is now referred to as Program-Related Investments to qualify toward meeting payout requirements. Although still only 1 percent of total foundation disbursements, Program-Related Investments provide a window for impact investors to operate within the protective incentives of foundation regulation.

Tax Breaks for Targeted Impact Investments

Impact investors may also find supportive policy in some specific areas of social concern. In the Netherlands, for example, a 1995 green investment policy lowered capital gains tax rates on investments in renewable energy and helped mobilize 5 billion euros of investment capital in its first ten years, though it is being phased out. The New Market Tax Credit system in the United States established in 1994 similarly provides tax credits and capital gains tax breaks to investors capitalizing projects in typically poor neighborhoods and has mobilized more than $16 billion directly, with estimates that these investments have leveraged an additional $200 billion.

For investors operating within the relatively limited areas these innovations cover, these adjustments are starting to provide a more supportive regulatory framework for impact investing. The program-related investment regulation allows a philanthropist who is looking to provide a low-interest loan to a nonprofit to get credit for the charitable intent of the investment. An investor in a Dutch wind farm or a housing development in a poor neighborhood in New York City receives a tax break that acknowledges the impact of the investment. Of course, if you do not live in a country with a program-related investment policy or targeted subsidies for impact investments, you're out of luck.

Although these innovations in the regulatory framework have so far been applied in a patchwork fashion, they point the way to potential holistic changes in investment regulation that could encourage impact investment while preserving its fundamentally social purpose.

Building the Regulatory System to Support Impact Investing

In most countries, regulations simply do not recognize and support the ambitions that social entrepreneurs and impact investors increasingly hold to create blended value through impact investing. As we discuss in the next chapter, the most intrepid pioneers are finding ways to make the existing system at least tenable. But regulatory systems that force people to jump through hoops will stifle impact investment. Those who lack the stamina to deal with these current frustrations may just give up and fall back to funding nonprofits through donations or maximizing financial return with investment. And impact investing will not become a widespread tool for addressing social challenges and deploying substantial capital.

For impact investing to realize its potential, regulators need to catch up to the reality that the twin assumptions underpinning current regulation of philanthropy and investment no longer hold, Instead, organizations can pursue both profit and purpose in an integrated way (so regulation that narrowly limits the profit-making potential of social purpose organizations is too restrictive) and investments can create profit and social value simultaneously (so regulation that narrowly focuses on protecting only the investors' financial interest does not make sense).

In this new world, regulation needs to enable organizations to execute business models focused on generating blended value, increase the flow of impact investments, and set an ambitious floor for what constitutes a high-impact investment. A patchwork quilt of innovation in specific subsectors, such as the Dutch green bonds, points to potential components of this holistic approach. But we cannot regulate by exemption. We need to weave these innovations into an overarching framework for regulating impact investing that can blanket the full range of activities where impact investors are addressing social challenges and the many new areas they will move into in the future.

Building this supportive framework for impact investing is not only a task for government regulators. Good regulation will emerge from the engagement of investors, entrepreneurs, and potential customers as well. As the controversy and disruptions to the microfinance industry in India in 2010 showed, everyone who cares about the future of impact investment has a stake in creating a more supportive regulatory environment. Getting too complacent by operating under the regulatory radar or through regulatory work-arounds is not sustainable.

At a high level, the contours of a regulatory and policy agenda for impact investing are clear. While we touch on an array of existing regulatory structures spanning investment oversight and social policy, we focus on three overarching approaches:

- Promoting social enterprise

- Promoting impact investment

- Shaping the marketplace

These approaches will be applied with different emphasis and flavors in specific national and local contexts. And when they are taken together, these advancements in regulatory structure will help create an enabling environment that increases the pace and scale at which we address social challenges by supporting additional capital flows into ventures that create blended value.

Promoting Social Enterprise

Most governments now recognize the utility of harnessing private activity to tackle social challenges and deliver basic services, and most have created corporate forms that recognize the interest of some enterprises to pursue social purpose rather than profit. These enterprises can incorporate as nonprofits or charities. Governments often subsidize these organizations directly with grant funds, create training and other support programs to improve their capacity, and encourage them through preferential treatment in procurement.

In many places, these social sector organizations are so pervasive that it's easy to forget how new the idea of the social sector is. Acknowledging that private organizations could be responsible for providing social solutions was a quiet revolution in twentieth-century governance. This revolution is now due for its next turn as governments begin to recognize that impact investors backing for-profit social enterprises can provide a similarly powerful social force. Just as nonprofit innovators developed theirs over the past half-century, these enterprises will need their own innovations in corporate form and state support.

Creating a New Corporate Form for Impact Enterprises

For an increasing number of enterprises and investors, the division into nonprofit and for profit no longer makes sense. A new corporate form that enables entrepreneurs to take on impact investment capital in order to pursue blended value will be the linchpin of a supportive regulatory regime. This will allow social entrepreneurs to focus on producing blended value rather than skirting the edges of corporate law. Creating a new corporate form may sound quixotic, but it is neither unprecedented nor unrealistic. The development of the joint stock company four hundred years ago, often heralded as the central innovation in unlocking the potential of modern capitalism, was not predestined but arose out of recognition of the potential to unleash progress through regulatory innovation. Since then, corporate forms have continued to evolve.

The new corporate form will need to recognize that impact investors seek protection of both the social mission and their financial interests. This corporate form will need to marry the twin imperatives of charity and corporate regulation while enabling corporations to pursue blended value:

- Ensuring socially focused entities hew to their social mission but without placing undue restrictions on their ability to make money

- Enabling profit-focused entities to capitalize themselves with investors whose financial interests are protected but without constraining their ability to pursue social objectives

Various initiatives are underway to develop new corporate forms that meet the needs of entrepreneurs, investors, and society. Going from conceptualization to regulatory reality is not easy for any of them. As Andrew Kassoy of the nonprofit B Corporation notes in "New Rules for a New Capitalism," passing any new corporate form into law requires strong advocates to muster unusual coalitions against forces of inertia.

Although none of these initiatives is perfect and none has achieved a critical mass of take-up and support, all offer important steps forward. Consider some of these more interesting developments gaining momentum now:

- *Community Interest Corporations (CICs).* The United Kingdom has gone further than most other countries with the creation of a national-level corporate form. Created in 2005, the CIC (pronounced "kick") designation frees for-profit entities to pursue a social mission without fear of being sued for violating the fiduciary responsibility to maximize financial return. This addresses the problem of our entrepreneur who worried about being barred from some socially focused activities. But the CIC regulation still reflects its origins in a fundamental mistrust of the profit motive. The equity value of a CIC is prelocked and unavailable for distribution, though the government has raised the ceiling on dividends to 20 percent annually in order to better balance the profit and social motives.

• *The L3C.* The low-profit limited liability company (L3C) in the United States provides a useful option for companies whose primary purpose is to provide a social good. The L3C is not constrained in its ability to make profits or to share profits with shareholders. However, because it has been created specifically to prequalify companies for Program-Related Investments under U.S. private foundations regulation, incorporating as an LC3 constrains the range of profit-seeking activity a company can pursue and, in practice, the returns it can offer investors. Some entrepreneurs and investors will find meeting these narrow criteria too confining.

• *Flexible-purpose corporation.* A group of lawyers in California introduced SB201, a proposal to establish a flexible-purpose corporation designation. As of this writing, the legislation is working its way through the State house. This legislation seeks to free company managers to pursue philanthropic activities or impact-oriented projects without worrying about lawsuits from investors. Its articles of incorporation make clear to any prospective investors that it is pursuing activities that are focused not only on maximizing shareholder value. If this law passes, a subset of flexible-purpose corporations could be interesting targets for impact investors. Without any requirement for third-party verification of social impact, however, this corporate designation could create confusion in co-branding companies that pursue impact as a core part of their operations with those that dabble in philanthropy but seek the goodwill that comes with it. Interestingly, various representatives of nonprofit associations testified against this legislation, expressing fear that this new corporate form could divert donor dollars into investment in flexible corporations.

• *B Corporations.* Another attempt to strike a balance between providing flexibility and ensuring social purpose is benefit corporation legislation also being pushed forward in the United States. (See "New Rules for a New Capitalism.") Benefit corporation status enables managers and owners to pursue profit and purpose while providing greater flexibility in their operations. In addition to pursuing social purpose in their business operations, benefit corporations (or B Corps) must also agree to levels of transparency and accountability that exceed minimum requirements for other companies and to mandate management to optimize the multiple interests of various stakeholders, such as employees and the environment, rather than solely the owners. This approach incorporates a company's social commitment and practice into measurement of its value rather than looking only at its financial performance. Impact investors can invest in B Corporations with greater confidence in management's ability to pursue social purpose and create substantial profits for investors if possible. Not yet a national standard, B Corporation (like the L3C) is available to companies registered in a growing number of states, with Vermont and Maryland leading the way with formal approval of the designation in 2010 and New Jersey following in early 2011.

In addition to these innovations in corporate form, various initiatives around the world are exploring ways to expand and adapt the centuries-old cooperative ownership model to broaden the share and stake that workers can gain from the enterprises they help build.

Subsidizing Impact Enterprises

Once a corporate form is in place that enables business owners to create blended value in a transparent and integrated way, governments will more easily be able to tap these companies. Many countries have already created a precedent for this in supporting targeted companies. The U.S. Small Business Administration, a fifty-year-old organization with an almost $100 billion balance sheet provides loan guarantees and investment subsidies to banks and venture capitalists investing in small businesses. It also offers technical advice to business owners and their investors. In India, the National Bank for Agriculture and Rural Development has played a similar role to support investment in rural businesses since 1982.

In these examples, policymakers have determined that a discrete area of investment activity—small businesses in the United States, rural enterprises in India—deserves encouragement from government. Governments could create similar programs to support enterprises pursuing impact in a much broader range of sectors and geographies. Programs currently focused on promoting companies based on their ownership structure (in the United States and South Africa, for example, for black- and woman-owned enterprises) could be complemented with those promoting companies based on their social impact. The Small Business Administration has seen this opportunity and in early 2011 proposed a $500 million commitment to support impact investors by putting capital to work in companies throughout the United States that create jobs in targeted low-income communities.

Promoting Impact Investment

The creation of a new corporate form for social enterprises and policies to support their growth will help seed an army of organizations ready to create blended value through market-based approaches to addressing social challenges. But how will they get capital to start up and grow?

Some social enterprises will be profitable enough to fuel their growth with mainstream investment capital. But mainstream markets will ignore many others even if they could produce substantial blended value if adequately capitalized. What can the government do to promote flows of impact investment into these enterprises—and should it?

One important promise of impact investing is that it will unlock substantial new capital flows to complement cash-strapped governments and charities to solve social problems. It may seem a bit odd, then, to urge governments to subsidize these investors. But well-formulated tax incentives and direct subsidies could be an effective way for governments to leverage their limited resources. In some areas, investment mandates from government will also be needed to shock markets out of structural inefficiencies.

Given the mixed history of government interference in private sector investment decisions, these incentives and mandates will need to be carefully constructed and recognize a fundamental distinction between impact investments that generate risk-adjusted market rate financial returns and those that do not. In some cases, structural barriers will keep investors out of geographies or sectors even if these investments could ultimately prove profitable. Impact investment may need to prime these markets, creating the critical mass of established business models, businesses, and networks that can subsequently support mainstream financial returns. In this case, government involvement may be temporarily necessary to induce investment, but the results could ultimately correct for a market failure and enable mainstream investors to enter. In these cases, government involvement can fall away over time.

Other enterprises might create substantial public good externalities but will not be able to generate enough profit from their activity to attract mainstream investors. In these cases, financial returns may never attract private capital beyond impact investors even if these investments generate substantial blended value. Investments in deep rural areas in most countries reflect these characteristics. Government can reduce the risk of investments in these sectors with guarantees and other support, or they can simply mandate these investments. In both instances, the concept of impact investment helps create the framework for understanding these dynamics and places these mandates within the broader regulatory structure that seeks to harness private markets to social purpose.

Broadening Tax Incentives

The tax code has been a powerful tool for steering private capital, and some governments are starting to use it to promote impact investing in targeted areas. This approach tends to have wide-ranging political appeal because it harnesses market forces and reduces tax exposure, which appeals to the right, and steers capital to support social and environmental priorities, which appeals to the left.

Current regulation provides the basis for a more holistic approach. Tax breaks for donations set a precedent that government can incent the contribution of private assets toward addressing social problems. Tax breaks for targeted sector investment, such as low-income housing development in the United States or green bonds in the Netherlands, extend this concept directly to for-profit investors.

Combining these concepts, governments can establish a broad regime of tax incentives for impact investments. Admittedly this would open up avenues for abuse by investors who are seeking a tax break without a real interest in creating impact. But the approach has the advantage of promoting impact investing in areas where market participants see opportunity for creating blended value rather than just the areas where the political process has determined impact investing capital is most needed.

More narrowly, creating broad rules that encourage private foundations to make impact investments could unlock a uniquely poised pool of capital. U.S. Program-Related Investment regulations (discussed at length in Chapter Nine) provide a good starting point by recognizing that private foundations can pursue social purpose through for-profit investment. Other countries that do not have similar policies should adopt them. But as currently applied in the United States, this regulation is too restrictive to support the practice of leading impact investors who are able to navigate more deftly the balance between pursuing profit and preserving mission than the regulations allow. Impact investors in foundations need to push the boundaries of what qualifies for Program-Related Investment status and ultimately seek more expansive guidance for what is possible under this regulation.

Expanding Subsidies

As is the case with tax incentives, policymakers may also draw on established practice as the basis for a broad regime of smart subsidies for impact investments. Entities such as the Small Business Administration in the United States and National Bank for Agriculture and Rural Development in India subsidize domestic impact investment to meet national goals through loan guarantees, concessionary capital provision, and training programs. Extending these programs and approaches to impact enterprises, whatever sector and geography they operate in, will unleash the power of impact investments to address a much broader range of social challenges.

These subsidies could be wasted on enterprises that do not generate social value. As we saw in the context of impact investing for international development, determining what constitutes an impact investment and aligning the incentives of fund managers to focus on impact is challenging. Making these distinctions (and determining who deserves government subsidy) is particularly difficult when impact investors operate alongside commercial investors.

A nationally recognized corporate form for designating and regulating enterprises focused on impact would reduce this risk. Government could also support data collecting and analysis that refines our understanding of what constitutes an impact entrepreneur and feeds back into regulations governing the requirements for investors and companies to earn the "impact" designation.

Mandating Impact Investments

Beyond the carrot of tax breaks and subsidies, governments can also wave the stick of investment mandates to steer investment capital into underserved areas. These mandates typically require banks to make impact investments in targeted communities to win the right to pursue (potentially more lucrative) business elsewhere—for example:

- The U.S. Community Reinvestment Act of 1977 (commonly referred to as CRA), which required banks to extend their lending in poor neighborhoods in inner cities. A multibillion-dollar industry of affordable housing development and community-based lending has materialized around the capital the law has unlocked.

- The Indian priority sector policies that, since 1969, have required banks to lend 40 percent of their total loan volume to government-designated priority sectors and, since 1977, require banks to open branches in underserved areas in order to gain regulatory approval to open branches in already-served areas.

- The South African Financial Sector Charter, adopted by industry in 2003 partly to preempt further regulation from government, which creates a set of impact investing mandates. These include a commitment to allocate a portion of profits to social investment and to set aside capital for investment in small businesses and black-owned enterprises.

Mandates can be applied both where impact investments could ultimately be lucrative for investors and where they create a substantial public good that the investor cannot realize. In the first case, the mandate will shock investors out of the biases and blindness that are currently keeping them out of a geography or sector. In the second case, it will ensure adequate capitalization for businesses that create social good. Admittedly this will constitute an operating tax on the investors given the mandate; it could be the most efficient way to generate a necessary social outcome, and ultimately it may be less expensive to the company than the costs of operating in a degraded social or environmental context if the outcome is not achieved.

Shaping the Marketplace for Impact Investing

Around the world, government subsidy, incentives, and mandates have underpinned the emergence and growth of new industries such as venture capital, private equity, and green technology. But even more important to the broader success of modern capitalism has been the role governments have played as the market shaper. By ensuring information flow, reducing uncertainty, and setting basic rules of market interaction, governments build the conditions that enable markets to function. Governments increasingly play this market-shaping role for philanthropists. But because impact investing falls between investment and philanthropy, governments have largely shirked their market building role here.

Governments can fill in this void of impact investment market shaping by taking on two essential functions: buffering investors from unintended regulatory harm and setting standards.

Buffering from Unintended Regulatory Harm

Reforms intended to strengthen the regimes that oversee charity and investment separately often create unintended consequences that undermine impact investment. Trying to cobble together subsector-by-subsector exemptions is an exhausting distraction to impact investors. Instead, financial services and philanthropic regulatory reform need to protect impact investing from the beginning. Regulatory reform is appropriate and crucial in the wake of the financial crisis. But reforms intended to protect asset owners from unscrupulous fund managers and investment banks, and society from excessive risk taking and tax avoidance, can also hamper investors from experimenting with impact investing.

Three major buffers would permit impact investing to flourish without compromising regulatory oversight of mainstream investment and donations:

- *Allow risk-taking flexibility*. Impact investment asset owners often want their fund managers to pursue innovative investment strategies and to take on risks in pursuit of blended value. Enforcement of the prudent-man rule, intended to ensure that fund managers serve the interests of the owners of assets whose funds they manage, needs to allow fund managers to honor this desire of asset owners. Fund managers, especially of private foundation assets, should not be restricted by regulators from making impact investments.

- *Modify restrictions on banks*. Banks should not be overly prohibited from using their capital to help seed impact investments. Reforms intended to reduce systemic risk by limiting regulated banks' investment in private equity operations make sense. However, they also threaten the participation of investment banks in impact investing. In the U.S. financial reform of 2010, the provisions limiting bank investment in private equity, commonly referred to as the Volcker Rule, recognized this threat and created an exemption for impact investments in U.S. small businesses. This type of exemption could be expanded to cover other impact investments as well.

- *Recognize that investment can serve a direct charitable purpose*. Philanthropic regulatory reform also threatens impact investment. Regulators should crack down on nonprofits and their donors who enjoy tax breaks for undertaking activities with dubious social value. But campaigns to crack down on such abuses could sweep up all impact investment–focused organizations. Governments need to set clear guidelines recognizing that for-profit impact investment can be both legitimate and effective in addressing social problems and protect them from these crackdowns.

Setting Standards

An efficient marketplace cannot form without standards for measuring the results of investment. The mainstream capital markets could not function without widespread agreement about the principles and terms that businesses and investors use to communicate and compare their activities. In most countries, governments recognize this and either directly develop and maintain reporting standards or delegate that responsibility to designated industry bodies.

Impact investors, however, operate without the benefit of similar standards and are left to assess potential social impact largely on a deal-by-deal basis. But these investors are now organizing to address this problem. The Impact Reporting and Investment Standards is the strongest effort yet to create a standard for impact measurement. Government could strengthen these standards by giving them official designation. The Generally Accepted Accounting Principles formed through government support to a process led by the accounting industry. In the same vein, government can legitimize the work of social impact ratings companies such as the Global Impact Investing Rating System as they have done for risk-rating agencies like Standard & Poor's.

Governments can also help set standards by simply adopting them when making their own impact investment. In many sub-markets, governments are the market-making impact investor with the scale to make others follow. In the realm of impact investing for international development, governments are already investing billions into investments for social impact. Many governments also manage substantial domestic impact investing programs. But as with the private markets, they are investing with fund managers and companies that adopt their own unique social reporting systems (if they report at all). Adopting a standard for how companies and fund managers that receive public capital must report on social impact would not cost much. Government would also benefit directly when the existence of a standard, and the efficiency and transparency it brings, improves the investment performance of these public funds.

Certify Impact Investment Managers

We often meet investors who are eager to place substantial assets in impact investing but hesitate to do so because they do not know where to place their capital. They ask us: "How will I know which fund manager is really creating blended value and which one is just telling me nice stories about impact?" We have our answers based on personal experience and networks, and others have a different set of favorites. The impact investing industry will take off only when all investors asking that question can go to credible sources that sort out the real impact investors from the impact posers. Government can also help address the information problem by leveraging its influence to certify impact investment intermediaries. Governments are well placed to work with industry leaders to write the rules that determine what it means to be an impact investor and to certify who meets these criteria. This is a role the U.S. government plays in the subsector of community development finance institutions. Working with investors, entrepreneurs, and the intended beneficiaries of impact investment, governments could extend this role into broader impact investing.

NEW RULES FOR A NEW CAPITALISM
Andrew Kassoy, Cofounder, B Lab, New York, New York

Jay Coen Gilbert, Bart Houlahan, and I met in college before going on to successful private sector careers. Bart and Jay built an apparel and footwear company, And1, into a $250 million global brand, and I became a private equity investor. By 2005 we were ready for second careers using our private sector skills to create public benefit. But how?

We knew that while government and the nonprofit sector were necessary for social progress, business had the incentives to attract innovation, capital, and talent to solve our greatest challenges. But businesses could do little more than maximize shareholder wealth. No standards or metrics existed to allow consumers, investors, or policymakers to judge the difference between a good business and just good marketing. And legal structures did not enable mission-driven businesses to maintain mission as they scaled. In fact, U.S. law specifically mandated company directors to maximize shareholder wealth to the exclusion of any broader societal considerations.

The result? While there was a huge market developing for mission-driven businesses—60 million consumers and over fifty thousand businesses in the United States alone—no marketplace existed to facilitate the development of these companies or the flow of capital to them. And so Bart, Jay, and I decided to make the creation of this market infrastructure our mission.

When we formed B Lab in 2006, the market for high-impact businesses lacked clarity, transparency, comparability, and standards. We decided to start by building a brand for high-impact businesses that could create a collective voice for entrepreneurs, easy identification by stakeholders, clear performance and legal standards, and a center of gravity for the growing market. The brand is a Certified B Corporation. B Corps meet high standards for social and environmental impact and change their corporate structure to ensure consideration of their stakeholders. By the end of 2010, there were almost four hundred Certified B Corporations.

But these businesses and their investors are still playing by old rules built for a profits-at-all-cost game. A new capitalism requires new rules. We need a new corporate form that allows companies to satisfy the demands of investors, employees, and customers who increasingly want corporations to consider the impact of their decisions on multiple stakeholders rather than maintain a singular focus on short-term profit maximization. Without a new corporate form, we will continue to see an endless string of well-intentioned companies sacrifice their mission the minute they require third-party growth capital or liquidity for founders.

We have therefore begun advocating for a new benefit corporation legal form with three main components:

- The corporate purpose of a benefit corporation is to create general public benefit in addition to shareholder value.

- Directors' fiduciary duty is expanded to include consideration of the effect of decisions on shareholders and employees, suppliers, customers, community, and the environment.

- Benefit corporations must publish a benefit report in accordance with third-party standards for defining, reporting, and assessing social and environmental performance.

Two factors have spurred support for the passage of benefit corporation legislation. First, this approach allows businesses and their investors to opt in to higher standards rather than imposing new regulations on all companies. Second, it provides policymakers an inexpensive way to restore public confidence in business and to spur economic development and bring quality jobs to their districts.

However, creating a new corporate form is not easy. In the United States, corporate forms have to be passed separately in each state, requiring significant resources and grassroots organizing. The movement requires a legislative champion in each state who understands both the big picture need and the subtleties of corporate legal reform. Lawyers' associations are also inherently protective of existing corporate law from meddling legislators. Getting them behind this movement requires finding lawyers to back the concept and making sure they see how many business clients support this innovation.

Benefit corporation legislation passed in Maryland and Vermont in 2010 and New Jersey so far in 2011. Eleven companies registered as B Corporations in Maryland on the first day the legislation

Overcoming Legacy Systems

Regulating impact investing effectively will be a difficult task. It requires a regulator who understands the power and limits of financial markets and the challenges and potential in mobilizing diverse constituents to address social challenges. Unfortunately, existing bureaucracies mostly separate the people tasked with overseeing investors from those tasked with tackling social challenges. They are not a natural place for the impact investment regulator to emerge. Just as impact investment banking is emerging as its own discipline with a unique set of skills, so will impact investment regulation require a new set of integrated skills and collaboration across government functions.

This is why regulatory reform cannot be left to the regulators. Everyone with a stake in the growth of impact investing for blended value has a role to play in supporting the development of a more conducive enabling environment. But as Andrew Kassoy's description of the challenges facing advocates for new regulations highlights, no one can do this alone. We cannot count exclusively on charismatic individuals like Bill Young in Canada to lead by example alone. Instead we need strong leadership that couples vision with collaboration. We need a coordinated effort to build the became effective. The legislation is now pending in seven other states as momentum behind the movement continues to build. Long term, we aim to make this new corporate form available in every state.

When this happens, every company will be able to practice business in a different way and provide an outlet for impact investors. Benefit corporations will allow business and the capital markets to take their place as a legitimate tool for alleviating poverty, restoring the environment, creating high-quality jobs, and rebuilding communities.

---

leadership platforms and career pathways that can expand impact investing from a potent idea to a social force. The next chapter examines the actions and attributes necessary to pull this off.

Chapter 7

HOW WILL WE CULTIVATE TRANSFORMATIONAL LEADERSHIP?

- J.P. Morgan announced the launch of a social finance unit in its investment bank in November 2007. This unit aims to build a profitable business for the bank, structuring and putting proprietary capital to work in investments that generate financial returns for investors and also tackle social ills such as poverty and environmental degradation. Within a week of this internal announcement, more than one thousand J.P. Morgan employees contacted the new unit's director to express interest in working with her team.

- At Harvard Business School, the largest opt-in student interest club in 2010 was not focused on investment banking, private equity, or management consulting. Instead more than four hundred graduate students joined the Social Enterprise Club. Similar student groups focusing on how students can apply business skills to solving social and environmental problems are similarly prominent at top business schools across the world.

- One young man in his early twenties is the grandson of a successful investor. His father took a different path, leading environmental programs and working to advance sustainable development. As the young man considered taking a Wall Street internship, his father voiced concern he would be corrupted by the "finance first" mind-set of the Street. But the son rejects this concern, opting to pursue a career that combines public service and investing: "My dad doesn't want me to go down the path of finance, and my grandfather doesn't really get the social agenda, but the point is that I want to make money and create positive change in the world. My future is not going to be about wealth or social justice—I want to create impact and make money and have passion about what I'm doing. Why is that so hard for them to understand?"

Every industry requires leadership to flourish. Effective leadership enables individuals and institutions to organize resources and attention to achieve a common task. Leadership exerted at the right moment helped create many of the opportunities we describe in this book. The early pioneers of international development finance, the innovators who experimented with new ways to lend to poor women, the community activists who pushed policies to bring commercial banks to low-income housing lending in the United States: all were charismatic and dynamic leaders carving out opportunities for impact investing at scale.

But for impact investing to evolve, leadership must move beyond the determined individuals who had the will to squeeze their aspirations and activities into existing systems. Instead, we need leaders who can transform the systems themselves. This transformational leadership will open the industry to a much wider pool of people, institutions, and resources. Breaking out of a founding phase in which only charismatic pioneers could succeed, the impact investing industry will be able to embrace all the passionate, peaceful warriors it can find.

The bifurcated systems that separate profit maximization and charity still keep most people out of impact investing. Colleges and graduate schools train students for careers as either profit-maximizing business managers and investors or socially focused civil servants and nonprofit leaders. Recruiting firms and human resource professionals match talented people who want to make money with private companies and those who want to pursue social purpose with nonprofits and government. And with few exceptions, trade associations, networks, and industry jargon facilitate collaboration and communication among leaders within these separate worlds, not between them.

But what happens when these separate worlds collide—when impact investing creates opportunities to generate multiple returns by leaders who can operate effectively as both profit generators and social problem solvers? How will we train the mutant managers who can pursue the both-and as opposed to the either-or value proposition? How will we establish career ladders for integrating profit making with generating social value? And how will we cultivate industry-wide collaboration that can accelerate impact investing's transition from a niche concept to a mainstream force?

We need to develop a new set of systems and approaches to leadership that foster successful integration between the worlds of profit making and social problem solving. Charismatic innovators operating in isolation, save for when they are presented at yet one more international gathering of the Good and the Great, will not get the job done on their own. Instead, the truly transformative leadership we need will arise through thoughtful collaboration among individuals offering new leadership within multiple communities.[1]

Leading Change, Transforming Leadership

So far, impact investing leadership has come largely from charismatic individuals pursuing relatively constrained agendas. Their work has revealed the limits of systems that enforce the notion that investment must focus only on generating financial profit and that social and environmental problems should be solved solely through charity and government intervention. But they have operated largely from within these systems. They have creatively built adapters that can connect the square pegs of investing with the round holes of charity. These adapters are the mezzanine funds that bring philanthropies and commercial banks together, the nonprofit management courses at business schools, and the occasional column on impact investing in mainstream investor journals.

For impact investing to enter its next phase, leaders will need to build new systems rather than just adapt to existing ones. This phase poses a fundamentally different leadership challenge than we are currently organized to understand and promote. At its core, visionary leadership pushes out the contours of what is possible. The first phase of impact investing created new possibilities within specific sectors such as microfinance, low-income housing finance in the United States, and international development. Now we can construct a fundamentally new set of systems that greatly expand the platforms for an integrated approach to generating blended value much more widely.

In its 2009 report on impact investing, *Investing for Social and Environmental Impact*, the Monitor Institute described how industries evolve through four phases.[2] As Figure 7.1 shows, we can also apply this framework to understand how the nature of leadership evolves. As an overarching industry, impact investing is emerging from the uncoordinated innovation phase shown in the figure. In this initial phase, leadership has been embodied by iconoclastic and charismatic individuals—for example:

- Klaus Tischhauser, who leveraged a career in mainstream asset management to build ResponsAbility, a Swiss-based social investment fund that has aggregated more than $1 billion into microfinance and broader impact investments

	Uncoordinated Innovation	Marketplace Building	Capturing the Value of the Marketplace	Maturity
Industry characteristics	• Innovative activities proliferate, driven by charismatic entrepreneurs	• Infrastructure is built that reduces transaction costs and supports a higher volume of activity • Centers of activity begin to develop	• Mainstream players enter a functioning market • Early leaders able to leverage fixed costs of previous commitments across higher volume of activity	• Relatively steady state as growth rates slow • Consolidation may occur
Drivers of leadership	• Charismatic visionaries create bold new organizations • Effective communicators spread word about inspiring anecdotes of isolated success	• Industry-wide research and benchmarking provide evidence of larger impact • Early pioneers band together to support industry-wide infrastructure (for example, networks and measurement standards)	• "Messengers" translate compelling evidence of success to mainstream audiences • Successful investors scale rapidly by mobilizing partnerships and investment syndicates	• Large-scale players with strong brands bring credibility and awareness • Attention turns to innovators who push the frontiers

Figure 7.1. Phases of Industry Evolution

Note: With impact investing evolving from the "uncoordinated innovation" through the "marketplace building" phase, leadership will shift from charismatic individuals to effective collaborators.

Source: Adapted from Monitor Institute, *Investing for Social and Environmental Impact* (Cambridge, Mass.: Monitor Institute, 2009).

- Willy Foote, founder and head of Root Capital, who quit Harvard Business School to start a nonprofit that lends to farmer cooperatives throughout Latin America and Africa, putting together a balance sheet of $50 million from traditional donor sources and large corporations

- Jacqueline Novogratz, who left the Rockefeller Foundation to start Acumen Fund, a nonprofit that invests in social enterprises in East Africa and South Asia

- Muhammad Yunus, the Nobel Prize–winning icon of microfinance who began to lend money to poor women near his classroom when he was a professor teaching standard economic theory in Bangladesh in the early 1970s

These people share the character traits most typically celebrated in discussions of iconic social entrepreneurs. They are passionate. They are risk takers. They abandoned established career paths to step out into the new territory between for-profit investment and charity. They are determined when it comes to confronting a skeptical world and bending the existing systems to create a space for their work. And they are also very, very rare.

Such charismatic people, and the pioneering institutions they have built, are typical of the innovators we expect to see in the first phase of an industry's evolution. And we could have a useful discussion about impact investing leadership by simply asking, "What can we do to cultivate more leaders like Jacqueline Novogratz and Willy Foote who can build inspiring organizations?"

That's not a bad question, and we explore some answers to it in this chapter. But constraining our discussion of impact investing leadership to charismatic individuals is ultimately limiting. Such an approach excludes the many more potential industry participants and leaders who, by temperament or circumstance, are not going to be pioneering innovators or bask in the international spotlight. A focus on charismatic leaders also does not meet the impact investing industry's current moment.

As the industry stands poised to move to a new phase in which it generates systemic change, we must turn our attention to an ultimately more important question: What can we do to cultivate the leadership required to build new *systems* for impact investment to solve social and environmental problems at scale?

From Charismatic to Collaborative Leadership

Impact investors tend to equate leadership with charismatic indi-viduals. These are the people we read about in business journals and meet on the speaking circuit. They are the lead characters in business school cases. This does not surprise us in an age increasingly dominated by celebrity culture and within an industry overrepresented by entrepreneurs and those who see themselves as bold investors. And it can be helpful. Movements go mainstream when their complex ideas can be embodied in a personal brand. Vice President Al Gore has been a crucial unifying emblem of the campaign against climate change. We have also seen how Muhammad Yunus became a powerful figurehead for microfinance.

Similarly determined individuals are popularizing impact invest-ing more broadly. But a single-minded focus on individuals obscures the crucial role collaboration and coordination need to play in impact investing's next phase. Impact investing will take off when its pioneers and newcomers collaborate effectively, building the infrastructure that will enable the next wave of talent and capital to join the field. In many ways, the elements of impact investing— microfinance, sustainable finance, social enterprise funding, and so on—currently represent separate block parties. These parties, while impassioned and meaningful, will not attain their full poten-tial until they spill off the side streets and flow onto the avenues where participants mix and match and see for themselves that it is all one grand parade with many moving parts and components.

Leadership of the Whole

In an established industry, success comes from beating competitors on a field with clear rules. In the emerging world of impact investing, success will come from setting the rules and creating a worldwide field to play on. The success of impact investing will necessitate transformation in multiple systems, from capital markets, to performance measurement, to public policy. No individual, however charismatic, will be able to create these transformations alone. It will be an especially tricky transition since it requires a focus on the "we" of sustained social change, not just the "me" of social entrepreneurship.

Fortunately, a new wave of industry builders is picking up from the early pioneers in this emerging spirit of collaboration. For now, the impact investing industry is young enough that collaboration is a win-win for many players. Thoughtful industry-building work will cause the pie to grow quickly enough to compensate for any loss in market share that collaboration could create. Leading investors are bringing others into deals, sharing data and networking aggressively. By definition most impact investors are in it for more than the money and are attracted to the idea of bold and innovative action.

Is this spirit of pioneering collaboration sustainable? Overcoming zero-sum thinking will not be easy as the industry matures, raising the stakes. Some charismatic individuals will be reluctant to let the light shift from their work to the industry's broader impact. And it will be all too easy for entrepreneurial leaders to prioritize their organizational agenda over the needs of industry growth. For example, a microfinance institution could easily feel threatened by the many other options that impact investing opens up for its investors.

For truly transformational change, we will need leaders to fight this institutional gravity. Individuals will need to build organizations to amplify and carry on their work. But these organizations will need to recognize and embrace their participation in the broader impact investing industry. And mainstream financial services firms will need to do more than simply reassign existing personnel to this new area of corporate activity; they will need to hire from outside their community to help infuse their emerging efforts with perspectives that come from beyond their corporate borders.

Building Global Platforms

In its emerging phase, the impact investing industry suffers from fragmentation with an increasingly crowded field of subscale players unable to rise above the noise. In this context, collaboration and consolidation are appealing and beneficial; so too is standardization of practice, language, and so forth. But forcing collaboration and standardization too soon will stifle innovation. We do need leaders to compete and innovate.

In established industries, participants develop formal trade associations to create the platforms that can strike this balance between collaboration and competition. The launch of effective collective action platforms tends to mark the arrival of an industry and position it for growth. The microfinance industry found its platforms in the Microcredit Summit and the Consultative Group to Assist the Poor, both launched in the 1990s at the beginning of the global microfinance boom. The community development finance movement in the United States found its collective action through the launch of the Local Initiatives Support Corporation in 1979 and Living Cities in 1991.

The launch of the Global Impact Investing Network (GIIN) in late 2009 may have marked a similar milestone for impact investing. As British investor Sir Ronald Cohen told the *Economist* at the time, "This reminds me of private equity in the early 1980s, just before it started to grow," when the formation of networks of early leaders presaged industry growth and consolidation.[3]

But investor-driven organizations such as the GIIN cannot stand alone. The impact investing industry also needs to give voice and influence to a wider range of actors. To this end, polyglot events that bring together representatives from nonprofits, social enterprises, governments, and academia are crucial. Events such as the SoCap "social capital" conferences (which began in 2008 in the San Francisco Bay Area as an annual gathering of investors, entrepreneurs, and thought leaders and expanded to Europe in 2011), the Social Enterprise Alliance (a convening of social entrepreneurs managing a variety of ventures), and the annual Skoll World Forum (an international gathering of social entrepreneurs and those who invest in them) in Oxford, England, are critical to advance the broad parade of the impact investing community, especially as they increasingly coordinate with traditional sustainable investing events which have been convened annually for decades, such as "SRI in the Rockies," which now brings together leading socially responsible investing professionals.

New Responses to Old Challenges

Imagine a world in which impact investing is established and widespread. That world will force us to rethink our responses to three interrelated questions:

- Who will tell our story?

- How do we educate the next generation of leaders?

- How do we hire and retain top talent?

Charismatic individuals will play a part in answering these questions. But the answers will require much more coordination and engagement with established institutions than charismatic individuals have exhibited in the past.

Who Will Tell Our Story?

Developing a vibrant impact investing industry will require effective communication and marketing. This task too will shift as the industry matures. In the past, visionaries have passionately and eloquently shown how for-profit investment can be an appropriate and feasible way to address social problems. Our challenge now is to bring this perspective from the fringe to the mainstream. The visionaries will play a crucial role, holding the industry to its founding principles as it becomes more diverse and engages more commercial interests. But we will also need to cultivate a new generation of advocates who can further popularize the message.

Impact investing builds on the vision of early leaders who explored the possibilities of deploying capital in new ways through the creation of experimental funds and enterprises. As these ideas become relevant to a much broader market, the storytelling task will shift in two ways. First, communication will flow not just from the iconoclastic and independent guru, but from the next generation of leaders able to take advantage of the growing infrastructure that can amplify their own message. Second, effective communication will not just describe the isolated success of inspiring individuals but will account for the collective impact of a wide-ranging global industry.

While we hope some of the early visionaries remain powerful voices, this shift needs communicators who act as mainstreaming messengers. These individuals will be the conduits that can absorb the lessons from visionary practice and communicate them effectively to much wider audiences. The influence of the writer Malcolm Gladwell is a good example of the power of effective mainstreaming messengers. By translating insights from the visionaries who developed the behavioral economics field over the past few decades, he has brought their ideas into broad social and political discussion.[4] By popularizing the term *philanthrocapitalism*, Matthew Bishop and Michael Green have similarly brought widespread attention to new approaches that modern philanthropists have developed over many years.[5]

How do we balance the needs of broad communication with the need to hold onto critical elements of the vision? A perfect message that only a few people hear is no longer good enough, but neither is a message that reaches millions with platitudes and banalities or, even worse, misrepresentation. The challenge is to tie the mainstream message closely to grassroots experience consistent with the deeper vision. Honest discussions in the blogosphere and social networking communities can facilitate this link. The development of industry infrastructure will also help facilitate this communication. In the microfinance industry, infrastructure such as the Microcredit Summit and the Consultative Group to Assist the Poor helped leading practitioners refine their thinking together and then communicate to a wider audience. For impact investing more broadly, emerging platforms such as the Social Edge blog and organizations such as the GIIN and SROI Network, similarly provide those doing the work with more efficient avenues for figuring out what we are learning and communicating those insights to a mainstream audience.

Successful collaborative leadership in telling the impact investing story will create a reinforcing cycle. With this message accepted in the mainstream, impact investors will spend less time making the case that impact investing is feasible and effective. We can instead use this time to develop and execute innovative approaches that can feed storytelling with examples of promising practice and lessons learned along the way.

How Will We Educate the Next Generation of Leaders?

The current system of leadership education reflects the historic separation of profit-making and society-improving activity. Business schools have traditionally treated societal engagement as a business constraint to be managed. Public policy and social work schools have typically treated business as an evil to be regulated and restrained, if not condemned outright.

To many students, this bifurcated mentality is increasingly anachronistic. Though they may sometimes lack the language to express it as "impact investing," these students crave opportunities to learn how to create blended value. At top business schools, this yearning manifests in widespread participation in social enterprise classes, clubs, conferences, and business plan competitions. At top public policy schools, students are challenging administrators and faculty to help them understand how to harness business for the public good.

We have noticed this dynamic in our own work. Jed's lectures on blended value are standing-room-only at top business schools around the world. Antony teaches an oversubscribed course on business and international development at Columbia Business School. When we give speeches at business schools, policy school students increasingly sneak in. When we speak at policy schools, business students show up. And increasingly, we cannot tell them apart from their interests, backgrounds, and aspirations. Faculty and administrators are responding to this student interest. Yet their initial responses echo the bifurcated worldview. Business schools began adding courses on nonprofit management in the mid-1990s, responding to a small group of students who sought to apply business discipline in nonprofit work. An explosion of interest in social enterprise has seemingly brought a closer integration between training in business and social problem solving. However, most course offerings continue to perpetuate rather than transcend the idea that running businesses and solving social problems should be separate activities.

This approach leaves many students frustrated. They arrive at school convinced they can integrate profit making and purpose throughout their careers but find that perspective validated only in rare exposure to charismatic entrepreneurs who represent exceptions to the norm. Despite the good efforts of initiatives such as the Aspen Institute's Center for Business Education and the New York University Reynolds Program for Social Entrepreneurship, a unique university-wide initiative targeting both undergraduate and graduate students, the curriculum and culture of business schools largely continue to pigeon-hole blended value creation into a small corner of activity, where it is overwhelmed by the overarching message that the core purpose of business is the pursuit of financial profit.

At public policy and social work schools, the situation is arguably worse. While some clear exceptions exist, administrators and faculty are generally nervous that for-profit enterprises will lure their students away from the career of public service for which they have trained them. This concern is not unwarranted after two decades in which management consulting firms and investment banks have reached increasingly aggressively into the ranks of policy school graduates for hiring. Accommodating student interest, some policy schools have begrudgingly embraced the language of social enterprise but tend to be comfortable only with enterprises that take a nonprofit, civil society, or public sector form.

Despite this general rigidity, graduate schools are taking gradual steps to accommodate exploding student interest in blended value. They are bringing lessons from the other side of the bifurcated world into their curriculum and programming. But they generally are not yet offering an integrated training for future impact investment leaders and the regulators they will work with. This is beginning to change. Some business schools have begun to integrate social purpose into the understanding of how a business leader generates value. And some policy schools are increasingly adopting a less defensive posture to engaging the private sector—and not seeing students who go into impact investing businesses as lost causes.

Curriculum Development

Impact investment courses have tended to follow the industry's trajectory, beginning with courses focused on pioneering subsectors such as microfinance and sustainability. The first courses explicitly labeled "impact investing," built out from these narrower courses, were taught in the 2009–2010 academic year. This trend is poised for rapid growth, with a consortium of impact investing business school professors launched in 2010 as part of Harvard's Initiative for Responsible Investment. Beyond the classroom, the first impact investing student business plan competition was held in early 2011. And the Indian School of Business in Hyderabad is creating an entire program centered on the role of business in providing basic services profitably to poor people. ("Building Awareness and Catalyzing Markets" describes the genesis of this program and its ambitions.)

Interschool Collaboration

To implement a blended value vision will require the skills and sensibility to work with an unusual array of people and institutions. Impact investors must learn to work with nonprofits, foundations, and governments in structuring, executing, and monitoring investments, and impact investment regulators must understand the creative potential of business. But providing such training is difficult within the confines of an educational program designed to attract one type of student and hold one type of discussion.

Some schools are responding to this structural challenge by creating special programs that orchestrate collaboration between students from different disciplines. The Blum Center for Developing Economies at the University of California at Berkeley is an early example of this approach. The center has staged a regular competition between in which teams comprising students from the business, policy, and engineering schools work together to develop models for sustainable economic development projects that include revenue generating components. Similar programs are emerging elsewhere.

Role Modeling and Meaningful Mentors

Given the importance of socialization in leadership education and the power of analogue to organize people's approaches, one important facet of training the next generation of impact investors is to celebrate role models. Historically business schools have exposed students to leading businesspeople who have exemplified a model life in which their business success was followed by a retirement enriched by charity work. Now the increasing popularity on business school campuses of impact investing pioneers is offering an alternative model for students to follow. Schools that recognize the importance of mentoring and role modeling will need to identify additional opportunities to expose students to similarly forward-looking role models. Beyond the charismatic entrepreneurs, role models can also come from the leaders of networks, standard-setting bodies and other industry-builders who will increasingly represent high-leverage leadership in the impact investing industry's next phase.

How Do We Hire and Retain Top Talent?

In the traditional, bifurcated world, career paths are relatively simple: if you want to work for social causes, you pursue a career in nonprofits or civil service, enjoying the noble sacrifice of a relatively low-wage life spent "doing good." If you are interested in business and investing, you pursue financially lucrative jobs in the hope that you can enjoy a retirement making charitable gifts, volunteering, and sitting on nonprofit boards. Nonprofits hire people with social work and policy training and retain them by offering "meaningful" work. Businesses hire people from business schools and retain them with ever-growing salaries and bonuses.

But for the emerging impact investing generation, life is more complicated—and frustrating. Top students are seeking to integrate business skills with professional purpose at the start of their careers, not in sequence. They are frustrated with companies offering the occasional nonprofit assignment as the only outlet for pursuing purpose. They are similarly disappointed with nonprofits that stigmatize engagement with business and application of business approaches. Yet most have had to suppress this frustration in the face of a job market that offers few alternatives.

The emergence of impact investing is beginning to change that. It is opening an increasingly wide outlet to channel this frustration into new career choices. The young professionals we meet are increasingly rejecting formerly irresistible jobs offering lucrative salaries in order to pursue integrated careers creating blended value from the beginning. They are the entrepreneurs exiting the mainstream corporate world to launch their own impact investing start-ups. They are the investment bankers leaving Wall Street or the City of London for impact investing funds. They are the top business school students rejecting offers from McKinsey for work with impact investing consulting firms. They are the J.P. Morgan bankers leaving a traditional career track to join the bank's Social Finance Unit.

In response, approaches to hiring and retaining leaders are adapting. Pioneering headhunting firms are building portfolios of impact investors and carving a niche serving the growing number of investors and businesses recruiting impact investing talent. And managers are beginning to poach top talent away from traditional career tracks by offering a credible way to integrate purpose and profit throughout a career. They are also retaining employees who a decade ago would have left their firms to pursue purpose through traditional nonprofit work.

Young professionals around the world often ask our advice about how to begin a career in impact investing. A few years ago, we encouraged them to gain mainstream business and investment experience to position themselves for a high-level transition into the nonprofit sector in five years. Now we're not so sure. With

BUILDING AWARENESS AND CATALYZING MARKETS
Reuben Abraham, Executive Director, Centre for Emerging Markets Solutions, Indian School of Business, Hyderabad, India

I think business schools are doing a fine job teaching all the traditional skills, but they do not actually impart knowledge on the incredible macrotrends remaking the world — for instance:

- In health care and education, private companies dominate in the low-income segment, and in countries like India, the government will commit hundreds of billions of dollars into public-private partnerships to deliver these services.

- Urbanization is the biggest macrotrend across Asia and Africa for the next thirty years. Businesses that figure out how to deliver decent housing affordably will have a market of hundreds of millions of customers.

I cannot think of a more interesting and intellectually challenging set of problems for a student to work with. Oh, and in the process, she may also end up doing a world of good.

But business schools must do a better job of making students aware of trends like these. That awareness will help students make much better choices in their careers, not to mention spot the arbitrage and entrepreneurial opportunities hiding in market inefficiencies in these sectors.

The skills these students need are not different from those for normal businesses or regular buy-side opportunities. In fact, I think it would be a mistake to think you need a different set of skills. Most of the solutions require good knowledge of the business sector. What's more, a lot of the innovation to make high-quality goods and services available to large populations in India will involve adaptation of proven technology models and new business models for affordable innovation, both of which should be core strengths at a business school.

What you need is a combination of regular skills along with the awareness of the sector and the incredible opportunities within, which are obviously harder to uncover. The real problem with talent markets is that most of the time, the pay scales are lower, so it takes someone who is genuinely interested in the issue to take a pay cut and work in this space. The upside is that this acts as a filter of sorts for the right kind of personality. As the risk is reduced in these sectors (there are more entrepreneurs willing to look at low-cost health care solutions today, for instance), the markets will find the right equilibrium between demand and supply.

Beyond what we teach, we catalyze these markets in other ways. I am a free marketer, but I don't believe in automatic market clearance. In a free, perfect market, market clearance is a given and opportunities find takers. Unfortunately, in emerging markets, perfection exists mostly in textbooks. Markets do get clogged and need a nudge to clear. The clogging happens mostly because of an overpricing of risk in emerging markets.

At the Centre for Emerging Markets Solutions, we have uncovered opportunities that paved the way for investors to enter various markets, including low-income housing, sanitation, and education. The question is: Why haven't people looked at this opportunity earlier? Part of the answer is that people were distracted seeking high returns in the high-income market, but there clearly was also a market that was left untapped. The average entrepreneur does not have access to the research and networks that can help define and capture the opportunities. Building this ecosystem is a high-leverage way for us to help these markets to clear. In our housing work, we spent $100,000 over a year and a half to conduct deep research, build networks, and identify strong institutions. Once we helped build this ecosystem, millions of dollars of profit-seeking capital have moved into this sector.

Students at the Indian School of Business are very interested in the field of market-based solutions. As they learn the tools of the trade, they also begin to understand systematically why India came to be the way it is and what can change the situation. Unlike previous generations, the current generation of Indians looks at business as a positive force for good. This applies equally to the application of business solutions for socioeconomic problems.

None of this is to suggest that students are flocking to jobs in the sector. By and large, students at Indian Business School are entering a consumerist phase and are certainly not posteconomic men and women. Even so, planting the seed in their heads is a very good idea, and we hope the seed will help them make the right set of choices even in a conventional business career and, most important, be aware that the economic growth of a country cannot be restricted to the elite.

---

impact investing positions opening up with more frequency, people increasingly do not need to give into their frustrations. To paraphrase the famous movie line: When you know you want to spend the rest of your life creating blended value, you want the rest of your life to begin now. And increasingly, it can.

Leading into the Future

Throughout this book, we describe how established systems and practices need to evolve in response to changing conditions and context. The nature of leadership with the impact investing industry is no different. The next phase of leadership will need to support an industry that is no longer the sole domain of charismatic individuals, but instead a complex ecosystem of global institutions across sectors that is building clearer career pathways, earning widespread recognition, and operating through dedicated networks and trade associations.

Talk about "collective infrastructure" and "mainstreaming the message" may sound deadly dull or distracting. The chance to tackle complex problems and even to be seen as on the fringe is precisely what has attracted many pioneers to this work. When impact investing becomes an established practice, it may well lose some of the allure early leaders have seen in the struggle to build something new. But the moment when impact investing becomes banal to some, it will also create exciting openings for others.

The future of impact investing will be shaped by a process of broad, transparent inquiry, experimentation, and pursuit of a vision sculpted from shared ideas, efforts, and passions. The charismatic social entrepreneurs and financial wizards engineering new investment products will play their part. However, the leadership model of the future will be the leadership of the whole—the outcome of individuals collaborating organically using social networking sites, regional networks, and working groups focused on specific, shared challenges. This will not be directed from above; rather, they will grow up from below, with roots set deep in the muddy middle between mainstream and new stream with the pursuit of singular agendas played out on a global stage.

What will happen when our world is led by a new generation naturally embracing the idea that investment can and should seek to maximize blended value? This world is more than a distant fantasy. The ground has been prepared for this leadership transition, with students increasingly manifesting an instinctual interest in a more integrated approach and universities and employers beginning to respond to this interest.

The young leaders we talk with today have been spared immersion in the bumbling bifurcated world. They naturally embrace a blended understanding of self, society, and success. As they take their seats at the table of investment committees and governing boards, they will not ask, *How did we do financially last quarter and how much extra cash do we have to do good?* Rather, they will simply ask, *How did we do?*

With that singular inquiry, the emperor will be seen for the nude jester he is. These new decision-makers will set aggressive new terms of success for their wealth advisors, fund managers, professors, employers, and employees. The implications for their generation and those yet to come are clear—but perhaps more intriguing is the implication these questions will have for current leaders who assume themselves to be guarding resources for the future and protecting the interests of their institutions. The real leadership challenge may not be about organizing the message and building the infrastructure but rather opening ourselves to let this new generation lead us.

Chapter 8

HOW WILL WE MEASURE BLENDED VALUE?

Only what we count counts ...

- More than one hundred business school students sat bleary-eyed in a New York auditorium for an early-Friday-morning panel on impact investing in which Antony participated in 2009. One of the panelists discussed his work at IGNIA Fund, a Mexico-based impact investor. He described IGNIA's investment in a company providing decent health care and health insurance to poor customers. He told the story of an investee company that was helping poor families build better and larger homes. He talked about another investee who was enabling poor farmers to export to the more lucrative organic market in the United States. Through these stories, the students sat nonplussed, still shaking off the early-morning haze. Then an audience member asked what financial returns IGNIA Fund targets. "We are targeting net IRRs of more than 20 percent," the panelist said. And suddenly, the room was alive with audible gasps and enthusiasm as the students sat up, eager to pay attention to this fund manager with a suddenly inspiring story.

... until it doesn't!

- A recent discussion between Jed and an impact investor turned to how he makes investment decisions. As he and Jed explored what factors drove his allocation of thirteen angel investments, totaling $1 million in 2010, he said: "I look at the numbers, and, of course, I consider the investment opportunity for what it is—the business opportunity it presents—but at the end of the day, I make my decision based on the story the entrepreneur tells. Is it compelling? Does it sound like it comes from a deep, personal commitment to the vision she describes? Is he someone I feel has real integrity and with whom I want to work over a number of years? These are all intangible factors—well beyond the numbers and the quantitative analysis. And these are the factors I use when making my final decision." Jed asked if he ever overrode the numbers and made a decision to invest based simply on his personal assessment of the individual or some other social factor, and he laughed. "All the time," he said, "Just like the big boys do in venture capital. They *say* it's about objective analysis and the market opportunity, but in reality everyone wants to be a part of the 'big deals,' everyone wants to be at the 'right' table and everyone invests with their gut. It's that way in traditional markets and that way in impact investing. Numbers play a role, but it's the story and the social element that drives the decision."

These two stories are being repeated around the world as the impact investing industry grapples with the challenge of developing tools to measure and describe blended value. The hard numbers impress, and the good rap compels. Yet neither provides the tool we really need to make the best investment decisions in a blended value world.

The social impact that the IGNIA Fund generates with its investments should have riveted the audience of social enterprise–focused students. But the simple phrase "net IRRs of more than 20 percent" had an unmatched focusing power. It provided the audience with a single number they understood, having been trained to know that "IRR" is the measure of annual internal rate of return. Just as important, they knew how to benchmark that number against a common understanding of relative performance. In contrast, to describe IGNIA's social performance, the fund manager could only tell stories. And these stories could not easily differentiate IGNIA's success from the similar stories from other socially focused enterprises.

Yet stories do influence investment decisions. As Jed's conversation with the impact investor brought out, mainstream investors are often driven by much more than simple numeric analysis. And a lack of standard metrics for quantifying social impact has not prevented early impact investors from raising capital and making investments. Some investors have been willing to stomach the higher costs it takes to measure and monitor social impact directly by commissioning custom impact reports or hiring specialist staff who assess social impact on a deal-by-deal basis. Others have been willing to let anecdotes substitute for analysis, asking impact investing fund managers merely to send photos and stories of happy customers.

But the substantial capital standing on the sidelines will not flow into impact investments until social performance data are transparently available for benchmarking and research. And even if substantial capital did flow, how will we know our investments are having the full impact we intend? Despite our good intentions, intent is not impact. Developing an effective measurement system is the price and prize of mainstreaming impact investing—as well as assuring ourselves that we are in fact having the impact to which we aspire.

Interest in reimagining how we measure value is growing. Philanthropists are becoming increasingly frustrated with their inability to see what social good their donations have created. Social entrepreneurs want to have their life's work assessed, and social capital allocated, on more than just the ability to tell a good story. They yearn to give more objective credit to their work and to differentiate their venture's impact from that of other social enterprises. Investors still stumble from the failure of standard approaches to protect their financial interests during the 2008 crisis. And even governments are catching wind of this zeitgeist, with prime ministers from Bhutan to France rejecting GDP as an effective measure of national well-being.

But beyond picking or choosing from the best of the nonprofit and business approaches, impact investors need to develop a new approach that allows us to recognize blended value in its integrated form. Even if we could reduce everything to the numbers, it would still not reflect the full value or impact of a strategy. Instead we need to build comprehensive systems that find a secure resting place between the competing pressures of the "greenwashers," who seek to dilute standards to make them easy to meet, and the metrics "wonks," who push a level of rigor that will be unrealistic to implement.

This chapter does not provide a simple guide to measuring blended value in an investment portfolio or enterprise. We do not offer a comprehensive review of metrics frameworks or approaches. There are certainly enough books, reports, and training conferences to support learning in that area. Instead, we offer a bolder vision of the impact investing metrics opportunity. We see it as just that: not a divisive challenge or insurmountable divide, but an invigorating opportunity to develop a more compelling way to capture the full value of our investments and track their multiple returns.

The Measurement Moment

For decades, voices on the fringes of both the nonprofit and business worlds have argued that standard approaches fail to measure value adequately. New realities are amplifying these calls and bringing them closer to mainstream attention. In the social sector, shrinking budgets in the face of growing social challenges are concentrating attention on the waste we have historically tolerated when donors and governments allocated billions of dollars to projects without reliable ways to measure their social impact and commensurate value.

In the business world, the financial crisis of 2008 revealed the problems of relying on complicated formulas to substitute for a more nuanced understanding of investment risk. The crisis also fueled calls for companies to manage the social aspects of their business more effectively; many have observed that a large part of the failure of corporate capital markets rests in the realm of governance, a centerpiece of traditional socially responsible investing and today viewed as an important consideration for any investor. Despite this new attention, the fundamental challenge remains unsolved: How do we develop a measurement system that offers an integrated understanding of blended value creation that matches the interest of the impact investor?

New Attention to Measuring Value

Practices for measuring and reporting on the social impact of both charity and investment have evolved considerably since the 1970s. A growing number of nonprofit organizations and their donors have advanced the field of impact measurement through an array of innovations. And some for-profit companies are managing social performance as a contributor to financial returns. These twin forces are creating new tools, practices, and attention that could transform the potential for measuring social value creation.

Maximizing the Social Impact of Nonprofits

When the current impact measurement movement for nonprofits began in earnest in the late 1980s, assessment was viewed largely as an exercise in contract fulfillment or compliance. Managers found themselves having to fill out monthly reports by hand, pulling from case files to tabulate figures of questionable integrity. "Objective" third-party evaluators visited a program for a day before passing judgment on the efficacy of a given intervention strategy. Program evaluation felt as if it had more to do with justifying past grants than with informing ongoing work—much less providing an informed predictor of future performance.

We are moving on from this sorry state of affairs. In many areas, evaluators now focus not simply on what metrics are most helpful to both manager and investor, but also on how best to create dynamic information systems that improve performance. Many of today's nonprofit managers have access to customizable, online performance and information systems for managing sustainability and social impact. These management information systems, referred to as Social-MIS, have helped facilitate reporting not only within a single organization but increasingly across portfolios of similar organizations. These systems create the basis for future comparisons of the blended value created by varying types of investments, whether in youth development, microenterprise, or for-profit social ventures.

Managing the Social Impact and Value of Business

Meanwhile, in some sectors of the for-profit arena, business leaders are engaging in discussions their colleagues would have had a hard time justifying only a few years ago. Some CEOs now manage the relative sustainability of a supply chain, support a nation's efforts at health care reform, or allocate employee time for community engagement. The concept of blended value, introduced in 2000 and widely promoted internationally over the past decade, has even found its way onto the hallowed pages of the *Harvard Business Review*, reframed by consultants Michael Porter and Mark Kramer, who now join others, including Stuart Hart, Lynne Payne, Rosabeth Moss Kanter, and John Elkington, who are envisioning a new form of capitalism advanced by companies pursuing what they term "shared value creation."[1]

The 2008 financial crisis accelerated this trend. The crisis loosened the conviction many people held regarding the immutable truth of traditional numerical measurement systems. In the span of hours and days that seemed like minutes, the numbers betrayed investor and fund manager alike. As mainstream capital markets slowly began to fray, then to unravel, and later to disintegrate, many marveled at the degree to which supposedly rational, quantitative markets revealed themselves to be driven by social factors such as panic and fear. And against this backdrop of value destruction, investors, regulators, and the general public around the world began to ask more regularly and with greater vehemence how investors could contribute to the social good instead of destroying it. The drive to answer that question has given new impetus to efforts to quantify and communicate the social impact of business.

Approaching a Measure of Value

Despite these advances, the metrics with which we work still reinforce the notion that financial return and social impact are distinctly independent outcomes of an investment decision. They seek to describe blended value but begin—and often end—with measuring its separate parts. This approach is grounded in an assumption that for-profit ventures generate quantifiable economic value, and nongovernmental organizations or corporate responsibility projects create social value that must be described with stories or pictures alone.

The problem with this approach is that it prevents us seeing true blended value. Describing the value of an investment only through the lens of its financial or social impact separately is like describing light with the assumption that only visible light exists. We can describe the reds and blues and greens that we see with our naked eye. But the majority of light falls well outside the visible light spectrum in infrared, gamma, and ultraviolet rays. We just can't see them with our naked eyes. Similarly, blended value exists where investments target social and financial returns in an integrated way. We just can't see it with existing metrics systems and stories that look at only a limited part of the spectrum.

Traditional investors know how to track and count a given unit of performance—a dollar, for example. Traditional philanthropists are getting increasingly effective at tracking the performance of an organizational unit—for example, a service hour or meal served. But we do not necessarily really know the full and true value of that dollar. An impact investor may provide a loan to a soup kitchen. With that investment, the soup kitchen may provide the investor a 5 percent annual return and also serve ten thousand meals. One plus one may equal two, but in this case, how much blended value is "two" ultimately worth?

You may be wondering: "Haven't economists and public policy professors already figured this out?" Not really. Unfortunately, standard approaches for measuring value do not travel well into the blended value world. One standard approach is to simply say that any given object—a doggie in a window, a company being sold, a bond offered in the muni market, those ten thousand meals—is worth its exchange value, that is, whatever price others will give up in exchange for that object. But exchange value has limited application to measuring social value because different people value social goods so differently. While we may create exchanges for diamonds or grain, we cannot create exchanges for the value or measure of a parent, though we may say, "That woman is a very good mother." There are no "good mother" markets or smile exchanges operating with the same level of liquidity as the New York Stock Exchange or NASDAQ.

Hedonic pricing has arisen as an alternative approach to valuing items that are not exchanged. Hedonic pricing argues that we can in fact value meadows and open range by virtue of assessing how much individuals are willing to pay for a given parcel of the meadow or a particular pleasure (for example, spending a day on the open range as opposed to being trapped within one more housing development built on that range), and adding up the sum of all the components.

Applying this approach to measuring the value of impact investments generates thorny methodological problems. The first is that blended value often comes with public and collective good characteristics. Like the meadow that creates a feeding ground for migratory birds, they often create value that is enjoyed by those who do not pay for it. They also often require coordination between both customers and others, such as a drinking water business that relies on many noncustomers to keep the aquifer where it sources the water clean.

Markets and surveys are also suspect at revealing the value of many social goods because of the great gap that can exist for many poor people between their desire and ability to pay for something like a hot meal or a doctor for their sick baby. Just because a family cannot pay ten dollars for the hot meal they receive from the soup kitchen does not mean they do not value the meal; they just may not have the money on hand or anything else to exchange for the service, even though that meal may have greater value for the hungry family than the satiated gourmand tucking into his expensive fourth course.

Advances on the Way

If we cannot apply tools from mainstream economics, where else can we look? Some interesting advances promise to lead to a deeper, more relevant discussion. Many intriguing innovations are taking place, and several of these stand out:

- One Report, based on the initiative and book by the same name, envisions companies issuing a single report that describes corporate financial performance and sustainable business practices in an integrated framework.[2] Pioneered by business professors Robert Eccles and Michael Krzus, this approach grows out of the idea that a company, enterprise, or organization's value can be adequately captured only in a unified manner. This notion fits well with the vision of many impact investors who are interested in structuring capital to maximize total performance and return.

- The European Alliance for CSR issued a valuation framework that seeks to advance a dialogue between business and capital market leaders regarding extrafinancial aspects of firm value. The framework promotes a common set of beyond-financial indicators and recognition that business performance and value are integrally connected to a firm's standing in and impact on society.

- The SROI Network and Heidelberg University's Center for Social Investment explore how to refine and promote social return on investment frameworks that integrate financial performance with social and environmental performance. For many years donors and some impact investors used the phrase "social return" in a metaphorical rather than practical sense. Then Jed led work at San Francisco–based REDF that culminated in the publication of the first formal Social Return on Investment (SROI) report in 1996, followed in 2000 by a methodology paper and related documents.[3] This approach augmented the classic cost-benefit analysis that many economists use with a complementary, integrated set of social metrics. The result is an analytical framework to inform cost-benefit decisions with social risk ratios and blended return analysis. A host of actors around the world have since standardized, refined, and promoted an SROI framework that presents investors and stakeholders with an integrated performance report describing the multiple impacts that capital can generate. Whereas cost-benefit analysis seeks to determine a single return on investment metric, the best SROI work offers a more integrated assessment of capital returns and organizational performance. The Center for Social Investing in Heidelberg is executing a broad agenda of academic research into the social aspect of an SROI framework that promises to complement the practitioner-focused work of the international SROI Network in new and powerful ways.

- The recent launch of the International Integrated
  Reporting Committee, endorsed by HRH The Prince of
  Wales, is advancing a variety of practices within
  mainstream corporations and financial services firms to
  promote more holistic reporting practices.

New approaches to describe blended value are going to need new
ways to display it. The classic two-dimensional risk-return frontier
curve for investments captures only the financial return (the y-axis)
and financial risk (x-axis). How will investors visually display their
portfolios and options when the social impact of an investment
matters? One approach is to map investment options and portfolios
in three dimensions, where a z-axis sums up the social impact of
an investment. In this approach, a three-dimensional efficiency
surface replaces the efficiency frontier. An impact investor could
be willing to accept more financial risk for an investment with a
strong chance of creating substantial social value.[4]

Spider graphs also liberate us from the old two-dimensional
confines of the risk-return chart, presenting multifactorial data
in an integrated, even dynamic manner. Sphere IT and other
practitioners solicit feedback on an organization's performance in
qualitative areas from various stakeholders (shareholders, management at different levels, and outside interest groups, for example)
and then present these factors alongside economic and socioeconomic indicators.[5] The resulting graph enables various users
to explore and debate the total value and returns that a firm,
organization, community or other entity creates.

What's Still Missing?

With this recent proliferation of new approaches and tools, you may
wonder, "Why the big fuss about measurement? Don't these new
approaches give impact investors what they need?" Unfortunately,
the poor state of measurement practice continues to threaten to
undermine the impact investing industry. Impact investing will

not attract substantial capital flows until investors can measure the social impact of their investments much more efficiently than they can now. And we do not see how we can gain this necessary efficiency without widely adopted measurement standards and recognized measurement providers.

The Central Importance of Standardization

Universally agreed definitions of terms such as *gross margin*, *net profit*, *income*, and *interest rate* are the water in which private investors swim. They are so central to the functioning of our capital markets system that we sometimes take them for granted and forget they are there. They allow us to easily compare the financial health and prospects of potential investments. Imagine how frustrated you would become trying to pick the best mortgage offer or savings account if every bank defined "interest rate" in a different way.

In contrast, investors and entrepreneurs in the currently disorganized, impact investment market are like fish out of water or at least fish in a very shallow and dirty pool: we each conduct our own research and undertake our own due diligence. We analyze proposed investments with our own systems that generate proprietary results, ask investees to report on the different social metrics we care about most, and track results with varied stamina based on our impact measurement appetite.

The inefficiency of this was brought home to Antony during two back-to-back consulting assignments in which he was involved in the early 2000s. In the first assignment, the consulting team spent thirty minutes with their banking client before deciding what financial metric to use in comparing strategic alternatives over the next nine months. In the second assignment, the team spent three weeks of a three-month project negotiating with their U.N. client how to define and measure impact for a program review.

Think about what the lack of standards does to impact investment fund managers. Antony met with a dozen investors in an

Indian impact investing fund a few years ago to discuss what social impact metrics the fund manager should track. The investors called the meeting in order to simplify the fund manager's life, to free him from having to produce a dozen different social impact reports each year. But by the time they had gone around the table explaining the metrics they wanted tracked, the fund manager was left to track job creation, business participation by women, carbon emissions avoided, technology spread to poor farmers, and so forth—all without any standards for what these terms meant or accepted ways to measure them.

Seeing Through a New IRIS

Fortunately, investors and other industry leaders are mobilizing to create measurement standards. The Impact Reporting and Investment Standards (IRIS) project, launched in 2009, is organizing the impact investing community to develop a common language to describe the social outputs they generate. These standards are available free and online.[6] If an impact investor seeks to improve health for poor people, IRIS defines what words like *clinic*, *hospital*, and *patient treated* mean so that an impact report for one health care investment can be consistent with the impact report of a different one. Without these standard definitions, an impact investor is left in the dark just as we would all be trying to choose between savings accounts that define interest rate differently.

Standardizing definitions is just the beginning. Working with Hitachi Corporation, IRIS has developed a system to create benchmarking reports that will allow investors to see the relative efficiency with which other similar companies are converting impact investments into blended value. This benchmarking would be impossible without adherence to standard definitions of impact.

The Need for Independent Measurement

Once IRIS adoption picks up, highly motivated investors willing to develop expertise in social impact measurement will be able to use data of comparable performance to judge the relative merit of different investment options. But highly motivated investors are not the impact investment market of the future. *That* market will be dominated, in terms of volume of capital deployed, by investors seeking to have social impact but untrained in measuring it and less interested in developing proprietary systems to do so. And these investors will need more than measurement standards. They will need third-party companies willing to take on the hard work of interpreting the standards without charging so much that they make impact investing too costly.

The need for independent impact measurement services has been brought home to us in various conversations with the gatekeepers of mainstream capital: the managers of multibillion-dollar accounts in private banks, pension fund managers, family office investors, and developers of retail financial products. With increasing frequency, they tell us they would like to create large impact investing funds but are kept back by their lack of in-house capacity to determine what investment products will deliver impact.

In a typical conversation in a typical glassed-in corporate suite in midtown Manhattan recently, a leader of one of the largest private banks swept his arm with pride as he gestured to a team of bankers working diligently at their desks in the open plan office: "I have twenty of the world's best investment professionals working for me. They are as good as anyone at creating investment products, but they don't have a clue how to measure social impact. Frankly, I wouldn't want them to try. But my clients are interested in impact investing and want us to create an impact investing product for them." This private banker is not going to create his own performance measurement system. Like many peers poised to tip billions of dollars of client assets into impact investing, he wants others to determine what investments are creating the best impact so his team can focus on raising and placing client money.

Moving into Higher GIIRS

The Global Impact Investing Rating System (GIIRS, pronounced "gears") is a bold initiative to provide the independent, outsourced social impact assessment service that the private banker and hundreds of gatekeepers like him need. GIIRS grew out of conversations among investors and social entrepreneurs eager to open the impact investing industry to new sources of capital that care enough about impact to want more than self-reported stories from investees but do not want to become impact assessment experts themselves.

Modeled on credit ratings agencies but structured to avoid the conflict-of-interest challenges they have faced, GIIRS offers investors a relatively low-cost way to access comparable and transparent assessments of the social impact an investment produces. Fund managers and social enterprises can receive GIIRS Impact Ratings, while investors can consider the GIIRS rating of a potential investment before deciding whether to invest. GIIRS does not replace the need for investors' due diligence or put those of us who have developed expertise in social impact measurement out of a job. For some investors, a GIIRS rating will be the starting point, not the end point of their impact investing due diligence. But GIIRS (and, eventually, a range of competitor systems and approaches) is a crucial step to open up the field of impact investing to the many other investors who are happy to have outside experts making these assessments.

How Are We Going to Get There?

We are not the first people to recognize the importance of social value measurement and the need to build a system with universal standards and independent measurement capabilities. Many people share our frustration at having to reinvent new measurement tools for each investment. Many people have felt the lingering uncertainty that comes with not knowing if we are really creating the impact we seek. Fortunately, after years of fits and starts, impact investors and social entrepreneurs seem galvanized to do something about it.

Principles for the Measurement Movement

We cannot predict exactly how the different efforts will ultimately come together to create an effective measurement regime. Nor do we have any magical prescriptions for what we need to build or how we're going to build it. But because an evolution of the measurement movement seems afoot, we offer our thoughts on the principles that the movement will need to follow and the contours of the path it can take.

Built for Users, Not Experts

The successful measurement movement will need to be built for users and remain clear-eyed in its appropriate use of quantitative analysis. It will need to find the balance that ensures its rigor and practicality and be built on a solid foundation of data integrity.

The people who use measurement systems don't tend to be the people who build them. Measurement systems tend to be built by people who have the appetite and capacity to spend days at metrics conferences and months or years developing systems. Entrepreneurs and investors are too busy making investment decisions or running enterprises to maintain a working knowledge of the latest literature on impact measurement and apply it to their work. So how do we make sure methods for measuring social impact make sense for investors, business owners, regulators, and customers who will ultimately need to use them?

Users and creators have a shared responsibility to strike the balance that incorporates the best thinking from within academic and other expert communities with the practicality that will promote compliance. The field of environmentally sound green building is a good example of how this could work. Over the years, a group of expert engineers, architects, and environmental scientists have worked together to develop standard recommendations for what building developers and managers should do to reduce their environmental impact. When a client now says to his developer, "I want our new office building to be environmentally sound," the developer does not have to be an environmental expert to find out what type of flooring, roofing tiles, and windows will meet the client's environmental concerns. Green building is going mainstream because there are now independent and easily adopted standards that allow people and companies to move into green buildings without having to become expert in green building themselves.

As one investment banker told participants in an impact investing conference, "My CEO has no idea what goes into the LEED Green Building Standards, but he does know that our new headquarters building is going to be LEED Gold." Similarly the private banker in the glassed-in office in New York City does not want to become expert in measuring the social impact of investment, but he does want to put his clients' money into impact investments that outside experts verify will deliver blended value.

Clear-Eyed But Not Blinded by the Light

Determining blended value is more complex than measuring financial return or even environmental impact. Overly simplistic quantification of projects that address such critical issues as health care, hunger, youth development, and education can certainly be dangerous. Those things we can count—patients treated, meals served, student test scores—will never be able to describe fully the way an intervention affects a community or influences the trajectory of an individual life. For example, the respect a nurse shows a poor patient will create ripple effects in the complex system of her own or the community's social health. The nurse's impact cannot be reduced to a single number. Moreover, many people who can become comfortable with a rating that compares the social impact of two hospitals will not be comfortable with the value judgments required to assess the relative usefulness of these hospitals compared to a food distribution business or low-cost school.

But sometimes the complexity and nuance can paralyze us. We need to avoid being overly reductionist, but we also need to embrace the power of reductionism to help steer our investment decisions. No system can perfectly capture every nuance of social change work. But we don't need perfection; we just need a system that efficiently allows us to allocate resources better among investments that can create blended value. Quantification will be one component crucial to spur that efficiency. But "measuring impact" needs to be about more than "counting outputs." We need to develop better systems of analytics that capture the qualitative components of blended value while tracking quantitative outcomes that matter.

Balanced and Transparent

The arena of impact assessment is not a place for the thin-skinned. Every measurement system is buffeted between critics who consider it too superficial to ensure social impact and those who consider it too onerous to implement. These winds of criticism will only grow stronger as more and more capital pours into impact investing and regulators start paying attention. In the end, the best systems may well be those no one likes. They will be rigorous enough to challenge social entrepreneurs and investors to spend more effort than they otherwise might, yet practical enough that they can be of real use.

Building a product you know will alienate your potential customers is not typically a winning strategy, but in the realm of impact measurement, not striking this balance is also sure to fail. Too many systems make impact investing too hard by creating burdens of proof for claims of social impact that cost too much to implement and risk distracting management from running their business. Others make it too easy by letting investors and companies claim to be creating impact if they are able to come up with an anecdote about a happy customer or if they sign a declaration.

Intellectually difficult and morally contentious judgments about the relative value of different impact investments will be an unavoidable feature of a comprehensive impact measurement system. Not every investor will agree with these judgments, but they will be much more likely to accept them if they are able to understand how they were made. Proprietary black box algorithms will not be a winning approach. *Transparency* is an increasingly overused term, but it will be a touchstone of successful impact measurement.

Built on a Solid Foundation of Data Integrity

None of the systems for assessing social impact will work if the data they interpret are not sound. Without solid monitoring and reporting systems, we cannot have real confidence in reporting, whether numeric or qualitative. But who will pay to ensure data integrity?

We will need an answer at the organizational and industry level. Many social entrepreneurs take the position that if the "new money" wants numbers, then *they* should pay for creating the systems that can gather and verify them. And some impact investors are willing to embrace only those measurement and verification systems that other institutions pay for. Even worse, we've heard of some investors using their relative inattention to social impact measurement as a selling point to potential investees whose other potential investors insist on rigorous impact measurement.

In the end, data integrity is an industry-wide public good that everyone interested in the future of the impact investing field will need to steward carefully. Public campaigns and industry-level mobilization needs to affirm the centrality of measurement as a prerequisite to participating in impact investing. Auditing and assurance firms will be eager to provide verification services, partly as a corporate responsibility commitment and partly out of the awareness that social impact auditing could become a major business line. Leading investors, entrepreneurs, and government regulators can harness this interest to create the tools and capabilities that can put the impact investing industry onto a solid foundation of data integrity.

Self-Improving Rather Than Self-Righteous

We do not know exactly which common standards and measurement systems will succeed in the coming years, but we do know they will share one trait: none of them will start out perfect. They will all need improvement and modification over time. So let's all maintain a level of self-deprecation and humility as we engage in this shared journey.

Unfortunately, in many measurement debates, the perfect is becoming the enemy of the good as measurement experts chase magical bullet-proof metrics and practices that all can embrace. Instead, we will need a continuous process of "dialing in" as our collective experience and exploration inform practices that evolve over time. We must be open to, as Tom Peters termed it, "failing forward" as we try out new approaches. We all must be committed to staying in the process even if the initial reporting results do not favor our firm or approach to value creation. And that reaffirms that only open and clear information management and reporting systems will enable us to understand and critique both processes and outcomes to ensure their improvement.

The Leviathan Rising from the Measurement Depths

Throughout this discussion of measurement, we have stressed the centrality of standardization. But with competing standards and measurement systems vying for attention and adoption in an industry peopled by charismatic entrepreneurs unused to collaboration, how will we ensure these standard systems take hold? The fragmented and chaotic impact investing industry needs a Leviathan—that mythic beast that rises from the sea and imposes order on a chaotic world. The managers of government investment funds and of the largest pools of private capital have a particular responsibility to step up to this role.

Governments have played this coordinating role successfully in the past. The Generally Accepted Accounting Principles (GAAP) began as a movement in the accounting industry to create standards. But ultimately the decision by the U.S. government to imbue these standards with quasi-legal status enabled them to become the standard for the United States and many global companies. Taking on this standard-setting role will be an important contribution governments can make to facilitate the broad growth of a productive impact investing industry.

Beyond government, we look to asset owners to coalesce around a system that could become an industry standard. A measurement system must be user driven, built through constant feedback from the business owners ultimately responsible for collecting impact measurement data and their customers. But business owners and customers will not be able to organize activity around a standard as effectively as the asset owners who are fueling the industry. Investors can tell investees what standards to use; investees cannot typically return the favor. Few investors today operate at a scale that could allow them to take on an industry-organizing role. But investors are beginning to aggregate through industry associations such as the Investors' Council of the Global Impact Investing Network that could help to coordinate activity among enough investors who collectively have the scale to make an industry standard stick.

Moving Metrics Forward: Creating a Shared Future of High Performance

Imagine the difference an effective system for measuring social impact will make to the people we have met in this chapter:

- The representative from the IGNIA Fund will be able to stun that audience of sleepy students with descriptions of the social impact his investments generate that are just as compelling as the financial returns they target.

BENCHMARKING SOCIAL IMPACT
Brian Trelstad, Chief Investment Officer, Acumen Fund, New York, New York

Most measurement and evaluation in the development sector is backward looking—kind of like an autopsy: very intrusive, often inconclusive, and definitely too late to help the patient. Instead, we need a balanced and timely approach that provides a coherent narrative about what the numbers tell us, what the customer experience is, and what we are hearing from management.

At Acumen Fund, we saw soon after we began investing how financial returns inevitably come to dominate our understanding of an investment simply because they are straightforward to measure. The measurement of social impact needs something similarly convincing to let us know we are getting our impact money's worth, so to speak.

Good measurement takes critical data points to tell a compelling story. I would rather have sparse data but a compelling (and accurate) narrative about what is happening than great data but no idea what is happening to the underlying performance of the company or the people it serves. But relying on narrative alone requires the entrepreneur or portfolio manager covering the investment to get it right, and there are limits to how well this intuition scales.

We needed a data collection system that could allow us to take the pulse of our investments, using simple measures that could give us a sense for whether things were on track. Working with volunteer engineers from Google, we built a functioning system in 2006 that we put to work in April 2007 for our annual portfolio reviews. It worked well and allowed us to generate a relatively comprehensive and integrated report on the financial, operational, and social performance of our investments.

But our system told us only about the investments in our portfolio. The thirty-five active investments in our portfolio are so disparate that we cannot benchmark the social performance of one investment against another. We cannot usefully compare the social performance of a hospital, ambulance company, and insurance provider.

A narrative about impact that can't be benchmarked against peer funds or independently verified is not good enough.

We realized that if we adopted the same measurement standards as other impact investors operating in our markets, we might be able to create benchmarks. We might, for example, be able to compare our investment in Lifespring in India with other maternity hospital chains in other portfolios.

To begin to put in place the building blocks of social impact benchmarking, we have rebuilt our data management system into a widely available tool that other investors can use. Now, in mid-2011, forty other impact investors use the tool, known as Pulse. We have also worked with other impact investors to develop a set of measurement standards, the Impact Reporting and Investment Standards (IRIS). These standards create consistency in how we define what we measure, a crucial input to facilitate benchmarking.

Developing Pulse and IRIS has required an insane amount of collaboration. We also imposed on a number of leading impact investing funds, such as E+Co., Root Capital, and Grassroots Business Fund to get them to share their perspectives throughout the development of the taxonomy. We learned a lot from the MIX Market, which has been gathering microfinance bank data using similar technology for the last several years. Trust and friendship made the collaboration work.

We have been pleasantly surprised at the willingness of so many industry leaders to give it a shot. Another surprise has been how quickly people have said they would be willing to adopt this new approach. Pulse adoption, for example, was nearly double what we thought it would be in the first year.

But many people remain skeptical that the data will ultimately be aggregated in a way that will be meaningful for them and that it will be worth the effort. Some brave early adopters are setting aside this skepticism to use the system and contribute their data. When we develop a strong business process for managing and reporting the shared data so that they are meaningful for fund managers, we will be on our way.

- The impact investor talking with Jed will draw on tools that merge his quantitative rigor with his emotional instinct instead of forcing him to abandon one or the other in making investment decisions.

- The private banker in Manhattan will launch his impact investing fund because he will be able to draw on companies like GIIRS to provide social impact assessments that make the insights of industry insiders accessible.

Building this system will not be easy. It will require balance, integration, and acts of grace. If you are an impact investor, you will need to demand more from investees than a few photos, crude numbers, or stories about social impact. If you run a social enterprise, you will need to embrace impact measurement as an opportunity to improve your performance—not begrudge it as a tax on doing business imposed by the self-righteous. The measurement system we build will need to be rigorous enough to matter and practical enough to implement. We will need to quantify as much as we can without losing sight of the social value that we cannot describe with numbers.

If this sounds daunting, consider the alternative. Impact investors can continue to swim in the murky puddles we currently inhabit where investors and entrepreneurs struggle to make our own judgments, fail to learn from each other, and watch the prize of capturing more mainstream capital continuously recede like the proverbial pot of gold at the end of the rainbow.

Chapter 9

HOW WILL WE UNLOCK PHILANTHROPIC CAPITAL?

Total Foundation Asset Management

- In the late 1990s, the board of the New York–based F.B. Heron Foundation asked a critical question: Shouldn't the foundation act as more than a privately held investment company that uses its "surplus cash" for charitable good as most U.S. foundations had for decades? Shouldn't it seek to use every tool at its disposal to pursue its institutional purpose, including the investments it makes out of its endowment? In response, the foundation has shifted more than 30 percent of its total assets into impact investments while maintaining financial returns that exceed most of its peers.

- The Kellogg Foundation, one of the largest private foundations in the United States, has for decades donated hundreds of millions of dollars to improve the health of children in the United States. More recently it has sought to understand how for-profit investment from its endowment can complement this and other grant making. It launched a $100 million mission-driven investment experiment in 2008 to make for-profit investments that can advance its social mission. Among many deals, from this fund it structured a $500,000 working capital line for California-based Revolution Foods, a company that provides healthy meals to more than twenty thousand school children. This credit line has enabled the company to expand despite seasonal revenue streams and delays in government payments.

- When Swiss-based businessman John McCall-McBain turned his attention to addressing climate change, he sought worthy grantees, as did many philanthropists before him. He contributed to advocacy campaigns in Europe that seek to block the development of new coal-fired power-plants. But he also recognized that existing coal-fired plants are major emitters of greenhouse gases. Advocacy campaigns could do little to reduce their emissions. But alternative, renewable feedstock would. So McCall-McBain invested $10 million through his for-profit investment fund, Pamoja Capital, to help build a wood-chipping business in Liberia. That for-profit business converts old rubber trees into renewable fuel for power plants, reducing their carbon footprint now, while the advocacy campaigns work for a greener future.

These are just three of many recent examples of how impact investing is transforming the almost century-old model of private philanthropy. Instead of organizing exclusively around the question, "How do we give well?" foundations and individuals are beginning to ask, "How can we use our total assets to address social and environmental challenges most effectively?" Answering that question is leading many to reorient around the practice of maximizing blended value in an integrated way.[1]

In a world in which for-profit investment can contribute directly to a foundation's mission and impact investments need not undermine financial performance, fulfilling a foundation's mission now requires more than just organizing the most effective grant-making program. Increasing numbers of philanthropists have realized they must be more than grant makers acting as charitable ATMs, churning out modest twenty-dollar bills in support of those working in areas of critical need, particularly in these times of economic stress. To paraphrase an old saying, "If your only tool is a grant, then the whole world is a charity case," but if your tools span grants to debt to equity investing, you just might be able to build something.

Although this approach is easy to describe, it is hard to implement, and there is no single correct way to do so. Adopting an integrated impact investing strategy requires foundations and individual philanthropists to embrace a new business model and exert strong leadership against a skeptical set of organizations and institutions with vested interest in preserving the status quo. Foundations need a new strategy that can deploy, monitor, and communicate efficiently the performance of a multifaceted portfolio that is inclusive of, yet goes beyond, grant making. This vision includes financial and extra-financial assets such as social capital, intellectual capital, and convening power. Given the topic of this book, we will focus here on the components of financial asset allocation and refer to this approach as *total foundation asset management* (TFAM).

This chapter describes the new possibilities TFAM opens up and the challenges the philanthropic sector faces in taking advantages of them. Foundations and family offices have a unique role to play in advancing impact investing innovation. Everyone has a stake in seeing them become more effective. Having said that, there is also a great deal to learn about the challenges they face and innovations they are developing as they embrace the promise of impact investing. This chapter is not exclusively targeting the rarified offices of foundation executives and trustees. We do not provide a technical guide for implementing this new strategy. (Others have written those guides which we reference in the Further Reading section.) Instead, we hope anyone interested in how society will unlock greater resources to address increasingly complex and overwhelming social challenges will find the ideas and tools here to be provocative and useful.

The Traditional Approach of Transactive Philanthropy

Historically, almost all donors have organized themselves around these twin assumptions:

- Social considerations in investment decisions will undermine financial performance.

- The only way to pursue a philanthropic mission is through giving grants or subsidizing charitable programs.

If these assumptions are true, then maximizing the social good from charitable assets is a relatively straightforward two-step process:

1. Invest all assets in mainstream, commercial market investments without any consideration of their social impact.
2. Take part of the financial surplus these investments generate and give them away as grants or spend them on programs.

And this is what most donors have done in the hundred-year history of modern philanthropy.

It should be no surprise, then, to learn that when donors discuss the social good they create, they focus on the grants that they make. This conception of philanthropy as a set of charitable transactions is an approach Jed has termed "transactive philanthropy." Transactive philanthropy sees donors as a source of grants and on the whole holds those involved in philanthropy accountable only for giving their money away with competence and effect. It does not necessarily hold them accountable for investing in impact.

The organizational implications of the transactional philanthropy approach are clear. A traditional foundation is intentionally a house divided: "program people" decide which potential grantees should receive donations and investment professionals in standalone units or external fund managers decide how the foundation's endowment assets should be invested. Each side of the house has clear and separate administrative direction: the program staff is charged with maximizing the social impact of grants, and investment professionals are expected to maximize the long-term size of the endowment. Program staffs typically see for-profit investment as morally suspect or irrelevant to their mission; investment staffs see social mandates as distracting and threatening to financial returns. The two sides rarely speak to each other and often report to different board committees.

Individual donors largely mimic this structure. Almost all high-net-worth families operate within the same divided house mentality. They allocate assets to an investment advisor charged with maximizing capital appreciation and then make grant decisions independently from financial considerations, sometimes following separate guidance from a philanthropy advisor. (While much of the following discussion is taken from the perspective of institutional philanthropy, the critique, alternative strategy, and suggested tools also hold true for individuals and family offices, a growing source of innovation and change within the impact investing arena.)

In relying almost exclusively on grants, transactive philanthropy greatly limits the assets deployed toward social purpose. Most foundations contribute the minimum required by regulation (in the United States, 5 percent of their total assets annually) while managing the vast bulk of their financial assets in pursuit of financial performance alone. For a foundation using the 5 percent spending rule, this means that for every dollar held in a foundation, five cents every year goes to achieving its mission. The remaining ninety-five cents invested through the endowment remain neutral or may actually undermine the institutional mission, such as when a foundation uses grants to fund antismoking programs while its endowment invests in tobacco companies.

The New Opportunity: Total Foundation Asset Management

Transactive philanthropy makes sense as long as we assume grants are the only way to create social value and believe financial return will suffer if investors take the social impact they create into consideration. But impact investing is upending both assumptions. The basic math of 95/5 doesn't make sense to a growing number of donors and trustees. It's what caused the F.B. Heron Foundation trustees to start to question their real purpose.

To be clear, effective grant making will always be a crucial tool of philanthropy. For-profit investments and the businesses they support will not alone solve all social challenges. But organizing a foundation, yet alone the entire philanthropic sector, around a focus on only one tiny portion of the assets it deploys is an underperforming strategy of philanthropic asset management.

It is clear we need a new strategy that enables foundations to consider how best to deploy all their assets toward mission attainment. Total foundation asset management describes this approach. Building on the work of others, this framework reimagines the potential of philanthropy with increasing appeal in a time of tight grant-making budgets and increasing need. This strategy expands both the sources of capital and the investment tools available to foundations. It may also alter how we understand the structure and leadership requirement of philanthropy today and into the future.

Consider two hypothetical foundations focused on homelessness and community development:

- Foundation A has an endowment of $600 million.
  Employing a transactive philanthropy strategy, it gives away

$30 million in grants each year and invests the rest of its assets without regard to its mission.

- Foundation B has $400 million in total assets. Employing a TFAM strategy, it gives away $15 million in grants each year, makes an additional $5 million of concessionary loans to housing development nonprofits, and invests $80 million from its endowment in market-rate impact investments in affordable housing projects and community development notes.

Which of these foundations is better run? Which has more social impact? Which is allocating its assets more wisely?

We do not have any easy answers to these questions. As we discussed in the previous chapter, measuring the social impact of investments is a complicated and nascent science and art. But no foundation can optimize the full return on its assets if it is unaware of the range of available tools. We begin with an overview of these investment tools before considering the challenges of leadership and organization required to wield them effectively.

Strategic Philanthropy

Impact investing focuses on investments rather than grants, and we will also focus our discussion on these additional instruments here. But if grant making, the core philanthropic approach of a foundation, is not managed in an effective strategic manner, then the impact investing strategy will be built on a base of sand. An effective foundation must develop and execute a thoughtful strategic approach to charitable grants, which may be viewed as nonprofit social equity investments. We do not need to revisit here the ideas and practices on this topic contained in countless books, other resources, and conferences. But as we discuss later, effective philanthropy makes up a key portion of a unified investment approach to TFAM and should not be ignored in our rush to advance the tools of impact investing.

Program-Related Investments

Beyond grants, the first formally codified tool available to the total foundation asset manager has been Program Related Investment, formalized in the 1969 U.S. Tax Reform Act. Commonly referred to as PRIs, these initially tended to be unsecured, low-interest loans to nonprofit organizations.[2] They now cover a range of fields, but have come to focus on education, the environment, arts and culture, human services, health, and church support. They include increasingly diverse investment instruments, from traditional loans and loan guarantees, to direct equity investments in companies, to participation in venture capital and private equity funds. Adoption of PRIs is growing in the United States, where they have formal designation, as well as around the rest of the world. In the United States alone, more than 120 foundations reported making $391 million in new PRIs in 2007 compared to $148 million by 89 foundations a decade earlier.

PRIs convey several advantages on the foundations that use them:

- They allow the foundation to recycle limited grant funds, since the dollars expended will be returned to the foundation if the investment goes well.

- They enable the foundation to support larger capital projects than grants alone might allow.

- They can leverage commercial capital to complement foundation assets when a PRI takes a "first loss" position, decreasing the risk for other investors like banks and making it possible to finance deals that would not close if they were structured as either pure philanthropy or pure market rate investment.

- They make it possible for the foundation to meet regulatory obligations to deploy assets to social purpose in deals that often move more money than typical grants do. This is a benefit in countries like the United States, where foundations are required to contribute a minimum amount of their total assets each year to charitable purpose and where PRIs qualify to meet that obligation.

- They may be structured as "convertible notes," whereby the initial PRI is a high-risk loan, which then converts to an equity position for the investor should the venture achieve certain social and economic performance benchmarks.

PRIs benefit recipient organizations as well by:

- Enabling them to tap into longer-term sources of finance that can be more stable and efficient to source than multiple short-term grants

- Building the organization's institutional credit rating and managerial capacity through debt management

- Potentially freeing them to provide more significant support to programs and projects

PRIs can be a powerful complement to grant making, but they are not without drawbacks. Few foundations are set up to use the PRI tool effectively right out of the gate. Because the legacy of transaction philanthropy has separated investment professionals from program staff, most foundation program officers are not trained to evaluate the potential financial risk of borrowers or to manage a portfolio of investments.

Many PRI recipients are also ill equipped to manage loans and investments. Nonprofit organizations that previously relied on grants exclusively may not be experienced negotiating with investors. They may not have the expertise to anticipate and manage the risk that a failed business venture or real estate deal could threaten their ongoing charitable activities. Furthermore, foundation investors may place covenants or performance requirements that add to the pressure on the nonprofit to focus on financial return.

Mission-Related Investing from the Endowment

PRIs offer a tool to take money that would have been spent on grants and make investments that count toward charitable distribution requirements. But what about the other 95 percent of the foundation's assets that are invested primarily for the purpose of generating financial return? Total foundation asset managers can put those assets to work as well through the even more disruptive innovation of mission-related investing.

Mission-related investment grows out of the realization that impact investments can generate solid financial returns. Assets from the foundation's endowment are placed into investments that target more market-rate financial return and also strong social impact, often in the same areas as the foundation's mission. With both old and new foundations embracing this approach, mission-related investments are being made across asset classes, geographies, and social issues, from the Kellogg Foundation's debt investment into a school food company in the United States, to John McCall-McBain's investment in the Liberian renewable energy company. The U.S.-based More for Mission campaign, launched in 2007 to spur and coordinate this activity, by April 2011 included ninety-five foundations representing $37 billion in total assets.

Interest in mission-related investment is booming from a tiny base, with most foundations initially dipping their toes rather than jumping in. But even small experiments can unlock substantial capital because mission-related investment draws from the endowment assets, which are typically twenty times the size of annual grant-making budgets. For example, the Kellogg Foundation's initial foray into mission-related investment left almost 99 percent of its endowment untouched but still committed $100 million. If U.S.

foundations committed as little as 5 percent of their endowments to impact investing, they would create a $30 billion investment pool that is as large as the entire U.S. venture capital industry.

Loan Guarantees

Foundations can also harness their assets without making direct investments through loan guarantees. In a guarantee arrangement, a foundation commits to cover any default that a nonprofit or social enterprise may make on a loan. Importantly, the guarantee need not cost the foundation anything beyond what it sets aside to cover the potential liability. Through guarantees, foundations can enable socially focused organizations to receive lower-interest loans or gain access to credit for which they previously may not have qualified. The Gates Foundation has committed $300 million to guarantees. In an early transaction under this program, Gates guaranteed $10 million in loans for KIPP, a nonprofit charter school operator, to build additional school facilities. This enabled KIPP to lower the rate of its bank loan by 3 percentage points. By saving the nonprofit (and, of course, its donors) $10 million in interest payments during the life of the loan, the guarantee provided the equivalent social benefit as a multimillion dollar grant and cost the Gates Foundation nothing—as long as KIPP repays its loan.

Adding Traditional Socially Responsible Investing to the Mix

While the primary tools of impact investing focus on private equity and debt transactions, most foundations will continue to hold assets in public equities. Foundation leaders intent on squeezing the most blended value out of all their assets can apply socially responsible and sustainable investment principles to this part of their portfolio. These principles can also target the foundation's specific focus areas. A foundation whose grant-making program seeks to tackle the obesity epidemic may choose to divest from companies whose main business is selling snack foods and soda.

Similarly, a foundation with a grant-making program promoting access to clean drinking water may join a shareholder advocacy campaign urging management to consider the effects its industrial water use has on local communities. Failure to make these connections between endowment holdings and grant-making priorities can lead to embarrassing questions, as the Gates Foundation found out in 2007 when an article in the *Los Angeles Times* used publicly available data about its investment holdings to question whether its investment practices were undermining its grant-making goals.[3]

The Nature of Returns: Moving Beyond Either-Or Definitions of Performance

To navigate this confusing landscape of new philanthropic tools, many foundations considering impact investment have found it useful to separate investment options into below market-rate and market rate categories. The F.B. Heron Foundation produced an influential chart (Figure 9.1), first produced by chief investment officer Luther Ragin, that lays out investment options along a spectrum of financial risk with these two categories of investments separated on the page. Building on this approach, the Monitor Institute's *Investing for Social and Environmental Impact* introduced the language of "social first" and "impact first" to describe the different motivations of impact investors willing to make below-market-rate investments and those unwilling to compromise financial return. This language has been picked up in, among other reports, *Solutions for Impact Investors*, released by Rockefeller Philanthropy Advisors, and the 2010 *Investing for Impact* by Parthenon Group and Bridges Ventures.[4]

This language has been a helpful bridge, framing the discussion of how to allocate funds for impact investing within a traditional mind-set that assumes financial and social components of value

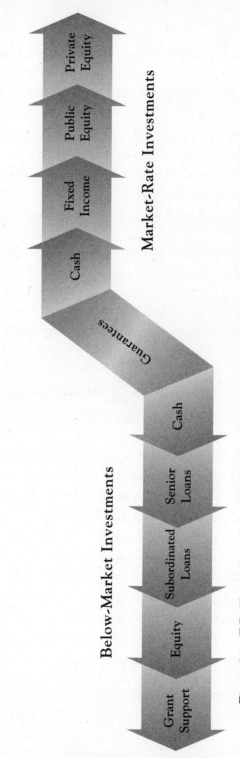

Figure 9.1. F.B. Heron Foundation Mission-Related Investing Continuum. Reprinted with permission.

are separate and competing. But this bifurcated approach will ultimately prove limiting for those seeking to harness the full power of TFAM. We need to roll up this approach into a more holistic understanding of capital structure and performance. Rather than dividing investment options into the two halves of "finance first or impact first" or "below market or above market," a unified investment framework assesses each investment option along multiple lines of financial and social performance and then constructs a portfolio that optimizes for the desired characteristics of total performance.

Our understanding of the performance of invested capital should ultimately go beyond a set of artificial trade-offs between economic and social interests. Rather, in the future we will come to see that a portfolio's measure of performance consists of an array of allocations across asset classes, with each generating a blend of multiple, integrated returns to investors and stakeholders.

Challenges of Implementing Total Foundation Asset Management

All of this may sound like common sense. But those of us working with and in foundations know that the TFAM approach is profoundly disruptive. The foundation sector is largely locked into a traditional set of business models and leadership modes that suit a much narrower view of the foundation as charitable grant maker. Even most of the new foundations tend to default to the transactive philanthropy model. To break out of these established ways of doing business will require profound vision and stamina. Developing an integrated organizational structure and expanding both the skill set and perspective of foundation executives will be critical.

How to Organize the Integrated Foundation

Total foundation asset management requires an integrated organization that positions managers on both sides of the organizational balance sheet to make savvy connections between grants and investments. In the short term in most cases, smashing the walls between program staff and investments officers is too disruptive. Instead, some foundations have sought to build an extension onto their organizational structure by creating a discrete third pool of impact investing assets, leaving most of the traditional investments and grant making untouched. They typically hire a dedicated impact investment manager or boutique advisor rather than expect existing staff to transform how they operate. This approach allows the institution to test management structures and build organizational capabilities while minimizing the disruption and threat to established systems.

Early pioneers are developing a range of approaches to creating effective organizational structures. Many are open about how they operate and eager to assist their peers in adopting similar approaches. Publicly available research provides step-by-step execution plans for setting up similar programs. In addition, a variety of impact investment advisory firms, impact investment marketplaces, fund-of-fund platforms, and industry experts are coming forward to support implementation by those interested in maximizing the value of their work and capital.

But the full power of TFAM takes hold only when investing and grant making integrate organizationally. A business model that integrates impact investing across a foundation or family office can build a virtuous feedback loop between grant making and investing. Investments can reveal what it will take to execute a social agenda, and grant making can identify new market opportunities for investments. At the Kellogg Foundation, the mission-related investment into Revolution Foods gave grant-making staff greater clarity about the regulatory reforms needed to improve the availability of healthier food in schools. This understanding led them to shift their advocacy program in this area. The relative discipline with which impact investment programs track social impact and manage risk also often sets a new standard for grant making.

And effective grant making can clarify where investors will generate real social impact rather than simply feel-good stories.

While few people give up their own room easily, when the walls do come down, they sometimes find their new rooms accommodate much grander ambitions as new roommates become inspiring friends rather than intrusive strangers making unreasonable demands.

How to Find the Foundation Leaders of the Future

Just as TFAM requires a new set of integrated organizational capabilities, it also requires a new type of foundation leader. In a transactive philanthropy model, philanthropic leaders are celebrated for their ability to execute an effective grants strategy. It should be no surprise that today's foundations are populated with talented individuals from academia and the nonprofit sector. But to deploy all of a foundation's assets in an integrated strategy will require what we call a mutant manager. Effective foundation executives will combine deep experience in and commitment to nonprofit work with skill and confidence in making investments that transform the assets and capabilities of individuals, institutions, and systems. Their profile is less institutional manager than entrepreneurial leader.

Where will we find these mutants? Probably not in too many traditional foundations, where most leaders are uncomfortable stepping outside their side of the house. Yet they are also not likely to be found among the ranks of the many successful businesspeople who too frequently succumb to hubris and overconfidence when they turn their attention to philanthropic work. Creating blended value through impact investment is too complicated to apply simple prescriptions learned in traditional business careers.

In contrast to either the philanthropic pterodactyl or the hard-charging corporate carnivore, the new mutants will have the omnivorous savvy to both envision and implement integrated investment strategies that generate blended value. Experience in running community ventures or educational institutions or in leading environmental justice initiatives will be as important in the future as demonstrated success in managing thriving for-profit corporations. But such a commitment will not be enough. These leaders also need to understand how to use all the investment instruments in the new tool kit of impact investing and apply them with a level of insight into their effects on communities to which traditional investors and philanthropists only aspire.

There are few mutant managers at gatherings of traditional foundation and corporate leaders, but that does not mean they don't exist. They are creatures of the impact investing forest that are often best seen on the fringe, coming out at either the beginning or end of the capital market day. They are out there leading innovative new investment funds and social enterprises. They are increasingly easy to spot at top business and public policy schools. And they are now frequently seen climbing the walls of the big city of finance and escaping into the dark woods to create a new blended future that maximizes the impact of their skill set. The extent to which foundations can unlock the power of all their capital will depend to no small extent on how effectively we identify and cultivate these managers.

How to Know Whether a Foundation Is Doing Well

With an integrated organization and effective leadership, the foundation of the future will be able to harness all its assets toward its mission. The size of the annual grant-making budget and the savvy of the grant-making strategy alone will become only one component in an understanding of a foundation's success. As we noted in Chapter Eight, a set of comprehensive measurement systems is emerging that will allow us to assess the total blended performance of companies and social ventures and, by extension, the capital invested in them. These will be useful in assessing foundations as well. Foundations will be able to manage unified portfolios of capital spanning strategic philanthropy, impact investing, and traditional commercial market investing using standards of practice such as the previously discussed Impact Reporting and Investment Standards and Global Impact Investing Rating System and sustainable finance analytics like Trucost. Additional tools such as SROI and Sphere IT will augment these standards and indicators.

The total foundation asset manager needs to develop a unified analysis of overall capital performance that integrates measures of financial return with impact. Such a unified approach will enable outsiders to assess the relative skill with which foundations are run and guide foundation managers in the construction of optimal impact portfolios consisting of investments and grants. Until the industry develops standards for this analytical approach, pioneering foundation leaders will need to innovate, building from established practices in grant making and mainstream investing. As in many other areas of impact investing, they will also need to draw in expertise from both sides of the bifurcated world. Creating blended value, yet alone measuring it, is simply too important a task for any one group to take on in isolation.

How to Build a Total Foundation

We have seen that implementing a TFAM strategy will not be easy. It requires upending established approaches to organization and leadership. The gravitational forces being exerted to revert to established modes of operating drag down even the most ambitious new philanthropists, not to mention the leaders of decades-old institutions. What will it take to sweep the philanthropic sector into the age of impact investing?

To begin, we must understand that foundations are legendary for their idiosyncratic nature. Philanthropists often joke that "if you've seen one foundation, you've seen … one foundation." But we can learn from the pioneers who have begun to reveal a path for those who wish to follow: individual philanthropists like

Bill Young, who become a reluctant expert on Canadian charity law on his own philanthropic journey, and Annie Chen, whose story is told in this chapter, and institutional leaders such as Tom Reis at the Kellogg Foundation and Luther Ragin at F.B. Heron. Each of these and a growing generation of other new leaders are advancing these ideas, developing successful track records, and demonstrating how these concepts of impact investing can get legs in the world of finance.

Implementing a TFAM strategy is like building a house. It requires the vision to see the opportunity and a combination of technical skills, organizational savvy, and stamina to capture it. Each house ultimately takes its own form, and building it means facing unique challenges and celebrating breakthroughs. But those who have built before us do provide some general lessons about what it will take to pull it off.[5] In breaking new ground, we need to go beyond analytical arguments, demand more from investment advisors, and share perspectives to overcome skeptical lawyers. Once we have the permission to build with a new approach, we need to develop impact investing capabilities, think like investors, and collaborate. Let's review each of these steps in turn.

Breaking Ground

Before you break ground, you need to think about what an impact investing strategy might look like for you and how best to execute it. In the world of foundations, you will require "permits" from foundation boards, investment managers, and the lawyers who advise them.

Target the Body, Not Simply the Heart or Head

Creativity and leadership will be crucial to overcome the emotional attachment many foundation decision makers have to the transactive philanthropy model. Often all the data in the world will not be enough to shake their convictions about the need to protect investment decisions from the social mission.

To spur the impact investing conversation at Oregon-based Meyer Memorial Trust, CEO Doug Stamm created a mocked-up version of the local newspaper with a headline condemning the trustees for investing the foundation's endowment in companies whose products contributed to obesity while the Trust made grants in support of an anti-obesity campaign. If such guerrilla tactics are not appropriate, take board members to visit other foundations that have embraced the new approach or stage visits to potential investees—whatever it takes. And recognize that the impact investing agenda threatens convictions that are emotionally as well as intellectually held.

Data analysis is especially unhelpful in addressing concerns about the relative financial return and risk of impact investments. While some impact investments are building solid track records, and traditional sustainable investing has proven its financial value, many new impact investment vehicles lack the decades-long historic performance many investment professionals will require before they accept that these investments are financially prudent. As long as the discussion remains focused exclusively on claims and counterclaims about the potential financial returns of an impact investing strategy, the status quo will win out. The advocate for an impact investing strategy is on more solid ground by shifting the argument to emphasize how impact investments will contribute additional value to the foundation's social or environmental mission, which makes the case for innovation more compelling. In the end, you need to target the whole organization by addressing both its heart and its head and showing how such an approach will play out through the numbers and the narrative.

Demand More from Investment Advisors

Even if you can secure the backing of management and trustees, in many foundations, investment advisors hold explicit or implicit veto power over investment decisions. Many resist mandates to build impact investing portfolios, and they will likely continue to resist until their incentives change. Foundations that do not want to miss out on the impact investing opportunity must be willing to shift their assets to new advisors if existing advisors and fund managers do not seek out and bring forward appropriate impact investment options.

Remember: you are the customer, and investment advisors respond to their clients. The 2010 decision by Rockefeller Brothers Fund to allocate 5 to 10 percent of its endowment for an impact investing fund spurred its investment advisor to seek out impact investment options, something the firm had not done in the past.

Share Clearer Legal Guidance on Investment Prudence

Even if you can win over the hearts and minds of management and trustees and convince investment advisors to find relevant investments, one more hurdle will stand before you when you set out to break ground on a new strategy: skepticism from traditional lawyers. A continuing and restrictive interpretation of the "prudent man" rule leads many legal advisors to reject any investment strategy that appears unusual.

The concept of fiscal prudence has advanced well beyond its early days when legislators for the State of New York prohibited the boards of trusts located within the state from investing in anything other than bonds issued by the state. And just a few decades ago, private equity investing was viewed as highly risky and outside the realm of common, prudent practice for foundation trustees.

But, with many foundations having lost 20, 30, and even 40 percent of their total assets in the 2008 market meltdown as the result of tried-and-true investment strategies, the relative discomfort with impact investing approaches is beginning to crack. The argument that trustees may actually violate their fiduciary duties by *not* investing on a sustainable basis is beginning to gain resonance in some corners. Hindsight is an unreliable guide, but it is certainly true that if more trustees had insisted on better corporate governance in investee companies prior to the 2008 meltdown— a cornerstone of sustainable investing—they could have limited their investment losses.

In the United Kingdom, the Charity Commission began a process in 2010 to revise guidelines to foundation endowment managers, but we need not wait for formal guidelines. The Further Reading section describes a few documents to inform trustees and their legal advisors. Although each institution should seek its own counsel, each need not begin the inquiry anew. Foundations adopting impact investing strategies are not entering some sort of legal limbo or no-man's-land where no one else has ventured and little legal guidance exists.

Beginning to Build

So let's say you have secured permission to break ground. You have overcome your trustees' fears, made clear to your investment advisors they need to find impact investing opportunities, and have convinced your lawyers that no one is going to jail over this. Now you need architects to design your new impact investing house, as well as carpenters and tradespeople to build the frames, lay the pipes, and pull the wiring.

Develop or Acquire Impact Investing Capabilities

Forcing either traditional program officers *or* investment professionals to become impact investors overnight will become a self-fulfilling prophecy of failure. Foundation staffs are expert at maintaining the operations of your current house, not building a new one. The impact investing program will either underperform financially (if program staff invest in ventures that are too risky) or stagnate in murky waters (if investment staff fail to find opportunities that meet their traditional underwriting criteria).

But many current staff members could be interested and useful in executing an impact investing approach. Foundation leadership will need to support current staff in developing expanded skills in structuring impact investments or complement them with appropriate outside expertise. Staff with deep programmatic expertise and knowledge should not be cast aside in the pursuit of this approach—unless, of course, they resist the future and undermine its advancement.

Think Like an Integrated Investor, Not a Program Officer

When it comes to philanthropy and social issues, foundation program staff are used to thinking in terms of program priorities—for example, "We fund education [or the environment or the arts]." Considering TFAM, however, staff members need to think like investors and diversify their holdings across broader issue areas. A foundation aiming at improving the lives of children, for example, needs to be expansive in considering the investment opportunities available to pursue its mission. Where do children live? What do they eat? Where will their children's children live? A grant program can focus only on funding early education for youth, but an investment strategy should also consider loans to sustainable farms that will help bring higher-quality food at a cheaper price into that child's region, microfinance bond notes that will improve the economic prospects of children overseas, or an equity investment in a company that improves the performance of teachers. A program priority is not an investment allocation strategy. Impact investing requires managers to join narrow interests to the larger web of economics, society, and investment opportunities.

Collaborate

You are not going to build your house alone. Foundations need to conclude a long history of viewing themselves as being the only ones capable of conducting responsible due diligence. This would facilitate more efficient allocation of grants as well as investments. It is especially important for the acceleration of TFAM because collaboration among early leaders could prepare the ground for much greater impact, expansion, and leverage over years to come. Platforms to share due diligence materials, syndicate investments, design new investment approaches, and benchmark data on social impact of investment are being developed. Foundation leaders

TOTAL FOUNDATION ASSET MANAGEMENT IN PRACTICE: "EVERYTHING IS PART OF A WHOLE"
Annie Chen, President, River Star Foundation, Hong Kong

I used to believe that if you had money and wanted to do good, you had to give your money away. But two "aha" moments led me to reconsider this approach.

The first was at a philanthropy conference in 2008, where I came across the idea of social entrepreneurship. I was intrigued by the spectrum diagram that showed social enterprises as something being supported in the middle ground between grants and commercial investments.

The second came when I listened to a keynote presentation by Stephan Chambers of the Skoll Centre for Social Entrepreneurship at a social enterprise conference in Hong Kong about two months later. He explained that the financial crisis arose in part from businesses not taking into account externalities such as the environmental and social costs of their activities. From that perspective, he argued, "Every [business] enterprise should be a social enterprise." After I heard that, I became convinced that business as usual was simply not sustainable in the long run. Who would feel good holding shares in a polluting company, or one where the welfare of customers is sacrificed in the pursuit of maximum (and sometimes outrageous) profit?

I spent the following months converting my portfolio into a socially responsible one that would still meet my financial goals and also started learning about impact investing. Initially I treated impact investing as a philanthropic tool and used sustainable investment screening principles to generate financial returns. Although I was beginning to see a common thread running through all these activities, I was still initially stuck in a traditional mentality and thought I would at some point divide the portfolio into two trusts: one for my personal use and one for charity. In the end, I decided to maintain a single portfolio, but for a long time, I felt quite perplexed about how to put all of these activities together and meet all my goals — personal, financial, and social — within the construct of a single portfolio.

My mental breakthrough came when I read Jed Emerson's concept of blended value. I began to see everything as part of a circle of interconnected activities that deliver a mix of social and financial returns, and it dawned on me that what I needed to do was to find the right mix for me. Whereas at first I struggled in my head to combine two very different purposes (personal and charitable) in a single portfolio, I realized later that an integrated approach can provide more options and leverage.

I thought converting my portfolio into a responsible one would be straightforward. In reality, I could not find an experienced and knowledgeable financial advisor in Hong Kong. I ended up retaining a specialist advisor from Zurich, who helped with developing the asset allocation model as well as screening appropriate products. With few locally sourced and regionally focused impact investment opportunities, I initially invested in international offerings, such as the Acumen Capital Markets fund, Dexia Blue Orchard Micro Credit Fund, and, more recently, ResponsAbility and Bamboo Finance's Oasis Fund.

Impact investing opportunities are still limited in East Asia, so I have made grants to support the development of the social entrepreneurship field here. I have supported established international organizations such as Ashoka and Grameen Foundation and their work in the region, and also supported local initiatives and ventures. I invested in SVhk, one of the first social venture funds in Hong Kong, and was a sponsor of the annual social enterprise conference in Hong Kong. These grants and investments opened up access to the social enterprise and impact investing community in Hong Kong and beyond. In the coming days, we will need to build local capacity among investment advisors and family offices to construct and manage integrated portfolios and assess the growing number of local deals.

Impact investing has allowed me to align my personal values across grants and investments in a single portfolio. Rather than feeling guilty about having so much while others have so little, I can invest my time, my skills, and my money for social impact and have fun doing it.

Who's Your Daddy? Impact Investing and Intergenerational Relationships

While a lot of attention within impact investing is given to larger institutional foundations and investment funds, in reality family foundations and individual philanthropists have driven much of the recent innovation in the field. With less cumbersome bureaucracy and stifling legacy, many family foundations are better poised to embrace innovation than their larger institutional foundation cousins. Younger family members tend to bring to the family foundation a sense of urgency and impatience with the practices of transactive philanthropy. Philanthropists and their family members increasingly tell us how impact investing has galvanized more productive discussions among family members, especially across the generational divide.

We should be clear that impact investing is not some financial remedy for poor family relationships, and it won't solve all the challenges that come with the management of significant wealth. That said, it provides a truly unique platform for families to discuss what each family member values and what strategies best reflect the shared legacy the family will have in carrying those values forward over coming generations.

Wealthy families and their advisors are increasingly attracted to impact investing for these reasons:

- It offers an excellent framework and vehicle for asking much deeper, more profound questions regarding the purpose of family wealth.

- Families come to understand the degree to which their interactions are a reflection of more significant understandings of the value (and values) of that individual family.

- It points out paths toward creating decision-making practices and new family leadership and mentoring relationships to sustain a family's values over time.

When done well, the process of exploring and executing an impact investing strategy offers families and advisors an opportunity for conversations about managing financial and extrafinancial family interests as opposed to a conversation that first addresses questions of how to manage family wealth and later raises questions regarding the purpose for which that wealth is being managed.

Families are dynamic, integrated, and complex systems — not linear, logical production and management processes. TFAM reflects the complexity of the family in a way many traditional wealth and philanthropic frameworks have not fully captured.

Impact investing is the avenue through which this conversation may take place since it raises issues of how a family thinks about the nature of its wealth, how it would like to structure its wealth to attain extrafinancial goals, and how various family members may work through a process of understanding what the answer will be for them as individuals and as a group. Growing numbers of families are using impact investing as the framework to have these discussions since it allows first-generation family members to talk with second- and third-generation members regarding a host of personal issues that are more difficult to explore in separate discussions about how to invest or how to give.

These ideas resonate strongly with many of today's young people who view their life goal as doing well and good, of having profit with purpose. Approaching the discussion of family preservation on this integrated basis opens the door for a parent to be viewed differently by the child (often after years of feeling that business or wealth creation comes first) while allowing members of the next generation to be heard as responsible adults with a new vision of the future — a future that the first generation is invested in creating with them.

would be well served not only to use these services but also to contribute to their ongoing evolution.

A New Approach for New Challenges

The philanthropic sector is undergoing more profound transformation now than at any other time since a handful of prominent industrialists created the modern philanthropy industry in the United States a century ago. The number of foundations is proliferating. The source of their wealth is shifting from legacy gifts of long-dead ancestors to commitments by living donors who have often built business empires. And foundations are appearing in Asia and Africa, regions that historically were philanthropy's beneficiary, not source.

At the same time, the world's social and environmental challenges seem to be mounting with relentless force and scale. Increasingly, foundations are responding to these challenges by looking for ways to harness more of their assets. Launching a PRI program or committing a small portion of the endowment to a mission-related investment strategy is a good start. And for many foundations it's highly disruptive to implement.

But these incremental approaches should not be confused with success. Making a modest allocation to mission-related investing risks positioning impact investing as just one more asset allocation, alongside fixed income and public equities. But the whole point of the TFAM approach is that all of a foundation's assets should be harnessed and managed toward the mission. This makes sense when you consider that ostensibly the sole reason any foundation is created is to advance the public and social good. In most countries, donors receive tax breaks for allocating their assets to a foundation and capital gains tax breaks on endowment investments. The public paying for these tax breaks has a right to demand that these tax-privileged assets pursue public good and common benefit.

Historically, that demand has been met in many countries through regulations that force foundations to give away a portion of their endowment each year. The public has neglected to scrutinize investment practices. This neglect made sense in a bifurcated world in which investments could not be expected to contribute to the public good. But in a blended value world, the public as well should demand to know how the other 95 percent is being invested.

So we now come to a relatively simple question: In the face of social and environmental challenges that seem to outpace our ability to address them and a global economy reeling from successive shocks, can we afford to have foundations hold on to a business-as-usual approach that leaves almost all their assets invested without concern for social impact and environmental factors?

If you think that giving away 5 percent or less of a foundation's assets in grants each year is good enough, then we hope those grants will be good ones. The world certainly needs effective grant makers. If, however, you believe a foundation must consider how to deploy all of its assets toward the pressing challenges of our time, then TFAM provides an increasingly clear blueprint to build approaches worthy of these challenges.

Chapter 10

HOW WILL WE MOVE
THE MONEY?

Rising to Their Customers' Challenge

• TIAA-CREF, one of the largest pension funds in the
United States, conducted market research in 2005 to
understand its customers better. The company had already
created socially responsible investment plans wherein fund
managers screen out ownership of stocks in industries some
clients do not want to support, such as tobacco and firearms,
and actively push public companies to improve their
social and environmental practices. But to their surprise, they
discovered many customers wanted more: the ability to put
their money to work in investments that seek to reduce
inequality, provide opportunity to poor people at home and
abroad, and improve the natural environment.

As a regulated pension fund, TIAA-CREF must meet legal
obligations to invest its clients' money in risk-adjusted market
rate investments and prudently pursue the highest financial
returns possible for a given asset class. But the leadership of
TIAA-CREF took up this challenge and in 2006 launched a
social and community investment fund with a mandate to
pursue a blended return of competitive financial performance
with social and environmental impact. In the past four years,

the fund has committed $600 million to a variety of impact vehicles ranging from equity investments in microfinance institutions, to loans to developers building environmentally friendly low-income housing, to deposits in community banks that in turn invest in local businesses and neighborhood families.

• In late 2003, leading Swiss banks and investment managers launched ResponsAbility, a company focused on mobilizing institutional assets into investments that could contribute to global development. With strong connections to Swiss and German banks and ultra-high-net-worth clients, Respons-Ability reached $200 million in assets under management in three years and $540 million by its fifth anniversary. When the capital markets crisis hit in 2008, other fund managers watched helplessly as clients withdrew their assets in the panic of financial meltdown. ResponsAbility's assets, however, grew 20 percent the following year and topped $1 billion in 2010. Its investments support microfinance, independent media, and fair trade enterprises in forty countries.

With the economic and social disruption of the recent financial crisis and deep recession still reverberating in 2011, it is tempting to join the popular chorus of vilification aimed at investment bankers and that shadowy villain, "The Capital Markets." We have certainly witnessed enough greed and smug self-assurance from mainstream investors to stoke our own fires of self-righteous disdain. The spectacular failure of the financial services industry in 2008–2009 should give everyone pause when we consider the role financial institutions should play in shaping the future of impact investing.

But we cannot afford to forget the crucial role bankers play in moving capital; we will not realize the potential of impact investing if we do not bring the capital markets into the cause. Microfinance would not have reached 100 million customers if not for the global capital markets and the financial engineers who built the bond structures that let microfinance institutions tap them. Despite this history, you may still argue that impact investors don't need global capital markets and the bankers and fund managers who make them work: "Let's just wash our hands of the whole corrupting enterprise of the modern finance services sector," you say. Well, we could. And you may not need capital markets—as long as you plan to withdraw cash from your personal account, get on a plane, hand that cash to the social entrepreneur who can use it, and then return to pick up a slightly heavier suitcase in a few years. For everyone else, however, the capital markets will be crucial to unlock the potential of impact investing.

Stripping away all the bells and whistles, the most basic function of capital markets is to take capital from its owners and place it with enterprises that can use it productively to create greater value than either the investor or the enterprise could generate alone. Because of capital markets, you don't have to get on a plane to directly invest your pension fund in a diversified portfolio or conduct in-person due diligence on a solar panel company in China before your savings funds may invest in it.

Historically the massive edifice that is the modern capital market paid little attention to impact investors. The multi-trillion-dollar financial services industry and its millions of employees are entrenched in the bifurcated world. But that is beginning to change. The examples of TIAA-CREF and ResponsAbility, when considered together with a growing number of other firms and initiatives, reveal cracks in this edifice. And they hint at how powerful established capital market institutions can be when they engage in impact investing.

We can accelerate this process by identifying the most promising areas where established players and start-ups will pool capital for impact investments and build the businesses that may successfully place this capital. From early experiments, we can also begin to recognize the emerging discipline of impact investing and the integrated skills and characteristics successful investors will need to develop. But we cannot stop when we have simply pried loose capital from its easiest sources. We need to widen the doorway of impact investing to create opportunities for everyday citizens to participate. We must take impact investing to the retail level where anyone who cares to invest in their future and their community may do so with the click of the mouse or a visit to their bank branch. Only when all investors can pursue blended value will impact investing not only unlock capital for social purpose but also transform how we manage society's assets in an integrated way.

Sourcing Capital

Global capital markets organize an estimated $80 trillion in assets and employ millions of people, from Wall Street traders, to Swiss wealth advisors, to Indian private equity fund managers. At this time, impact investing is not an important activity for any of the major players. Even TIAA-CREF's $600 million impact investing fund is less than 0.2 percent of its total assets under management. But impact investing initiatives are starting to pop up with increasing frequency in many of the mainstream finance firms. They may not register as more than a footnote in the balance sheet of trillion-dollar companies, but they are increasingly important in the modest but burgeoning impact investing capital market. They represent innovation within these companies where traditional analysts and fund managers are learning about the impact investing market, understanding more about its operations, and developing new strategies for creating impact and generating profit for their clients.

Existing capital market leaders face profound structural challenges in responding to the impact investing opportunity. Their massive scale makes it hard for them to interface with a still nascent and fragmented sector. A firm with two thousand brokers will struggle to launch a $50 million impact investing product that is available to only some of its clients. Institutional investors and asset managers also operate under regulation that reinforces the bifurcated view of investment, constraining innovation in impact investment products. And now more than ever before, people are skeptical of bankers and quick to see nefarious intention in any move they make.

Entrepreneurial start-ups are rapidly taking advantage of the opportunity to serve impact investors in ways the mainstream firms cannot. New enterprises are popping up in all corners of the capital markets, providing impact investors with dedicated banking, advisory, and fund management services. Compared to the massive mainstream players, these new enterprises are tiny, but many are thriving. New players in any market have an inherent innovation advantage: they can apply single-minded focus on serving new clients and move nimbly to capture new opportunities in a dynamic marketplace. And, frankly, they are simply cooler, attracting attention and intrigue as the "next big thing." Inspiring social entrepreneurs like the founders of kiva.org make compelling subjects for talk shows; midlevel bankers building a new asset management product in a Wall Street giant generally do not.

In the end, both innovative start-ups and established players will be crucial to building the impact investing capital markets of the future. While we celebrate the charismatic entrepreneurs, it will be much easier to take impact investing to scale if we can harness the immense resources and established position of existing capital markets leaders. The story of two microfinance funds illustrates this point.

You may have heard of kiva.org before reading this book. This Internet start-up became a sensation in social enterprise and microfinance circles, tapping a previously unknown enthusiasm for peer-to-peer microloans. In its first five years since its founding in October 2005, it facilitated approximately $200 million in lending. We doubt you heard of ResponsAbility until you started reading this book. In its first five years, from 2003 to 2008, ResponsAbility moved almost three times as much capital as kiva.org and continues to grow apace.

Kiva.org is an inspiring innovation. But ResponsAbility hints at what will be possible when we harness existing capital markets infrastructure that is already allocating $80 trillion. Established capital market leaders are waking up to the interest their top clients and top talent are showing in impact investing. And financial services entrepreneurs are not waiting around; they are responding now to the frustrations many impact investors and social entrepreneurs feel. Between them they will pool impact investing capital and create the investment structures that can channel it efficiently to firms that can best create blended value.

Key Actors for Moving Capital

We are inspired by the potential for impact investing because we know the world has enough capital to address many of our most fundamental challenges. With an estimated $80 trillion moving through global capital markets, unlocking only 1 percent for impact investing will create a capital pool four times larger than all current annual official donor flows and almost three times greater than the total of U.S. annual charitable giving. But most of that $80 trillion is locked up in investment structures that will not be unlocked for impact investors. The key will be determining where the high-potential capital pools sit, understanding how to motivate their managers to redeploy them, and supporting them to do so.

A quick survey of the capital markets indicates we need to target those assets in the sweet spot of scale and flexibility. To unleash their full force, capital markets need to progress from innovative deals to replicable deal structures, to funds and platforms that achieve scale and offer liquidity to investors. Eventually they need to establish infrastructure that can manage these new markets effectively. For impact investing to follow this trajectory, we need to identify pools of capital large enough to enable their managers to build a marketplace when they make a move, but small enough so that their original owners are still closely connected to investment decisions and able to push innovation.

The manager of a pension fund can move markets with the billions of dollars at her disposal. But she is trapped in a bureaucratic and regulatory framework that makes it all but impossible for her to engage with relatively tiny impact investment innovation. On the other extreme, you can do whatever you want with the five dollars in your wallet, but what you do with it is not going to seed a new industry. Fortunately, the capital markets include institutions like family offices and private banks that operate between these two extremes. We'll begin the hunt for capital markets allies there.

Family Offices: The Sweet Spot of Current Innovation

Family offices have historically been a good place to start the search for pioneers in financial services innovation. These investment companies manage the assets of a single family (or, in a modern variation, multiple families). They typically hold more than $100 million in assets, which can be large enough to anchor the creation of new products and investment platforms. But they are also independent enough to move quickly, responding to the interests of their asset owners, even if those interests are outside established investment practice.

Family offices have taken advantage of this unique role before. The idea that an investor should back a portfolio of very early-stage companies, many of which would fail, initially seemed crazy to mainstream investors. It was left to U.S. family offices to seed the creation of the venture capital industry, with many backing the first venture capitalists in the 1950s and 1960s. Mainstream investors, and especially pension funds, did not begin to invest in venture capital until U.S. regulatory guidance in 1978 gave them explicit cover to do so.

Family offices are now repeating this pioneering role in impact investing. They led the capitalization of the first commercial microfinance funds. The family offices of Atlanta real estate developer Bob Patillo and eBay founder Pierre Omidyar helped seed the first microfinance investment vehicles. As they did with venture capital, institutional investors have followed family offices into microfinance, benefiting from the investment infrastructure they helped create. And, as of late 2010, more than two hundred microfinance investment vehicles had channeled more than $6 billion, including investments from pension funds and other institutional clients.

Beyond microfinance, family offices are playing pioneering roles in other impact investing subsectors. Capricorn Investment Management, initially capitalized by eBay's first employee, Jeff Skoll, is making large investments in sustainable agriculture and renewable energy around the world. In Great Britain, the family office of Lord Sainsbury has seeded new companies and fund managers focused on African agriculture. And these early movers are being joined by increasing numbers of others who see the opportunity and are flexible enough to address it.

In addition to nimble size and client motivation, family offices have another incentive to move into the impact investing arena. By definition, families are made up of various generations. As we discussed in the previous chapter, impact investing is an opportunity for first-generation family members to engage with second- and third-generation members in a new discussion about stewarding the family legacy. The interest of family members in their twenties and thirties in environmental issues, education, and antipoverty programs represents opportunities for the larger family to join together and explore new ways of connecting around areas of shared concern.

Private Banks and Their Clients: Poised to Play

Family offices can play a crucial role in pushing the envelope of financial innovation, but they are a relatively small part of the overall financial services industry. In contrast, private banks oversee trillions of dollars in assets. Though typically less nimble and responsive to passionate asset owners, these banks could also help transform capital markets if they set their sights on impact investment. And in 2011 they appear poised to do so.

Private banks invest capital for clients with multimillion-dollar accounts. These clients have enough money to focus on long-term asset preservation and growth rather than short-term gains and liquidity. Historically, many private banks have been relatively conservative in how they manage clients' money. But the private clients served by such banks can afford to test new investment approaches and increasingly are asking their bankers to place their capital into impact investments. Before and during the financial crisis beginning in 2008, top private bankers repeatedly told us they were intrigued by the idea of impact investing but could fulfill their clients' interest in generating social good by offering philanthropic advisory services alone. That changed in 2010. Private bankers around the world began telling us about a steady drumbeat from top clients interested in impact investing. And a 2010 survey of high-net-worth investors in the United States found half were interested in exploring impact investing.[1]

Structural challenges are slowing the private banks' response to this interest. Many private banks have a hard time placing impact investing products through their current structures as they are organized to operate in a bifurcated world, with investment teams separated from philanthropic advisory divisions. They also struggle with the burden of scale. Often managing many billions of dollars of capital for thousands of clients, they cannot afford to dabble with investments in the tens of millions of dollars that are relatively expensive to execute and not available to all clients. Private banking relationships are also sticky, and few private clients will fire their bankers because they do not offer impact investing options—at least in the short term.

Despite these structural barriers, momentum behind impact investing is finally pushing private banks to respond. A few of the leading private banks are responding to client interest with a toe-dipping approach of creating an impact investing fund or two. However, given their scale, toe dipping can still result in significant funds moving into impact investing. As of this writing, one major financial services group is exploring how to move a small segment of its investment dollars through an impact investing platform. The amount is $400 million. For an emerging investment category, this is a meaningful commitment of capital. As others follow this path, the market will grow, additional actors will be drawn to it, and additional capital can then be accommodated by the market. These initial steps will lay the flagstones for others yet to come.

Still others are setting themselves up for a longer-term and structural engagement with impact investors. Venerable Swiss bank UBS established the integrated Philanthropy and Values-Based Investing unit in its wealth management division in 2010. This unit consolidates philanthropic advisory, the UBS foundation, socially responsible investing, and impact investing into a single platform. The senior bankers who pioneered this approach within UBS eloquently articulate the blended value vision: building a business in the belief clients will increasingly seek advisors who can have a single, integrated discussion about how all of their assets can be aligned to their values. Morgan Stanley Smith Barney is also responding to growing interest for impact investing among the millions of clients it serves through one of the world's largest brokerage forces.

While Annie Chen, profiled in Chapter Nine, has executed her unified investment strategy in the absence of formal institutional support, future asset owners will increasingly turn to UBS, Morgan Stanley, and other financial services firms positioning themselves to meet the needs of this market. These firms are not attempting this in a vacuum. A growing number of banks are developing partnerships to bring impact investing industry expertise to join with their internal capacity to create new investing vehicles that may then be offered through the banks' distribution channels to thousands of investors. In this way, impact investing is increasingly moving from Wall Street to Main Street.

While we anticipate movement from the larger firms, the cutting-edge innovation may still be found in start-ups and smaller firms. Wealth management companies dedicated to impact investing are beginning to win mandates to manage at least parts of the assets of an increasing number of private clients. Even as total assets shrank in 2008 and 2009, many of these start-ups saw their balance sheets grow, especially in northern California and Northern Europe, where impact investing is particularly popular.

Institutional Investors: Turning the Ocean Liners

The largest prize in capital markets today is the institutional investors who control the world's pension funds, insurance funds, and major endowment assets. Together they control more than $30 trillion in investible assets. And pockets of innovation show that regulatory and customer pressure can induce them to embrace impact investment despite their naturally conservative tendencies.

Pension funds are an obvious place to start. True, most people leave the management of these retirement savings to professional firms and pay little heed to how they are invested. And the vast bulk of institutional investors will wait for impact investing fund managers to establish firm track records and other investors to coalesce around the opportunity before they jump into the impact investing pool. But the implicit connection between pension savings and a concern for the long-term future creates a hook on which to hang a discussion of long-term investor interest in blended value. A forty year old who is saving for retirement in thirty years can easily see why a strategy for generating returns that also advances environmental sustainability and greater social equality will be better for her long-term life and legacy. This sensibility is what motivated TIAA-CREF to create its impact investing unit in 2006. Dutch pension funds have also led the way, especially in embracing investments directed to environmental sustainability.

A subset of values-inclined institutional investors is already beginning to move. Values-inclined investors match investment strategies with social purpose in various ways that reflect the reason for their interest in blended value. For example, some public pension funds pursue impact investing strategies that support local economic development. The California Public Employees Retirement System, the largest public pension fund in the United States, directs approximately 10 percent of its assets to investments in California. Pension funds managing labor union members' savings are also increasingly looking to put their capital to work with companies that promote job opportunities and workplace standards from which their members could benefit. And a growing number of managers of pension funds mobilized through religious communities are following a centuries-old tradition that sought to align a religious group's investment practices to its values.

Beyond pension fund management, other institutional investors are particularly susceptible to the community and political attention that can promote blended value sensibilities. Sovereign wealth funds have emerged as an increasingly important institutional investor in the past decade. These pools of capital, managed by governments on behalf of their citizens, now total close to $5 trillion. Although none has embraced impact investing with gusto, political pressures and native values of countries like Norway (whose oil exports have capitalized a sovereign wealth fund with more than $400 billion) are leading its fund managers to examine the social and environmental consequences of their investment. In the case of Norway, an independent entity evaluates the social and environmental practices of companies and makes recommendations to the fund's managers regarding how various corporations in its portfolio hold up under sustainability and equity analysis.

University endowments could also play an important role in capitalizing early impact investment innovation. Though relatively small in the context of the multi-trillion-dollar global capital markets, these endowments have been prominent battle grounds in the socially responsible investment movement in the past, as activist students and alumni rallied for changes in their university's investment practice. Impact investing may not elicit the same passion on campuses as the anti-apartheid divestment movement did in the 1980s. But as awareness of impact investing spreads among students and alumni, they could pressure endowment managers to implement blended value strategies. A number of actors and organizations are targeting endowments, including the Responsible Endowments Coalition, which is working to bridge the generational interests of students and stakeholders with the fiduciary interests of trustees in light of the reality that all are concerned with advancing both the financial and institutional integrity of the schools with which they are affiliated.

Finally, a quirk in U.S. tax law has created a high-potential pool of assets that sit in donor-advised funds. These are funds that individuals have established for eventual donation but sit in investment products accruing capital gains while waiting to be given away. Approximately 150,000 individuals own donor-advised funds totaling more than $25 billion in assets. Impact investing offers a potentially enticing enhancement to the social value a donor-advised fund can generate. Instead of waiting until the eventual donation for the assets to generate social value, they can generate value along the way if they are placed in impact investments. Maryland-based Calvert Foundation and San Francisco-based RSF Social Finance have pioneered impact investing with donor-advised funds. We expect many others will soon follow.

Actors for Moving Capital

With all of these potential capital sources, the notion that we could mobilize 1 percent of the world's capital into impact investments does not seem so outlandish or far off. And in fact, our goal is not simply to move just bits but rather the whole of the world's capital markets into both sustainable and impact investing practices. And while that will happen in time, for now let's start at the beginning.

Let's say we do move 1 percent into impact investments—$800 billion. Who is going to structure and place it all? There's no way around the fact that we are going to have to engage investment bankers.

Emerging Impact Investment Bankers

With family offices, private banks, and institutional investors mobilizing assets, investment bankers are awakening to the impact investing opportunity. A confluence of motivations has spurred this move in recent years. In the wake of the financial meltdown, investment banks around the world face public pressure to explain why they are good for society. Committing more money to their corporate foundations has proven relatively ineffective at winning public support. In contrast, impact investing offers an opportunity to highlight how the core work of an investment bank may generate social and environmental value. Similarly, impact investing inspires top talent, especially younger employees who hunger for opportunities to use their professional skills to create social good (in addition to more traditional opportunities to join coworkers volunteering at the local soup kitchen or tutoring group). Finally—and perhaps most important—impact investing can be a good business line for banks with a long-term vision.

These motivations have led major investment banks to make increasingly interesting impact investing commitments. In the United Kingdom, investment banks have responded to public pressure to raise taxes on banker bonuses with various proposals to put their skills and capital to work more directly for social benefit. In the United States, regulatory mandates in the late 1970s brought many banks into community development investing work. Investment banks such as Deutsche Bank Americas have placed hundreds of millions of dollars into community development loans, deploying a range of capital from grants to concessionary loans to market rate investments. The conversion of investment banks such as Goldman Sachs into bank holding companies in the throes of the financial meltdown brought more investment banks under the regulatory regime that will require them to make similar community-development-focused investments should the political will to make such demands continue.

Impact investing is also an increasingly good business line for investment bankers. The J.P. Morgan Social Finance unit was born in 2007 out of the realization that the fast-growing social enterprise sector needed dedicated investment bankers. Two years earlier, Citibank launched a global microfinance unit after a similar recognition that for-profit and nonprofit microfinance enterprises could be strong clients of the bank rather than just grantees of the corporate foundation. In 2010 Citi Microfinance linked up with its community development arm to create an integrated capability to pursue impact investments targeting low-income customers across emerging markets and the United States. Impact investing is also good business for investment banks that want to motivate employees. When J.P. Morgan announced the launch of its Social Finance unit, one thousand company employees contacted the unit within a week to express interest in participating in the work.

Despite these motivations, established investment banks share similar structural challenges as their private bank counterparts when it comes to developing impact investing practices. The largest investment banks are set up to execute only large deals that allow them to offset their high personnel costs. Goldman Sachs and Deutsche Bank were able to put teams of bankers to work in structuring the innovative International Finance Facility for Immunisation (IFFIm) because the bond issue raised more than $1 billion. But few deals of this size are available in the early phase of impact investing.

In response, boutique investment banks are springing up around the world to serve the smaller clients the large banks cannot. Unpublished Rockefeller Foundation research in 2010 identified more than forty institutions globally that were offering investment banking services to impact investors and social enterprises. Most had sprung up since 2007 as either independent companies or new business units. Some, like IFMR Trust in India, offer capital-raising services to social enterprises. Others, such as Imprint Capital in the United States, help identify, structure, and manage impact investments for foundations and family offices. And the Goldman Sachs bankers who put together the IFFIm have set up their own investment bank, Lion's Head, to enable them to work on impact investing deals that could not justify their attention at an established firm.

Governments too are beginning to recognize the value of impact investment banking services and the likelihood that this market will not reach its potential without support. The United Kingdom in 2011 launched a major public-private partnership to create an investment bank for domestic social enterprises that is capitalized with hundreds of millions of dollars from dormant bank accounts and U.K. bank investments. This bank aims to improve the efficiency with which both government and private capital is put to work addressing social challenges. A long-time advocate for this bank, private equity legend Sir Ronald Cohen, helped launch a scaled-down, private sector version of this bank in 2008. This regulated investment advisor, Social Finance, has been the driving force behind the first social impact bond (which we highlighted in Chapter Five), among other innovations.

Impact Investment Fund Managers

Beyond investment banks, the surge of capital into impact investing is creating opportunities for investment fund managers who can figure out how to efficiently direct impact investment capital into the best businesses for creating blended value. Private equity fund managers are central to this development as the greatest opportunity to optimize blended value for many investors still comes from providing capital directly to privately held companies.

Fund managers with experience in particular subsectors are well placed to take advantage of the wider impact investing opportunity. As we discussed in Chapter Two, the international development arena has used impact investing vehicles for decades, creating a range of fund managers capable of generating blended value. Fund managers spun out of government agencies, such as the U.K. firm Aureos, have recently worked with a range of investors to create new impact investing funds focused on emerging markets. Some dedicated microfinance fund managers have also begun to broaden their offerings. ResponsAbility launched an impact-focused enterprise fund in 2010 following the example of Jean-Philippe de Schrevel, the founder of microfinance fund BlueOrchard who launched impact investment–focused Bamboo Finance in 2008.

The unique needs of impact investors are also creating opportunities for start-up fund managers who combine financial skills with social commitment. Mexican-based IGNIA Fund raised $102 million from development finance institutions, private foundations, and family offices. As IGNIA founder, Alvaro Rodriguez Arregui notes in Chapter Five, IGNIA occupied a no-man's-land that hampered its fundraising efforts—too commercial for traditional philanthropists and too social for traditional investors. But that no-man's-land is shrinking as interest in impact investing spreads among a growing array of asset owners.

Some impact investors interested in building a solid foundation for the new industry are particularly focused on capitalizing new fund managers. Family offices and private foundations such as Omidyar Network and Soros Economic Development Fund are seeding new fund managers such as the previously mentioned Indian-based SONG fund, often working in partnership with other impact investors. They are also supporting existing managers to create targeted impact investing products. For example, impact investment pioneer F.B. Heron Foundation worked with Florida-based Community Capital Management to develop a bond product that allows impact investors to target specific low-income communities in the United States.

Leading mainstream fund managers are beginning to play in the impact investing field, sometimes unwittingly. Big-name private equity and venture capital firms are brushing against impact investments as they move aggressively to place capital in fast-growing emerging markets. Though not entering these markets as impact investors, these profit-driven firms are increasingly pursuing sectors of substantial interest to impact investors such as low-income housing, health care, and microfinance. Legendary Silicon Valley venture capital fund manager Sequoia found itself thrust into the impact investing cauldron in 2010 with the controversial IPO of SKS microfinance in India, a company its India fund had backed aggressively. Traditionally, where asset owner interests go, the private equity fund managers soon follow. As an early sign of what will likely become a gathering trend, private equity behemoth Carlyle Group has recently formed a sustainable investment practice.

Other Pieces of the Capital Markets Puzzle

The capital markets puzzle also includes many pieces of supporting infrastructure in the form of research firms, investment advisors, ratings agencies, and accountants. Their opinions and products substantially influence investment decisions and will help define the trajectory of impact investing. In fits and starts, they too are starting to respond to client interest and organize around the impact investing opportunity.

These capital market players have begun to consider investment criteria beyond traditional financial risk and return, largely as a result of the socially responsible investment movement. That movement is spurring institutions to collect data and provide analyses on a range of issues related to corporate governance, social impact, and the environment. National campaigns to require public companies to disclose their carbon footprint and potential environmental liabilities have led some investment advisors, ratings agencies, and accountants to develop expertise in environmental issues. Investment information giant Bloomberg has created a comprehensive data platform to track environmental social and governance data, and Deutsche Bank has launched a prominent climate change research group.

Like their banking counterparts, accounting firms, ratings agencies, investment advisors, and researchers are beginning to dabble in the more targeted impact investing markets as well. They face increased public scrutiny to prove their value and pressure from top talent to provide opportunities for integrating work and social purpose. However, as long as impact investing remains largely a private market activity, the investing pool will be too small and the cost of acquiring information too high to make a strong business case in the short term.

Even absent short-term profit motives, these firms have multiple incentives to develop impact investing capabilities. These efforts allow them to rebuild goodwill from regulators and the public. They also provide inspiration to recruits and current employees. Finally, as we've seen in related areas, impact investing offers an intriguing new arena for rapid business growth. Imagine the growth potential for all these players if they can add new business lines auditing impact statements, rating social impact, and advising and researching the new universe of impact investment products.

Impact Investing as an Emerging Discipline

Pushed by clients or pulled by other compelling business reasons, capital market institutions are finding their way into the world of impact investing. But how well equipped are they to flourish here? Impact investing is not just another derivative product or investment structure that investors from a different field can easily understand and manage. Instead, it requires a unique blend of professional skills and sensibilities. Whether referring to the investors with these skills as hybrid professionals (the term used by Kellogg Foundation's Tom Reis) or mutant managers (which we described in Chapter Nine), industry leaders are quickly realizing that impact investing is emerging as its own discipline.

This discipline requires time to refine and integrate. For years, many of us have looked forward to the day when mainstream investors would come to the impact investing table. To our pleasure, recent years have seen the entry of many individuals with just that skill set and talent. However, in some ways, the pendulum has swung too far to the side of "only financial analysts need apply." The impact investor of the future will need to combine the analytical rigor of a traditional investor with the political insight, collaborative instincts, and social sector understanding of the effective social change agent.

The Winning Traits of the Impact Investor

While impact investing opportunities span a wide range of sizes, structures, capital types, and sectors, certain characteristics are common among them. Some characteristics are typical of investing in an emerging subsector; others are unique to impact investment.

Operating in a new sector or geography inevitably requires investing without the comfort of rich industry research, benchmarking data, and competitor analysis. Investors in new areas must learn how to distinguish talented fund managers where few have a track record. They often must build fund management and investment capabilities where they are lacking. These are common attributes in frontier market investing and broadly define the current state of the impact investing industry.

But even when the industry matures to fill investors' spreadsheets with reams of data on fund manager and investment performance, impact investors will still face unique requirements (and opportunities). In most cases, impact investors will need to collaborate effectively with a diverse range of partners, including governments and nonprofit groups that will provide complementary skills as well as capital. These partnerships will be crucial to expand and maintain the impact investors' license to operate in politically contentious subsectors.

Not surprisingly, investors with a background in frontier market investing can transfer their skills more easily into impact investments. They are comfortable and savvy making investment decisions based on assessing the potential of an investee rather than the caliber of his or her track record. They understand how to bring more than just capital in support of investees who often need hand holding to build their businesses and fund management platforms. Frontier market investors are the leaders of the "just like" chorus who get excited about impact investing because it feels "just like when I began investing in Eastern Europe in the early 1990s" or "just like when we brought venture capital to Europe in the 1970s" or "just like India a decade ago."

But impact investing is not "just like" anything that has come before. When the frontier market dynamics fade, the unique attributes of successful impact investors will stand out in sharp contrast. Impact investors need an unusual capacity for empathy. They also need to cultivate instincts for understanding the complex interests and perspectives that could be at play in any deal. A traditional business education does not prepare an investor to work with a mobilized community group, a government investment fund, or co-investors with a wide range of impact goals.

Successful impact investors also need to be savvy to capture opportunities to create social value and persuasive in communicating it. Especially when investing in companies that interact with low-income communities, impact investors are always one misstep away from being vilified for "exploiting the poor." Avoiding this label will require more than good marketing. Impact investors need the political insight to understand how to build and sustain the support that can ensure their long-term interests. This is not just about appeasing governments and community groups. As IGNIA Fund's Alvaro Rodriguez Arregui points out, impact investors also need the empathy that can win the trust of social entrepreneurs whose skepticism about a potential investor cannot be overcome by offering the entrepreneur more money.

Finally, at this early stage of expansion, impact investors require unusual amounts of patience. Creating blended value is not a game for the flighty or easily frustrated. Holding complex partnerships together through their inevitable ups and downs can be unnerving. Convincing skeptical partners from very different worlds to recognize your good intentions can be trying. And maintaining internal support for a new business unit in an institution organized for a very different purpose can be lonely.

Finding the Blend Beyond the Balance

Close your eyes and think of a "typical investment banker." Now think of three adjectives to describe this person. We'd bet the price of this book—and more—that the words *empathetic*, *socially motivated*, and *patient* are not on your list. But we would also take a bet that traditional nonprofit leaders and social activists with only these traits would fail as impact investors. Impact investing needs to find integrated professionals who can complement traditional investment savvy with these atypical attributes.

Early impact investors bring exposure from both sides of the bifurcated world. The impact investors you have met in this book exemplify this experience: Root Capital's Willy Foote worked on Wall Street before spending two years reporting on rural poverty. J.P. Morgan's Christina Leijonhufvud worked at the World Bank and in Central Asia before her career in investment banking. IGNIA Fund's Alvaro Rodriguez Arregui worked in the nonprofit ACCION and with microfinance enterprise Compartamos alongside his corporate career.

As impact investing matures, career paths will open up that allow professionals to skip the need to work in the bifurcated world at all. They will hone their character in impact investment business units after receiving formal training that integrates the skills they need. Alternatively, the skills and character needed to be an effective investor and social change agent may prove too difficult to integrate in most people, just as pitching and hitting in baseball are so specialized that no major league professional excels at both. In that case, integrated capabilities will exist among teams of individuals chosen from different worlds, just as baseball teams pair great hitters with great pitchers.

Impact Investing's New Tool Kit

Beyond developing new skills, impact investors also need to bring new investment approaches to the capital markets. To date, impact investors have largely taken traditional investment structures and applied them to a set of investment opportunities screened for social impact. This made sense when impact investment bankers and fund managers needed to convince skeptical asset owners that these investments could work. The first commercial microfinance funds and deals like the IFFIm bond sold only because their creators intentionally dressed them to look just like mainstream deals and investment instruments.

This was a good start. And for some subsectors it has proven powerful and effective. But standard investment structures were not built for impact investment. In many sectors, impact investments require greater patience than a closed-life private equity fund can offer. The best impact investment management teams may respond to incentives other than participation in profits. And many opportunities to create blended value require entirely new relationships between governments and investors.

Imagine you invent a screw in a world that has seen only nails. In this world, the carpenters will only have hammers, so to get started, you need to figure out how to make your screws look like the nails they are used to hammering. But to make the most of your screws, you will eventually need to start making screwdrivers. Impact investors are now beginning to modify the hammers of standard fund structure to use the screws of impact investment better. They are offering compensation tied to social as well as financial performance and management fees structures that recognize the additional work an impact investment fund manager must take on.

This modification of existing structures will work for some areas, but the most exciting impact investments are fundamentally different. And in the end, we will have to forge many entirely new tools for creating blended value. The social impact bond we described in Chapter Five is a promising example of deep innovation in investment structuring. The concept draws on fundamental investment banking insight but offers a radical new approach to fund basic social services. Similarly visionary variants of this approach include the quality markets concept being pioneered by Social Futures Exchange in Peru and the diverse ecosystems marketplaces cropping up around the world.

Together these experiments show the promise of innovation that starts with the problem we need to solve rather than the existing standards we need to accommodate. While capital raising will be easier in the short term for fund managers like IGNIA Fund that provide capital markets with a structure they are used to seeing, the impact investing industry will be well served in the long run to push against the constraints of precedent and establish new standards built to match the tool of investment management to the task of creating blended value. Only these fundamental innovations will open impact investing to the full range of opportunities before us.

Widening the Doorway

How wide will the doorways we enter through ultimately have to be? We have so far dwelled exclusively in the realms of the ridiculously rich and the ludicrously large. Family offices with their $100 million holdings, private clients with their $50 million accounts, and pension funds with their $100 billion balance sheets are leading the impact investing charge. But few opportunities exist now for ordinary investors to participate.

Figuring out how to take impact investing retail will be crucial, but perhaps not for the reason you might think. If it is just about finding the capital for investments, the very rich and the very large have more capital than the impact investing industry may be able to put to work. But impact investing has always been about more than the money. It is about creating a more integrated relationship between our assets and our values. It is about transforming what society values and how we organize all our resources to achieve it. True integration and societal transformation cannot happen if impact investing remains the domain of a select few.

Developing Retail Products

The capital markets offer three democratizing channels that will be crucial to open the doorway of impact investing to a wider world. Most accessible are retail financial products, such as the certificates of deposit and money market products you may buy in your local retail bank branch. With low minimum purchases, these products are accessible to most people who can afford long-term investments. Impact investors are beginning to market retail products. In the United States, the leader in this market has been the Calvert Foundation, whose Community Investment Note offers low-single-digit financial returns and a report on the social impact that investments generate when placed into microfinance institutions and low-income housing developers, for example. In the United Kingdom, Charity Bank similarly uses client deposits to lend to charities and service providers. Triodos Bank in the Netherlands is successfully developing its balance sheet by offering a range of impact investment options for depositors and investors. And increasingly, retail products are available online through companies like Microplace.com.

Mobilizing retail assets around communities of common interest appears to be another promising area for democratizing impact investment. French food company Danone capitalized a $10 million impact investing fund to support early-stage investments in impact-oriented joint ventures by soliciting investments from its employees in France. That 25 percent of all the company's employees in France invested in the fund hints at the untapped energy in large corporations whose employees yearn for a deeper connection to their work. Such innovations represent an exciting step beyond traditional corporate philanthropy or corporate social responsibility initiatives.

Engaging Brokers

Between retail products and private banks stand the millions of brokerage accounts and financial advisors who could potentially become a powerful channel for democratizing impact investments. Realizing this potential is difficult because in the brokerage business, simplicity sells. Wealth advisors have to navigate a complex array of new product offerings and help clients make investment decisions during very short conversations. Most advisors cannot afford to take every client on journeys of discovery in the blended value woods.

But the payoff is also potentially great for advisors who can meet this growing customer interest. They can build new client relationships and deepen existing ones as they expand their offerings into new areas that combine client financial interest with related areas of concern. Impact investing allows advisors and their clients to discuss the purpose of wealth, not just its quantification. Many find this to be a transformative experience that improves their connection to their work and the likelihood of retaining clients.

Few financial advisors are equipped to implement impact investing strategies, so entrepreneurs are building enterprises to serve their needs. ImpactAssets, a nonprofit U.S. financial services firm launched in 2010, seeks to act as a translator between the impact investing field and mainstream wealth managers and asset owners. ImpactAssets fills this role by aggregating new thinking and knowledge about what is happening in the impact investment arena and works with wealth managers and family offices to create multi-manager investment vehicles. In 2011 the firm launched ImpactAssets 50, a designation of top-performing managers across asset classes and impact themes. These leaders are selected by a panel of experienced impact investors who assess prospective firms against a host of financial and impact criteria. The designation gives investors a starting place for exploring what firms may best fit any given investor's impact profile. In the United Kingdom, Investing for Good pioneered the practice of helping wealth advisors navigate impact investing options and has now merged with Charity Bank. Other platforms are emerging to help financial advisors and other investors navigate the growing range of impact investment options. Initiatives such as ImpactBase and GATE Impact offer prospective investors data to facilitate initial review of potential investee companies and funds.

Donor-advised funds are a particularly interesting target for financial advisors interested in deploying impact investments. These are highly impact-poised pools of capital as their owners have already prededicated these funds to charity but invest them in for-profit investments while waiting to determine where they will donate them. Most investment managers and brokers now offer clients the ability to set up donor-advised funds with as little as a few thousand dollars, making them accessible to many more customers than typical private bank products. When the mass market wealth managers like Schwab and Fidelity follow the lead of ImpactAssets and others in offering impact investment options for donor-advised fund clients, the doorway into impact investment will widen considerably.

Building Social Stock Exchanges

Beyond retail products and brokerage services, a new group of "social stock exchanges" are being launched to tap investor interest in more direct access to impact investments. Many of these self-identified "stock exchanges" are really philanthropic brokers who solicit donations for worthy charitable projects. But some do focus on impact investment and aim to lower the search costs for impact investors by aggregating investments on a single platform. Early prototypes are coalescing around two business models: the regulated exchange and the facilitating exchange.

Regulated exchanges enable both the public listing and secondary trading of impact investments. These will attract social entrepreneurs eager to raise public equity capital but reluctant to list on a standard exchange whose listing requirements hamper the management team from pursuing a social mission. The exchanges will provide a credible assurance that listed companies qualify as impact investments. They will have the substantial spillover benefit of making early-stage impact investments more attractive by providing a more realistic chance of timely exit. The Social Stock Exchange in the United Kingdom and Impact Investment Exchange-Asia, based in Singapore are leading the charge to launch regulated exchanges.

Facilitating exchanges typically focus on connecting investors with local social enterprises. Responding to a backlash against the hyperglobalization of the modern capital markets, these initiatives often seek to connect investors with local companies and nonprofits seeking relatively small loans and equity investments. These exchanges could dramatically lower the time and cost for investors and social enterprises to find each other by creating online deal clearinghouses. Through the transaction efficiency of the Internet, these exchanges may ultimately enable investors to make a twenty-dollar investment in the local food pantry, after-school program, or housing development. New York–based MissionMarkets, South Africa–based Nexii and the Toronto Social Venture Exchange are early innovations in this area. These pioneers were recently joined by GATE Impact, a new impact investing marketplace targeting institutional investors that promises to open wide avenues of capital flows for impact investing.

The Future of Capital: To Fit In or to Transform?

This discussion has highlighted the complexity that character-izes modern capital markets. Impact investing is asserting itself as another dimension of this complexity. But how will impact invest-ments fit in? Will they become recognized as a new asset class? Or will the spirit of impact investing infuse itself throughout the capital markets? This is more than an academic debate in that it highlights two fundamentally divergent visions within the impact investing community.

In one camp stand those who believe impact investing is becoming its own asset class. Like impact investors, hedge funds make a wide range of investments across debt and equity. But they are increasingly recognized as an asset class because of the unique set of investment skills they require, the standards and benchmarks they have developed, their fee structure, their dedicated trade associations, and, perhaps most important, the way that investors allocate a given portion of a portfolio of investments into the hedge funds category. To explain the title of their 2010 research note, "Impact Investments: An Emerging Asset Class," J.P. Morgan and the Rockefeller Foundation argued that impact investment now shares these characteristics with hedge funds and other recognized asset classes.

Examples in this chapter corroborate the view that impact investing is becoming its own asset class. Mainstream investors are creating business units dedicated to impact investing that span traditional asset classes. The TIAA-CREF impact investing unit organizes debt, private equity, and cash investments under an impact theme. UBS's Values-Based Investing unit similarly gathers under one roof the skills and perspectives required to generate and communicate blended value, as does J.P. Morgan's Social Finance unit and Morgan Stanley's Global Sustainable Finance group. The Global Impact Investing Network supports collaboration among a web of similar organizations.

HARNESSING THE CAPITAL MARKETS
Christina Leijonhufvud, Managing Director, Social Finance unit, J.P. Morgan, New York, New York

After ten years on Wall Street advising sovereigns and managing sovereign risk, I became increasingly motivated to return to focusing on sustainable economic development. (Prior to J.P. Morgan, I worked for the World Bank and in Central Asia.) I had grown intrigued by investment models like microfinance that seemed to be having significant positive impact on the lives of poor people, and at a greater scale than donation alone could support.

So in 2006, I took a sabbatical to work as an advisor to Ashoka, the world's largest network of social entrepreneurs. I became convinced that the social enterprise field was poised to take off and that the capital markets could be harnessed to support its growth. That realization led me to propose that J.P. Morgan launch a business unit in the investment bank aimed at providing financial services to social enterprises, investment funds, and interested investors. In 2007, the Social Finance unit was born.

Initially the obvious opportunity appeared in the fast-growing microfinance sector where dedicated private investment vehicles were proliferating. We invested in a moderately sized but highly reputable microfinance equity fund and helped place the fund with large institutional investors. That demonstrated to senior management the serious interest among investment bank clients for investments that explicitly target social impact. That said, we were quite cautious in our approach; we kept the team lean and relied a lot on interested employees around the firm.

One of the most inspiring aspects of the Social Finance unit has been the enormous outpouring of interest and enthusiasm from employees of J.P. Morgan. In the week that followed the internal announcement of our launch, nearly a thousand Investment Bank employees e-mailed or called us to express their interest in contributing in some way. We immediately realized that we needed to create volunteer programs to channel some of these skills to the broader social enterprise market. Our interest list has now grown to several thousand employees.

From the start, we have run Social Finance as a business rather than a part of our corporate foundation. As soon as one moves away from grant giving to expecting any level of return on an investment, the staffing skill set, diligence requirements, systems, and governance cannot generally be found in a typical foundation setting. This has been critical to attract employees who can structure deals and make investments. It also signals to our employees and prospective investors our vision to establish impact investments as a recognized asset class among investors.

That said, our business unit is unique in targeting both social impact and financial return. It requires a tailored governance and compensation structure. Social Finance unit staff are not paid like mainstream investment bankers. Moreover, the hurdle for expected returns on investments is lower than in other parts of the bank. We also collaborate with public sector and foundation partners to bring in the subsidy or first-loss capital often required to make deals work at this stage in the industry's evolution.

Since 2010 we've seen a surge of interest in impact investments among clients of J.P. Morgan's Private Bank. We believe these high-net-worth individuals will propel impact investments to a new level because they are not as restricted by fiduciary or regulatory constraints. Still, substantial work remains to manage client expectations and identify and source investment products that align well with the interests of individual clients.

Making our business model work is not easy. It is difficult to source viable investment opportunities at sufficient scale to justify the structuring, diligence, and distribution costs. Impact investing remains largely a private placement market, where deals are highly bespoke and tailored to specific social or environmental issues. The track record of business and fund managers is limited. Investment infrastructure, such as third-party systems of social impact measurement, which is just beginning to emerge, will make the market more efficient.

Above all, we must see more deals that demonstrate social impact. In the end, only great deals can ultimately transform the emerging enthusiasm for impact investing into sustainable momentum that will enable us to harness the capital markets to address social challenges at scale.

But some leading impact investors object to the asset class designation based on both facts and aspirations. Some are purists who revert to traditional definitions of *asset class* as defining a set of investments with similar financial characteristics. Perhaps more interesting are those who worry that defining impact investing as an asset class is dangerously limiting for impact investing itself. These people argue that the asset class designation pigeonholes impact investing into a safe niche in an investment portfolio when the ultimate point is to infuse the spirit and practices needed to capture blended value in all investment decisions. Investors we have met in this book corroborate this point of view as well. Annie Chen seeks ways to generate blended value across her entire portfolio. Canada's Bill Young sought a legal structure that would allow all of his private foundation's assets to be put to work for impact. So too do leading family office investors such as Raul Pomares of Springcreek Advisors, who structures diverse portfolios of impact investments across asset classes for his clients.

Both camps are right. In this case, where you stand really does depend on where you sit. For mainstream institutional investors, the asset class designation is both appropriate and powerful. The designation is galvanizing the industry to organize around the opportunity and create the bureaucratic space in which teams can develop the skills, practices, and networks they need to build impact investing into a viable subsector.

However, for an increasing number of individuals, committed families, and the advisors who serve them, the asset class designation will be limiting. There is certainly a danger of unintentionally ghettoizing impact investing, condemning it forever to the 1 percent allocation made to quiet the critics and demonstrate that investors can be motivated by "more than money." In fact, numerous asset owners and asset managers have told us that they want to infuse impact investing throughout their portfolio. For example, Bonny Landers, head of The Sterling Group family office in Hong Kong, sees her responsibility to maximize impact across the portfolio.

One way to describe this difference is to recognize that these investors aim to create an impact portfolio, while those focused on impact investing as a single asset class seek an impact allocation. Both impact portfolios and impact allocations will provide important impetus to established firms and entrepreneurs to build the new structures and systems for an impact-focused global capital market. A growing number of investors are creating sustained value by investing in companies managed not for short-term performance but for long-term sustainable growth. This public market approach is coming around the bend to meet impact investment strategies that aim to generate blended value in earlier stages of venture capital or private equity. Ultimately, instead of adding one more tent to the reception, impact investing could take its place alongside these other socially responsible investors at the head table under the big tent of values-driven investment innovation. If that happens, impact investors will infuse the blended value spirit throughout their holdings; they will have an impact not only on how some assets can be unlocked for addressing social problems but also our core understanding of the nature of value and the purpose of investment.

Chapter 11

HOW WILL WE SEE THE FOREST *AND* THE TREES?

Creating the New Ecosystem of Impact Investing for Blended Value

This book describes exciting events and introduces you to pioneering characters living inspiring lives. But ultimately, impact investing for blended value is more than just the sum of these experiences. It is an integrated system of thinking and practice, springing forth in a world where a different system dominates.

When systems clash, opportunities and frustrations abound. But once we realize impact investing is a systems-building task, we can draw on the lessons from history and theory about what it has taken to secure similar change in the past. These lessons tell us great change is possible when people unused to working together collaborate to combine existing ideas into new possibilities. They teach us we cannot change a system with persuasive analysis alone but must apply the full range of our emotional and spiritual intelligence. These lessons remind us to recognize the power systems have to mold all of us—as well as the power we each have to participate in changing them.

Building this new system will not be a linear process of following directions from point A to point B on a well-trodden path.

Rather we will cross a distant ridge only to find it to be a pass that brings us into another unknown valley. We will define strategies and execute steps toward goals, but we will also live through ebbs and flows, forward movement with lateral drifts. We will get there, but it will take time, focus, and commitment. And impact investing will always involve a precarious hike along the ridgeline at the apex of profit and purpose.

Impact investing is not about bumper-sticker solutions to feeding the billions or saving the planet. Poverty will not end tomorrow as a result of how you manage your pension account or reallocate your investments in the weeks to come. The new systems will spread at the organic pace of deep capital invested in communities, where milestones do not appear with the frequency of quarterly earnings reports.

Rather than revelation, we have sought to provide reassurance for what you already know to be true, to help you see more clearly the new paths that impact investing creates. Let us review a few truths:

- There is more to your life and your legacy than the amount of your wealth that remains when you're dead.

- You cannot pursue financial returns without generating or destroying social and environmental value. How you make your money is as much a reflection of who you are as is how you give it away.

- You can execute investment strategies that achieve an appropriate level of financial performance while simultaneously generating social and environmental value. Only you can define an appropriate mix of financial and social return for you. You do not need to give up financial returns to generate impact, but flexibility on financial expectations and risk appetite will expand the investment options available to you.

- Capital markets are created and maintained by people.
  They were not passed down from the hand of God. You
  influence them every day with how you manage your
  investments, talk to your children about money, make
  demands of your asset managers, and pursue your career and
  passions.

Standing on the Edge: Two Visions of Our Future

Throughout this book, we have described how pioneering impact
investors are planting seeds of new solutions to social and environmental challenges. Some are surviving, and even thriving, despite
their emergence into a hostile environment. But just like trees on
the edge of a plain, if enough of these solutions survive, they can
begin to alter the environment around them. They can precipitate
a new ecosystem that nurtures those who follow. Let's consider
what the world we want to create looks like and how we are going
to get there.

Scenario One: The Verdant Woods of Blended Value

Let's stand at the edge of our field and imagine what we could see
in a decade or two walking through these verdant blended value
woods. Early experiments have grown into towering oaks of success,
improving the lives of millions of people. Cool streams of capital
flow easily through the woods, sustaining the herds that have been
here for decades and providing fodder to new migrants. Pathways
through the woods are clear and safe so that anyone can venture into
them, not just the brave few with nothing to lose. In these woods:

- Almost all children, even those living in the world's poorest
  cities, attend decent schools each weekday morning because
  an affordable school movement provided loans to build
  thousands of schools, allowing public resources to be
  targeted more effectively.

- Formerly homeless people find gainful employment through a wide array of for-profit and nonprofit social enterprises providing supported employment, social services, and housing.

- Where there used to be darkness, the landscape at night is a constellation of lights powered by solar panels distributed by private companies capitalized by investors receiving a competitive, risk-adjusted return on their solar development bonds.

As these woods have expanded, they have absorbed the farmers who used to toil in the fallow fields of philanthropy and the city dwellers trapped in the dirt and chaos of blind pursuit of wealth. These farmers and city dwellers have not had to abandon their work but have also benefited from new opportunities:

- Top talent joins and stays in investment banks because they can rotate through impact investing units and pioneer new financial structures that inform traditional practices.

- Wealth advisors build profitable businesses offering clients integrated advice on how to align their values with their investments across a spectrum of philanthropy, impact investing, and sustainable commercial market allocations.

- Private foundations harness all their assets, financial and human, directly to the foundation's mission.

- Pension funds recognize their mandate to steward a better future for their members, not just to maximize the size of their retirement account.

- Legislators create new corporate forms that let entrepreneurs step out of the confines into which they have contorted themselves and instead stretch as high as they can to build businesses that create wealth, respect their employees, and deliver better products and services to communities that need them.

- Billionaires pledge to use the full command of their assets to address pressing social and environmental challenges rather than just give away half their fortunes.

- Widely recognized standards of measurement allow us to identify the most fertile ground and promising new developments and to assess and protect the health of the woods as a whole.

It is a new day.

Scenario Two:
The Scorched Earth of Business as Usual

Impact investing has gathered enough momentum that it is unlikely to go away. But that does not mean the vision of a healthy and sustainable ecosystem will come to pass. A less optimistic vision could also come to pass.

We can see new trees sprouting and the pathways beginning to form under the feet of adventurous pioneers. But blind to the possibility of a better life in the woods, some farmers are encroaching. They are ready to raze these woods so they do not cast any shade over their existing crops of business-as-usual. And the sun still shines harshly on the seedlings sprouting up on land not yet protected by the shadowy canopy. Stands of trees dot the landscape here and there but have not yet formed into a single ecosystem. Travel between them remains difficult.

Standing on the edge of these woods, we could envision a much bleaker future in which the woods wither, the streams dry up, and the fertile soil of innovation and excitement is blown away by the winds of complacency and inertia. In this future:

- Investment bankers abandon their attempts to build impact investment capabilities, chasing easier returns when the economy booms and retreating to sell traditional products during the inevitable downturns.

- Wealth advisors satisfy client requests for impact investment options with traditional investments repackaged to look as if they have impact.

- Private foundations cannot overcome the structural resistance to impact investing, and remain satisfied meeting their charitable payout requirements through grants, leaving the rest of their assets to the profit-only investing logic of the past.

- Politicians rally a skeptical public against businesses and bankers who "exploit the poor," protecting their monopoly over social service delivery.

- Collaboration and innovation take a back seat to the winner-take-all drivers of traditional thinking and practice among investors, enterprises and communities.

Tomorrow looks like an even worse version of today because we cannot build the new systems required to match the increased scale and complexity of our global challenges.

Realizing the Vision of an Integrated System

So which vision will come to be? How you walk, where you look, what you do: all these will have the power to influence the future and your place within it. We cannot tell what the future holds, but we offer a few closing observations for you to mull over as you continue your journey.

Square One, Squared

The world's opportunities and challenges are so vast as to be unimaginable from where we stand now. The systems we are building will ultimately engage trillions of dollars and millions of people.

But how will we bring new people into what has to this point been an insider conversation? We will inevitably have to go over old ground many times, and each addition requires us to go back to square one. A growing body of reports, papers, and shared knowledge may ease this process. But if the past twenty years are any indication, many newcomers will not know what they do not know. They will ask many old questions. And some proponents of "new" ideas will blissfully ignore previous work and emphatically make points that have been raised and addressed many times in the past.

Often the best perspectives will come between the silos our current systems have built around us: professional or market segments or generational rifts, for example. They could be found in between countries and cultures or lodged in between organizational structures, such as in the gaps between for-profit, nonprofit, and hybrid forms. Either way, entrepreneurial ideas will emerge from individuals and groups that are not part of the mainstream yet still able to see the larger flow of culture and commerce. Seek out ideas and collaborators in these hidden spaces as much as you reflect on the opportunities within the defined areas we know.

Get ready for the long haul, and have patience for we may well return to square one again, and again, and perhaps again.

Avoid Becoming the "New Them"

The radical work of systems change brings out the passion in people who believe they have found the truth in a world of lies. This passion drives and emboldens us and enriches our global community. But it also threatens to blind us to the vision of what we are seeking to create and to the humility and collaboration it will take to get there.

We have seen this creeping blindness. Microfinance leaders trade public attacks about the righteous and unholy uses of *their* tool. And socially responsible investment leaders dismiss impact investing as a "distinction without a difference."

We should certainly hold each other accountable. And we will no doubt witness more bouts of back-and-forth recrimination and debate. But when we turn our attention to fight off those standing closest to us, we lose sight of the long journey we all need to make together. Let us resist the temptation to react to new ideas by complaining, "There's nothing new about that; we were talking about that years ago!" Instead, let's ask, "How can this advance our work, and how can I contribute to that progress?" And let's never become the "new them"—so confident we have found the truth that we resist stepping aside when better systems become possible.

And Then Something Blows Up

Impact investing will encounter its bumps in the road. No communities or systems are immune to blow-ups. In the same way traditional investing has had to deal with the Madoff scandal and the spectacle of investment houses making money on both the capital meltdown and the market's rebound, impact investing will have its bumps in the road. Anticipate them, and protect yourself and those you're committed to from the damage they may cause, but do not be dismayed by the setbacks. Remember that ships in port are safe, but staying in port is not what ships were built for. Get out there and explore the oceans of financial innovation as you sail the rolling waves that are sure to come.

Separate the Winter Wheat from the Spring Chaff

All that is new is not necessarily better. In today's world where anyone with an Internet account can rapidly promote an idea as the next best thing, an appropriate level of investor caution is called for. We must support innovation through early-stage investments and passionate discussions. But let's resist succumbing to *premature celebrationitis* that leads us to promote new ideas as successes before they have had the time to be tested, refined and proven. Shiny new ideas can distract us from the important task of patiently refining and proving existing ideas and strategies.

In the context of impact investing, the passion to be in on the social capital market's version of the next Google or Facebook should not take precedence over the need for considered due diligence and reflection. When we pursue new ventures that have not been well vetted, we could take funds away from other ventures in need of precious capital or, worse, risk doing real damage to communities we seek to assist, causes we live to advance, or social entrepreneurs we aim to support.

Watching the Grass Grow

The pioneers of the American West enjoyed grand adventures and encounters with the unknown. But they also sat through interminable periods of looking out across the plains' endless waving grasses. Their diaries reveal how often their central challenge was simple boredom and the repetitive tasks of daily chores. In this spirit, impact investors must ready ourselves for similar tedium as we work to find consistency and scale within social capital markets, introduce standard investment products, and advance the narrative numeracy needed to assess the true measure of blended value. We will need to attend many meetings, read through many more reports and engage in seemingly endless discussions on the mundane and the minute.

Take note: There will be boredom.

But also take heart: you do not need to attend each meeting or conference or review every draft report. You are part of an increasingly integrated global investor community building new markets and pursuing new opportunities. Trust your colleagues, and give yourself a break.

Make New Mistakes

While we each tend to believe our own generation is uniquely gifted, do not forget the lessons of the past. Bubbles happen. A fad is not a trend. Hubris is a harsh teacher. We can draw important lessons from previous investors, social innovators, regulators, and entrepreneurs. Listen to their stories and learn from their wisdom as we all work to create a new understanding of what we know. When we make inevitable mistakes, let's make sure we are not just repeating the mistakes similarly well-intentioned people made in the past.

Beware of Idea Inflation

Impact investors want to fund innovative and sustainable solutions to critical social and environmental issues, and that's great! But this interest in innovation can also lead to an unhealthy focus on only the new and different—sometimes to the detriment of the tried and true. While many folks are waiting to see the impact investing equivalent of the next Google, it's important to remember that hundreds (if not thousands) of solid, worthy investment opportunities lie within existing companies, social enterprises, and investment funds seeking growth and expansion capital. As we ride out what to some may seem an impact investing gold rush, we risk setting off multiple rounds of "idea inflation" wherein ideas that are good end up being over-promoted as the "great impact hope"—at the expense of other, less flashy investment ideas also worth exploring and investing in. We need to be cautious not to overvalue the new and undervalue the steady, deliberate and sometimes incremental innovations that are the bread and butter of creating sustainable enterprises and long-term value.

Break Molds and Challenge Mind-Sets

As impact investing is increasingly becoming a mainstream option for asset owners and investors, there is still great room for capital markets innovation and transformation. By definition, this means change—change in thinking, in investment practices, and in how we understand the very nature of the value we seek to create.

While we should not act recklessly, we must also not allow our options to be defined by existing systems. We must take steps to move outside the safety of what we know. We must break the existing molds that define our present reality and challenge the mind-sets that determine what is right.

The Role for You to Play

As the morning fog slowly dissipates, we can see more clearly that a new system is springing up in response to frustration about what has been and excitement about what is possible. But these are early days. And money has a funny way of changing people and the systems they create.

Wherever you stand, you are not a passive observer of this new system. By choosing to jump in or stand back, you influence the system in which we all live. The question is not, "How can I influence the system?" The question is, "What result will my influence create?" We all have a role to play:

- If you are a pioneer deeply engaged in this new system, build your enterprise with focus and verve, but embrace a competitive framework that is collaborative.

- If you are an asset owner or manager, challenge your advisors and fund managers to create and bring to market investment products and platforms that offer integrated returns.

- If you manage capital or advise its owners, take responsibility for leading your principals and portfolio companies to pursue blended value.

- If you have influence over policy and regulation, clear the space that will allow social entrepreneurs and their investors to come out from where they are hiding.

- If you take responsibility for educating the next generation of leaders, honor their interest in learning how to create blended value.

- If you are starting out in your career, resist the temptation
  to follow the well-trodden paths that you know in your
  heart do not lead where you truly want to go.

Each of us who shares a vision of blended value needs to communicate that vision clearly to others. We need to make an open
and honest case for the fact that impact investing is both morally
legitimate and economically feasible. We must do this not just with
our words but with our actions; we need to hold each other accountable to making, measuring, and celebrating investments that address
social and environmental challenges as well as generate returns for
investors and stakeholders alike.

Let's explore and cultivate these teeming woods together.

Notes

Preface

1. Jed Emerson and Fay Twerksy, *New Social Entrepreneurs: The Success, Challenge and Lessons of Nonprofit Enterprise Creation*. The book, one of the first to explore the concept of social entrepreneurship, is available in PDF for free download at the REDF Web site, under Publications. http://www.redf.org/learn-from-redf/publications/117

2. Jed Emerson, *The Nature of Returns: A Social Capital Markets Inquiry into Elements of Investment and the Blended Value Proposition*, Social Enterprise Series 17 (Boston: Harvard Business School, 2000).

Chapter Two

1. Antony's conversation with Mohammed Ibrahim, Mombasa, Kenya, 2005.

2. Its first deal, a $250 million loan to France in 1947, remains its largest single transaction in real-dollar terms.

3. The institution commonly referred to as the World Bank actually comprises two entitities. The International Bank for Reconstruction and Development (IBRD) lends primarily to middle-income and credit-worthy low-income countries at

market rates. The International Development Association provides highly concessionary loans, guarantees. and grants to low-income countries. In 2010, IBRD lent $44.2 billion while the IDA disbursed $14.5 billion.

4. Julie Abrams and Damien Von Stauffenberg, "Role Reversal: Are Public Development Institutions Crowding Out Private Investment in Microfinance?" (Arlington, Va.: Microrate, 2007).

Chapter Three

1. Xavier Reille and Jasmina Glisovic-Mezieres, "Microfinance Funds Continue to Grow Despite the Crisis" (CGAP, May 2009).

2. Bhakti Mirchandani, "Microfinance Overview" (Lehman Brothers, 2008).

3. Celia W. Dugger, "Debate Stirs over Tiny Loans for World's Poorest," New York Times, Apr. 29, 2004.

4. The fact that the Indian government ran a competing microlending program in Andhra Pradesh was an important contributor to the crisis there. This angle, largely ignored in the international coverage, was described eloquently by the Indian consulting and investment advisory firm Intellecap in "Indian Microfinance Crisis of 2010: Turf War or a Battle of Intentions?" (Oct. 2010).

5. Lydia Polgreen and Vikas Bajaj, "India Microcredit Faces Collapse from Defaults," New York Times, Nov. 17 2010. This front-page story was typical of the international coverage and ran alongside a photo of a woman whose daughter had fled her village after taking on microfinance loans she could not repay.

6. CGAP published a fascinating paper that examined whether early donor support for an organization that eventually made such a lucrative exit for investors was appropriate and effective

and also the likely effect that public equity investors would have on the social benefit Compartamos could create. "CGAP Reflections on the Compartamos Initial Public Offering" (World Bank, June 2007).

7. "Compartamos IPO: Microfinance Doing Good, or the Undoing of Microfinance?" *Microcredit Summit News*, 2007, 5(1). Elisabeth Malkin, "Microfinance's Success Sets Off a Debate in Mexico," *New York Times*, Apr. 5, 2008.

Chapter Four

1. We are not going to waste our energy or your time wading into the debate over the definition of *social entrepreneurship*. We simply observe that social entrepreneurs lead both for-profit and nonprofit ventures, and they advance business models that can use earned income as well as grant revenue.

2. Matt Flannery, "Kiva and the Birth of Person-to-Person Microfinance," *Innovations*, Winter–Spring 2007, pp. 31–56.

Chapter Five

1. International Finance Corporation, "The Business of Health in Africa" (2007).

2. The 2010 J.P. Morgan/Rockefeller Foundation research note, "Impact investments: An Emerging Asset Class," identified an investment opportunity between $214 billion and $786 billion required to build housing for urban residents who could afford to pay for a basic home.

3. "The Recession-Proof Business Opportunity in Low Income Housing" (Monitor Inclusive Markets, 2009).

4. Hernando de Soto, *Mystery of Capital: Why Capitalism Triumphs in the West and Fails Everywhere Else* (New York: Basic Books, 2000).

5. Woody Tasch, *Inquiries into the Nature of Slow Money: Investing As If Food, Farms, and Fertility Mattered* (White River Junction, Vt.: Chelsea Green Publishing, 2010).

6. "Give to the Soil Trust" (June 10, 2010).

7. Ashish Karamchandani, Mike Kubzansky, and Paul Frandano point out in "Emerging Markets, Emerging Models" (Monitor Inclusive Markets, 2009) that large corporations with existing business tend not to focus on innovations for poor customers when they have rich customers to worry about. It should not be surprising that no microfinance operation within an existing retail bank has reached significant scale; every large microfinance operation was built as part of an independent organization.

8. The metaphor of the "Apple IPO" in the context of the impact investing industry first surfaced during research by Monitor Institute for its 2008 report, *Investing for Social and Environmental Impact.*

Chapter Seven

1. In this case, *community* refers to community of interest, organization, and/or geography.

2. Monitor Institute, *Investing for Social and Environmental Impact* (Cambridge, Mass.: Monitor Institute, 2009).

3. "A Place in Society," *Economist*, Sept. 29, 2009.

4. Malcolm Gladwell, *The Tipping Point* (New York: Little, Brown, 2000).

5. Matthew Bishop and Michael Green, *Philanthrocapitalism* (New York: Bloomsbury Press, 2008).

Chapter Eight

1. Michael Porter and Mark Kramer, "Creating Shared Value," *Harvard Business Review*, Jan.-Feb. 2011.

2. Robert G. Eccles and Michael P. Krzus, *One Report: Integrated Reporting for a Sustainable Strategy* (Hoboken, N.J.: Wiley, 2010).

3. There are a number of sources with information about SROI methodology. The original SROI Framework was published by REDF as part of its Box Set released in 2000 and available from its Web site. The New Economics Foundation, based in the United Kingdom, has published several pieces on SROI that highlight the role of stakeholder engagement. The SROI Network maintains a Web site with current methodology and resources. And Social E-Valuator offers an online tool to calculate SROI—though it is oriented toward generating a single figure as opposed to an integrated set of indicators reflecting the vision of the original approach. Brian Dunn, of Aquillian Investments, explored this concept in 2006 in "Modern Portfolio Theory—with a Twist: The New Efficient Frontier" (Aquillian Investments, 2006).

4. Recently released "ImpactAssets Issue Brief #2, Risk, Return and Impact: Understanding Diversification and Performance within an Impact Portfolio" explores these ideas in greater depth.

5. The Web site of Sphere IT (http://www.spherit.com/), founded by Phil Lawson, offers a good introduction to this approach.

6. The IRIS metrics and an explanation for their use are available at http://iris.thegiin.org/.

Chapter Nine

1. Interestingly, this is not a recent phenomenon. Benjamin Franklin established a two thousand dollar revolving loan fund for young artisans, a concept that, Rick Cohen has pointed out, "would today probably be touted in the *Chronicle* [*of Philanthropy*] as a foundation innovation." Rick Cohen, "A Call for Mission-Based Investing By America's Private

Foundations" (Washington, D.C.: National Committee for Responsive Philanthropy, 2005), p. 5.

2. Though nothing in the U.S. tax code explicitly precludes using PRI capital to make a more lucrative investment or investment in a for-profit entity.

3. Charles Pillar, Edmund Sanders, and Robyn Dixon, "Dark Cloud over Good Works of Gates Foundation," *Los Angeles Times*, Jan. 7, 2007.

4. Steven Godeke and Raúl Pomares, "Solutions for Impact Investors" (New York: Rockefeller Philanthropy Advisors, 2010). Tracy Palandjian, "Investing for Impact: Case Studies Across Asset Classes (Boston and London: Parthenon Group and Bridges Ventures, 2010).

5. The More for Mission Campaign, the PRI Makers Network, the Global Impact Investing Network, and other forums offer resources and support for foundation leaders interested in adopting impact investing strategies.

Chapter Ten

1. Hope Consulting, "Money for Good" (San Francisco: Hope Consulting, 2010). Nick O'Donohoe and others, "Impact Investments: An Emerging Asset Class" (New York: J.P. Morgan Chase & Co. and Rockefeller Foundation, 2010). NESTA UK, "Research of Investor Interest," http://www.nesta.org.uk/home1/assets/features/new_research _maps_supply_and_demand_for_social_finance.

Further Reading

Writings on impact investing are proliferating as fast as the industry itself. This list, organized by chapter, sets out the writings and sources that informed our own thinking or spurred wider debate in the field of impact investing. Many provide trailheads to paths of thinking you can productively follow on your own.

Introduction (Chapter One)

- The Global Impact Investing Network's Web site (www.thegiin.org) provides a comprehensive list of news clippings and research reports on impact investing; see its "Resources" section. The monthly "Investor's Spotlight" provides an insightful series of interviews that describe the strategies and challenges that pioneering impact investors are facing across a wide range of institutions, geographies, and investment perspectives.

- The Monitor Institute's "Investing for Social and Environmental Impact" (2009) provides a solid theoretical framework for understanding the impact investing opportunity that proved pivotal in popularizing the concept in 2009–2010.

- In April, 2011, NESTA-UK published three significant reports that will be of interest to impact investors: "Understanding the Demand for and Supply of Social Finance," "Why and How Wealthy Individuals Respond to Social Investment," and "Twenty Catalytic Investments to Grow the Social Investment Market."

- The consulting firm Parthenon Group and British impact investing pioneer Bridges Ventures documented case studies of impact investing deals and funds in "Investing for Impact: Case Studies Across Asset Classes" (2010).

- J.P. Morgan's research department teamed up with the Rockefeller Foundation to coauthor a research note on impact investing in 2010: "Impact Investments: An Emerging Asset Class." This report describes impact investing as a new asset class and provides the first-ever assessment of financial return expectation and bottoms-up market sizing in specific subsectors.

- Before the phrase *impact investing* described this activity, Jed coauthored a report for the World Economic Forum in 2006 with Josh Spitzer that described a range of investment deals and funds putting the principals of blended value into practice. "Capital Opportunities for Social and Environmental Impact" remains an important overview of investment opportunities and investor motivations. In addition, Jed's 2000 working paper from Harvard Business School, "The Nature of Returns: A Social Capital Markets Inquiry into Elements of Investment and the Blended Value Proposition," together with the 2003 production of The Blended Value Map, outlined the contours for much of the subsequent research and debate in this arena. Finally, Jed and Spitzer's *"From Fragmentation to Function: Critical Concepts and Writings on Social Capital Markets Structure, Operation and Innovation"*

(2007) includes a lengthy annotated bibliography of work advancing numerous concepts important to foundational thinking regarding impact investing. Jed's other writings on themes related to impact investing, metrics, and strategy may be found at www.blendedvalue.org.

International Development (Chapter Two)

- C. K. Prahalad's *Fortune at the Bottom of the Pyramid: Eradicating Poverty Through Profits* (2005) galvanized international attention around the idea that poor people in emerging markets can be customers, not just charity cases. Although subsequent research has identified the limits to which multinational corporations will drive innovation in this area, this book helped widen the arena in which today's impact investors play when they pursue profit by providing basic goods and services to poor customers in poor countries.

- Any discussion of the private sector's role in economic development in emerging markets must take into account the argument of Peruvian economist Hernando De Soto in *The Mystery of Capital: Why Capitalism Triumphs in the West and Fails Everywhere Else* (2000). This seminal work challenges economists (and, for our purposes, savvy investors) to consider the legal and social dynamics that underpin and constrain private sector development.

- After serving as a senior manager at the U.S. development finance institution OPIC and as U.S. ambassador to the African Union, John Simon coauthored, with Julie Barmier, "More Than Money: Impact Investing for Development" for the Center for Global Development (2010). This report provides an overview of impact investing internationally and discusses the implications for private and public development efforts.

- A 2007 paper from the nonprofit MicroRate, "Role Reversal: Are Public Development Institutions Crowding Out

Private Investment?" focused on the role of publicly funded development finance capital in the development of the microfinance market. The broader questions raised about the principal of additionality are important beyond microfinance.

• The United Nations Development Program waded into the private sector and development area when it convened the Commission on Private Sector and Development. Its 2004 report, "Unleashing Entrepreneurship: Making Business Work for the Poor," is more remarkable for its origins than its insights, but it provides a good overview of how private sector can best be harnessed for development.

Microfinance (Chapter Three)

• The debate between the commercial and nonprofit camps of modern microfinance is chronicled in Connie Bruck's compelling 2006 *New Yorker* article, "Millions for Millions" (Oct. 30, 2006).

• The Compartamos IPO in 2007 unleashed a prolific and emotional debate online, in popular newspapers, and among microfinance insiders. The best data-driven analysis (interesting if you have even a small appetite for accounting and finance) came from Rich Rosenberg at the Consultative Group to Assist the Poor. His "CGAP Reflections on the Compartamos Initial Public Offering: A Case Study on Microfinance Interest Rates and Profits" (2007) delves into a relatively detailed assessment of Compartamos's financial record to answer the questions of whether the organization's exceptional financial performance undermined its development impact and whether donor support was appropriate for a company that ultimately enriched its owners so handsomely. The founders of Compartamos, Carlos Danel and Carlos Labarthe, covered similar ground from a different perspective in their 2008 "Letter to our Peers," available on the Compartamos Web site: http://www.compartamos.com/wps/portal.

- Three years after the Compartamos initial public offering, that of SKS Microfinance in India created an even larger media storm and precipitated regulatory action that temporarily threatened the microfinance industry in the Indian state of Andhra Pradesh. The Indian advisory firm Intellecap wrote an incisive white paper on the controversy as it unfolded, "Indian Microfinance Crisis of 2010: Turf War or a Battle of Intentions?" (Oct. 2010), that highlighted the political origins of the crisis. Various articles about the Andhra Pradesh microfinance crisis provided sobering reminders about the skepticism most people still hold for the idea that for-profit investing can be a morally legitimate way to extend basic services to poor people. A front-page story in the *New York Times*, "India Microcredit Faces Collapse from Defaults" (Nov. 17, 2010), typified this coverage.

- In *Portfolios of the Poor: How the World's Poor Live on $2 a Day* (2009), Daryl Collins, Jonathan Morduch, and Stuart Rutherford describe how families in Bangladesh, India, and South Africa engage in sophisticated financial management. These descriptions challenge simplistic notions of microcredit as a silver bullet and highlight the importance of providing savings and insurance.

Social Enterprise (Chapter Four)

- *The Nonprofit Entrepreneur* (1987), by Ed Skloot, is an early important piece of work on social enterprise. This was followed in 1996 by the Roberts Enterprise Development Fund's "New Social Entrepreneurs: The Success, Challenge and Lessons of Nonprofit Enterprise Creation," which documents the experience of the Roberts Fund's initial work in social entrepreneurship from 1990 to 1995. It remains an important document of the development of social ventures in San Francisco and is available online at www.redf.org.

• *Enterprising Nonprofits: A Toolkit for Social Entrepreneurs* (2001) and *Strategic Tools for Social Entrepreneurs* (2002), both cowritten by Jed with Greg Dees and Peter Economy, are important fundamental books on social entrepreneurship.

• Although no single book covers the social enterprise movement comprehensively, David Bornstein has written extensively on the topic. His 2004 book, *How to Change the World: Social Entrepreneurs and the Power of New Ideas,* is a landmark in the mainstreaming of writing on social enterprise. His new venture, dowser.org, is a platform for identifying and describing cutting-edge social enterprises.

• A number of useful resources are available regarding social enterprise in Great Britain. Useful papers may be found at http://www.tsrc.ac.uk/Publications/tabid/500/Default.aspx. And a paper produced by the Skoll Center, "The Landscape of Social Finance: A Holistic Typology" by Alex Nicholls and Cathy Pharoah (2007), is a useful overview of social finance as it relates to social enterprise.

Future Directions (Chapter Five)

We have not yet come across any references that provide alternative predictions about the near-term trajectory of impact investing, though we would not be surprised if they have been published by the time you are reading this. If you are particularly interested in specific subsectors we mention as possible areas for near-term growth in impact investing the following are good sources to start for more in-depth analysis:

• *Health care:* The High Level Taskforce on Innovative International Financing for Health Systems concentrates on

mobilizing donor aid but covers financing mechanisms that
could tap into impact investing capital, such as front-loading
bonds and advance purchase commitments. The report of its
second working group, "Raising and Channeling Funds"
(2010), is particularly relevant.

• *Affordable housing:* The Monitor Inclusive Markets group
has conducted substantial research on low-income housing
business models in India. Its analysis and reports on pilot
projects are a good starting point to understand the broader
opportunity. http://www.mim.monitor.com/mbs_housing.html

• *Education:* James Tooley, a British academic and
entrepreneur, has driven the research agenda on affordable
private schools. In addition to academic articles, he
synthesized his views in his book *The Beautiful Tree: A Personal
Journey into How the World's Poorest People Are Educating
Themselves* (2009). For a more academic examination of the
topic, see *Private Schooling in Less Economically Developed
Countries* (2007) by Prachi Srivastava and Geoffrey Walford.

• *Agriculture:* The recent surge in foreign investment in
agriculture in poor countries has set off substantial debate,
especially in Africa. In addition to numerous articles in the
press, a few research efforts have sought to understand
the phenomenon and its broader implications for both
investors and development. The International Institute for
Environment and Development teamed up with the United
Nations and World Bank to produce a report examining
international land deals in Africa: "Land Grab or Development Opportunity" (2009). The Global Impact Investing
Network's Project Terragua works with impact investors
operating in the sustainable agriculture field in Africa and
compiles and distributes news and research on the topic.

- *Restructured social spending:* Interest in the concept of "social impact bonds" or "pay-for-success bonds" exploded in early 2011, especially in the United States and the United Kingdom. The U.K.-based organization Social Finance has produced a series of publications on social impact bonds targeting various levels of detail and practical advice. Its 2009 paper, "Social Impact Bonds: Rethinking Finance for Social Outcomes," is the organization's best general overview. Jeffrey Liebman's "Social Impact Bonds" (2011), a paper for the Center for American Progress, analyzes the opportunity from a U.S.-focused perspective.

Regulation (Chapter Six)

- *Impact Investing: A Framework for Policy Design and Analysis,* released in 2011 by Ben Thornley at Insight at Pacific Community Ventures and David Wood of the Initiative for Responsible Investment at Harvard University, provides a framework for regulatory policy and outlines sixteen examples of national policy reform in thirteen countries. Further country-specific research is underway in 2011.

- The United Kingdom's Social Investment Task Force, which ran from 2000 to 2010, recommended five reforms to create a more vibrant and efficient impact investment sector and to unlock entrepreneurial approaches to addressing national social challenges. The task force has produced regular reports on its progress. It has also served as a model for other similar reports, including the 2010 report of the Canadian Task Force on Social Finance, "Mobilizing Private Capital for Public Good."

Leadership (Chapter Seven)

- For more on transformational leadership, see Jed's Harvard Business School working paper, "The Nature of Returns: A Social Capital Markets Inquiry into Elements of Investment and the Blended Value Proposition" (2000).

Measurement (Chapter Eight)

• One prominent example of the trend to rethink GDP as the basic measure of national progress is "Report of the Commission on the Measurement of Economic Performance and Social Progress" (2009), chaired by Professor Joseph Stiglitz.

• The Wealth Creation in Rural Communities, project run by Yellow Wood Associates, has developed and collected a comprehensive set of measurement approaches and practical tools for understanding blended value creation in rural communities in the United States. They are available at http://www.yellowwood.org/wealthcreation.aspx. Many of these approaches could be transferred for broader application elsewhere.

• Jed's "Mutual Accountability and the Wisdom of Frank Capra" in *Foundation News and Commentary* (Mar.–Apr. 2001) discusses the ways in which funders can amplify the impact of their financial support when implementing systems of evaluation and working with grantees effectively.

• Richard Heeks and Alemayehu Molla offer a framework for understanding different approaches to impact measurement in their "Impact Assessment of ICT for Development Projects: A Compendium of Approaches" (2009). From the corporate perspective, Marc Epstein and Bill Birchard's *Counting What Counts: Turning Corporate Accountability to Competitive Advantage* (2009) remains an excellent resource among the many books and articles written on this topic.

• For an overview of the Social Return on Investment approach, a good place to start is "Social Return on Investment Collection," (2000, which synthesizes five years of writings, including a methodology paper from REDF. The New Economics Foundation in London has complemented this work (including "A Guide to Social Return on Investment" (2009)). The "SROI Guide" (2009) is a compendium of work compiled by the SROI-International network and available on its Web site.

Total Foundation Asset Management (Chapter Nine)

• Jed first presented the concept of total foundation asset management in a 2002 Stanford paper, "A Capital Idea: Total Foundation Asset Management and the Unified Investment Strategy." His 2003 *Stanford Social Innovation Review* article, "Where Money Meets Mission: Breaking Down the Fire Wall Between Foundation Investments and Programming," developed this thinking. The concept of transactive versus investment philanthropy builds off the concept of transactive social capital initially proposed in Jed's "The Blended Value Proposition: Integrating Social and Financial Returns" in *California Management Review* (2003).

• Rockefeller Philanthropy Advisors has produced a series of monographs on impact investing aimed at private foundation executives and trustees. "Mission-Related Investing: Philanthropy's New Passing Gear" (2008) provides an overview of impact investing for trustees and an outline for developing a foundation's impact investing strategy. "Solutions for Impact Investors: From Strategy to Implementation" (2009) offers more targeted advice for moving from interest to implementation. The Rose Foundation and As You Sow Foundation have posted online resources for foundation trustees and executive interested in exploring impact investing with endowment assets. An early European perspective on this issue can be found in the EIRIS Foundation's "Investing Responsibly: A Practical Guide for Charity Trustees" (2005).

• A case study on the Oregon-based Meyer Memorial Trust by eight students at the Harvard Kennedy School provides an interesting insider's perspective about what it takes to spur interest in impact investing and to overcome trustee skepticism: "$650 Million Ain't What It Used to Be: The Meyer Memorial Trust Considers Mission Related Investing" (2010).

• The PRI Makers Networks maintains a comprehensive online resource center (http://www.primakers.net/) that includes references to articles and books on program-related investments, as well as tool kits for members, such as sample term sheets and other deal documents. The Foundation Center's *PRI Directory* (3rd ed., 2010) lists foundations making PRIs with high-level investment criteria and sample deals.

• The Swedish MISTRA Foundation has long practiced mission aligned investing. Its 2011 report, "360-Degrees for Mission," authored by David Imbert and Ivo Knoepfel of onValues, offers an up-to-date overview of mission investing practices by European foundations.

• Various research and advocacy efforts have challenged foundation trustees to consider a more holistic approach to their fiduciary duty overseeing foundation investment decisions. Jed explored this in his 2005 paper with Tim Little and Jonas Kron: "The Prudent Trustee: The Evolution of the Long Term Investor." FSG Impact described how U.S. foundation trustees have greater flexibility in investment decisions than often recognized in "Risk, Return and Social Impact: Demystifying the Law of Mission Investing by U.S. Foundations" (2008), by Anne Stetson and Mark Kramer.

• The Investor Environmental Health Network collects and publishes research reports exploring various ways in which long-term fiduciaries need to consider environmental risks in investment decisions.

- On the policy front, the United Nations Environment Programme working with top U.K. corporate law firms produced "A Legal Framework for the Integration of Environmental, Social and Governance Issues into Institutional Investment" (2005).

- Recent surveys have highlighted the generational shift that is leading younger donors to reject the bifurcated philanthropic model. The University of Pennsylvania's Center for High Impact Philanthropy 2010 survey identified the eagerness for an innovative approach to philanthropy. The British firm Barclays Wealth identified similar dynamics among five hundred donors in the United Kingdom and the United States in "Tomorrow's Philanthropist" (2009).

- For readers interested in the general topic of family wealth management, a good starting place is James Hughes's *Family Wealth: Keeping It in the Family* (2004). The Family Office Association in Greenwich, Connecticut, is a valuable resource for family members and the professionals who work to meet their needs.

Moving the Money (Chapter Ten)

Much of the discussion regarding how to move mainstream investing toward impact investing products and structures builds on work done by leaders in the socially responsible investing movement as well as community development finance. Although a large number of publications and organizations have advanced work in these areas, Amy Domini and Peter Kinder's *Ethical Investing* (1986) remains a standard for the field, as does other work produced by various members of the Social Investment Forum. Mark Pinsky, executive director of the Opportunity Finance Network, has led the way for many years in the community development finance arena and worked through a variety of outlets to inform our thinking in impact investing. Finally, the publications section of the *UN-Principles for Responsible Investing* Web site (http://www.unpri.org/) has a wide array of offerings of interest to readers.

For more targeted writing on impact investing and the capital markets, we recommend the following reports:

- The U.K. Commission on Unclaimed Assets made an eloquent case in 2007 for the creation of a social investment bank. Although it focused on dysfunction in traditional approaches to funding nonprofit social services in the United Kingdom, the clear diagnosis and prescriptions resonate more broadly. The commission's core recommendation helped galvanize national support for the launch of the Big Society Bank in 2011, described, along with other recommendations, in the British Cabinet Office's *Growing the Social Investment Market* (2011).

- In *Up from Wall Street: The Responsible Investment Alternative* (2009), Thomas Croft describes investment options available to U.S. institutional investors interested in using investment allocations to promote local community development and jobs creation, with a particular focus on union pension funds.

- The Milken Institute's Center for Financial Innovations publishes and collates research on a range of issues relevant to unlocking impact investment. The center's director, Glenn Yago, collected some of this thinking in *Financing the Future: Market-Based innovations for growth* (2010), coauthored with Frank Allen.

- With gathering momentum in 2010, private banks have become increasingly engaged in impact investing. While typically less than effusive by their nature, some have begun to describe their motivations and vision in this area. The UBS

Values-Based Investing unit describes its vision for integrated asset management on its Web site: http://www.ubs.com/1/e/ wealthmanagement/philanthropy_valuesbased_investments/ value_based_investing.html.

- *The Future of Finance: The LSE Report,* from the London School of Economics (2010), summarizes discussions held by leading academics, reporters, and bankers in the wake of the financial crisis. Some of its chapters are relevant for readers interested in a fundamental consideration of the role of capital markets and financial services institutions as a foundation for understanding the impact investing opportunity.

The Authors

Jed Emerson has long been recognized as an elder in the field of impact investing. As originator of the term *blended value*, he has spent over a decade exploring how investors and entrepreneurs can maximize value and performance that are both financial and environmental/social in nature (www.blendedvalue.org). He is executive vice president of ImpactAssets, a senior fellow with Heidelberg University's Center on Social Investing, and a senior advisor to the Sterling Group (Hong Kong). He was founding director of REDF, a founding board member of Pacific Community Ventures, and founding director of Larkin Street Services in San Francisco. He has served as a senior fellow with Generation Investment Management and the William and Flora Hewlett Foundation and has held appointments at Harvard, Stanford, and Oxford business schools. Emerson has coedited three books and scores of articles and papers on topics such as social capital markets, unified investment strategies, and sustainable hedge fund investing, among many other subjects. He has presented his work at the World Economic Forum, the Skoll World Forum, and numerous other events around the world. He resides with his wife in New York City, but lives in Colorado and Norway.

Antony Bugg-Levine is widely recognized as a leading figure in the emergence of the global impact investing industry. He designed and leads the Rockefeller Foundation's impact investing initiative and oversees its program-related investment portfolio. He convened the 2007 meeting that coined the phrase *impact investing* and is the founding board chair of the Global Impact Investing Network. He previously ran TechnoServe, a nongovernmental organization, in Kenya and Uganda, where he helped develop and implement business solutions to rural poverty. Earlier in his career, as a consultant with McKinsey, he advised Fortune 100 clients in the financial services and health care sectors and helped develop new frameworks for incorporating social dynamics into corporate strategy. A native of South Africa, he served in the late 1990s as the acting communications director at the South African Human Rights Commission and as a speechwriter and media strategist for the African National Congress's 1999 election campaign. He is an associate adjunct professor in the Social Enterprise Program at the Columbia Business School. He lives in New Jersey with his wife, Ahadi.

Disclosure

In describing a field as dynamic as impact investing, we have had to leave out far more than we can fit between the covers of this book. We have strived to offer an objective account of the most exciting developments without tilting the narrative unduly to favor the ideas and organizations we have personally supported (and have aimed to keep each other honest along the way!). That said, our account inevitably oversamples from the work we know best and reflects the personal perspectives we have gained through our participation in different aspects of the impact investing industry. A few specific caveats and disclaimers seem worthwhile to allow you to judge our objectivity for yourself.

Jed is executive vice president of ImpactAssets, a senior fellow with Heidelberg University's Center on Social Investing, and a senior advisor to the Sterling Group of Hong Kong. He has been a major driver of the SROI framework for measuring the social impact of investment. As the leader of the Rockefeller Foundation's Harnessing the Power of Impact Investing initiative and Program-Related Investments program since 2008, Antony has supported numerous organizations and projects mentioned in this book. Most prominent has been his support for the Global Impact Investing Network (on whose board he sits) and its Impact Reporting and Investment System project. He has also funded the core work of B Lab (though not its policy advocacy work) and the Global Impact Investing Ratings System. Through the Rockefeller Foundation Program-Related Investment portfolio, he has invested in IGNIA Fund, the first social impact bond structured by Social Finance in the United Kingdom, and the Acumen Capital Markets Fund. He is an adjunct professor in the Social Enterprise Program at Columbia Business School.

A full list of the grantees of the Rockefeller Foundation's impact investing initiative and the investees of its PRI program can be found at www.rockefellerfoundation.org.

The opinions expressed in this book are those of the authors alone and do not represent the views of any institutions with which they are associated.

Index